CLOSER TO GOD

Reading the Bible in the power
of the Holy Spirit

STRUIK CHRISTIAN BOOKS

Closer to God is edited by Scripture Union (SU) in South Africa, using local writers and material produced for international use by SU Publishing, London. This edition of *Closer to God* is a joint publication of Scripture Union and Struik Christian Books Ltd.

Struik Christian Books Ltd
(A division of New Holland Publishing (South Africa) (Pty) Ltd)
Cornelis Struik House
80 McKenzie Street
Cape Town 8001

Reg. No. 1971/009721/07

Text copyright © Scripture Union 2001
Copyright in this edition © Struik Christian Books Ltd 2001

Scripture quotations taken from the Holy Bible, New International Version.
Copyright 1973, 1978, 1984 by the International Bible Society.
Used by permission.

All rights reserved. No part of this publication may be reproduced or transmitted in any form or by any means, electronic or mechanical, including photocopying, recording, or in any information storage and retrieval system, without the written permission of the publisher.

DTP by June van Aswegen
Cover design by Christian Jaggers
Cover reproduction by Hirt & Carter Cape (Pty) Ltd
Reproduction, printed and bound by CTP Book Printers
PO Box 6060, Parow 7501

ISBN 1 86823 490 8

Contents

Welcome to Closer to God		5
How to unlock the power of the Bible		6
Foreword		7
Signs of Life	Paul Harcourt	8
Friendship	Alfie Fabe	15
Lord, my faith is wobbly	Fiona Watson	22
Times of testing	Fiona Watson	29
Power for all the people	David Evans	36
Forgiveness	Costa Mitchell	43
The love of God in Jesus Christ	Cynthia Richards	50
Living proof	Belinda Pollard	57
Of icebergs and Babylon	Trevor Hoek	64
Christmas trees and shepherds	Trevor Hoek	71
God's promises are 'Yes' and 'Amen'	Don Phillips	78
Worship – gaining perspective	Sam Troost	85
The cross	Donovan Coetzee	92
The gospel from scratch	Martin Hodson	101
Righteousness from God	Martin Hodson	108
Mud, mud, glorious mud	Colin Veysey	115
A bigger Jesus	Clio Turner	122
Stark choices	Sheila Pritchard	129
A matter of life and death	Sheila Pritchard	136
God, where are you?	Jennifer Rees Larcombe	143
Old life versus new	Martin Hodson	150
God's mercy	Martin Hodson	157
Love's young dream	Walter Moberly	164
Living as God's people	Walter Moberly	171
Jesus in his people	Paul Hartwig	178
Dreaming dreams	Alfie Fabe	185
The hour approaches	Mark Stibbe	192
Which way?	Mark Stibbe	199
Amazing grace	Roger Witter	206
Faith in action	Andrew Marsden	213
Singleness/marriedness	Christine Platt	220
A gospel for all people	Sue Sainsbury	227
The perfect church	Mary Moody	234
Words of comfort	Ann Nias	241
State of the heart	Jennifer Rees Larcombe	248
Tantalising glimpses	Jeremy Clampett	255

Visions of destiny	*Jeremy Clampett*	262
How to live	*Martin Hodson*	269
Keep it going	*Martin Hodson*	276
Joy despite everything	*Jennifer Rees Larcombe*	283
Enjoying grace	*Jennifer Rees Larcombe*	290
God moves Israel forward	*Duncan Buchanan*	297
Can there be a king in Israel?	*Duncan Buchanan*	304
Praying for change	*Alison Bourne*	311
A new king in Israel	*Duncan Buchanan*	318
Why do Christians fast?	*John Hewitson*	325
Divine intervention	*Alf Friend*	332
The time has come	*Peter Pollock*	339
New beginnings	*Sheila Pritchard*	346
God's book of remembrance	*Paul Hartwick*	353
Busyness	*Costa Mitchell*	360
Christmas presence	*Belinda Pollard*	367
How good is our God	*Alf Friend*	374
365 Days of praise	*Belinda Pollard*	375

Welcome to Closer to God

Closer to God helps you to explore the Bible in fresh and stimulating ways. It is compiled by Christians who believe in reading the Bible regularly, and allowing God to speak through it so that we can receive the power of God to live like Jesus.

Closer to God is divided into weekly sections with introductory and closing articles. In most weeks we'll be going through a book of the Bible, but there are also several theme weeks. These include friendship, forgiveness, intercession, fasting and busyness.

A normal week contains:

- An introduction to the theme for the week, giving a foretaste of what's to come, as well as a pensketch of the contributor.
- Five main Bible readings with notes and two extra Bible readings for the weekend at the end of the reading for Day 5.
- 'Going deeper', which gives you a chance to experience the Bible theme of the week on a deeper level, as well as a conclusion to round off the week with a final thought or challenge.
- 'The Bible in a year', which appears at the bottom of each page for Days 1–5. These readings will enable you to read through the whole Bible in one year.

How to unlock the power of the Bible

The Bible is alive. Its covers contain the most powerful force in the universe: the Word of God. That's why, when we read it, the words can leap off the page and speak to us personally. These words have the ability to bring about radical change.

The Bible is the handbook for life. Although it doesn't have a precise answer for every question we might ask, through reading the Bible we come to know God's perspective and are able to make the right choices.

By reading your Bible with *Closer to God* you're part of a worldwide family of people who read the Bible. To get the most out of the Bible, you need to do two things: read it *expectantly* and read it *regularly*. *Closer to God* is designed to help you do this. The notes that accompany each reading are structured around the headings below. Many have found these to be helpful for meeting with God in his Word.

Prepare yourself to hear God's voice. Open your life to him. Ask his Holy Spirit to give you an understanding mind and a responsive heart.

Read the passage carefully, listening for what God has to say to you.

Explore the meaning of the passage before you read the comments in *Closer to God*, asking yourself: What is the main point of this passage? What is God showing me about himself or about my life?

Respond to the passage in prayer, worship, decision and action.

Extra Reading for the weekend.

Foreword

Closer to God is written by a mixture of South African and British writers. The eighteen South African contributors cover twenty-five weeks. They come from all walks of life. There are several clergymen, two psychologists, two retired school principals, a heart surgeon, an ex-Springbok cricketer and a retired bishop, to mention a few. They are invariably busy people carrying heavy responsibilities, but they have given freely of their time and creativity to guide us through a week or more of readings.

The aim of *Closer to God* is to take you through the New Testament verse by verse, while making sure that the major themes of the Old Testament are covered. Those who want to 'fast forward' their reading can follow 'The Bible in a year' at the bottom of the page.

How impoverished Christians are who don't make time to dig deep into God's Word! My prayer is that you will unearth 'treasures of great price' as you explore the deep things of God.

Alf Friend
Editor
Cape Town
October 2001

JANUARY 1–6

Signs of life

John 2–3

There was a book recently that caught my eye. I didn't buy it, and I haven't read it, but the title intrigued me: *What if Jesus had never been born?* The back cover said that the book looked at the impact of Jesus' life down through 2 000 years of human civilisation. Countless millions of people have been changed by Jesus and inspired to make a difference in their moment of history, in ways large and small. Some of their actions helped shape whole cultures, others perhaps were seen by God alone.

Having just celebrated Christmas, many people will move on into the new year, forgetting about Jesus until next reminded of his birth. That tendency to pack Jesus away with the Christmas decorations underlines our need to focus not simply upon Jesus' birth but also on what he came to do.

The Bible explains his mission in a variety of ways. In John's Gospel, Jesus himself summarises his role: 'I have come that they may have life, and have it to the full' (10:10). John organises his material to show us what it means to find fullness of life through Jesus. Commentators usually agree that, after the prologue (1:1–18), John's Gospel divides into two main sections, beginning with 'the Book of Signs' (1:19—12:50). In this section, which includes our readings this week, John highlights seven miracles that act as 'signs', revealing Jesus' glory and complementing his teaching about the nature of the life that he brings. Let these readings draw you closer to Jesus and inspire you to live a new life.

Thankfully, we don't have to worry about what life would be like if Jesus had never been born. We can simply embrace with joy the difference that he makes!

Because we start January with a six-day week, I have provided only one extra reading.

Paul Harcourt is curate at All Saint's with St Andrew's, Woodford Wells, Essex. He is married to Becky, and they have a son, Joshua. Paul is a Norwich City FC supporter.

JANUARY 1–6

DAY 1

Abundant life

Is there something in your life that you feel particularly short of at the moment? You might think of things like time, energy, patience, love, friendship or health. What would it feel like to suddenly receive an abundance?

John 2:1–11

It's important to remember that Jesus worked his miracles and delivered his teaching amidst the ordinary events of life. I find it enormously encouraging that he was so often found at parties and celebrations with ordinary people like us. It would have meant so much to this couple if later they came to realise who had been at their wedding reception. However, it was nearly remembered as a disaster. Imagine being forever known in a small village as 'the couple who couldn't even organise their own wedding properly'!

Jesus' seeming reluctance to help (v 4) is probably his way of checking that Mary realises that he is not at her (or anyone's) 'beck and call'. However, knowing his heart, Mary confidently gives good advice to the servants (v 5), and to us! The sheer quantity (vs 6–7) and quality (vs 9–10) of Jesus' solution to this couple's need speaks volumes about the life that he wants to give us. John's intention in highlighting a number of Jesus' miracles in his Gospel is to describe to us what this life is like. What does it say to you, that this should be Jesus' first miracle?

Jesus was neither too busy nor too important to attend this couple's special day. He still has that same desire to enter into every aspect of our lives – and the same compassion that drove him to intervene miraculously when their needs were brought to his attention. What do you need to bring to him today?

The Bible in a year: Genesis 1–2; Matthew 1

JANUARY 1–6

DAY 2

Consecrated life

When were you last angry? Did you feel later that you had let yourself down? My personality type means that I rarely get angry. However, as I grow as a Christian, I'm finding myself increasingly aware of times and situations in which perhaps I *ought to have been* angered by what I saw or heard – and maybe let myself (and Jesus) down by not reacting. Can you recall any situations where that might have been true for you also?

John 2:12–25

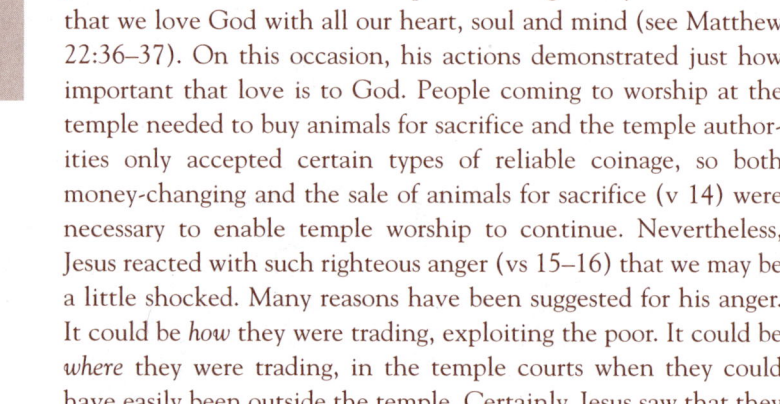

Jesus said later that the most important thing in any of our lives is that we love God with all our heart, soul and mind (see Matthew 22:36–37). On this occasion, his actions demonstrated just how important that love is to God. People coming to worship at the temple needed to buy animals for sacrifice and the temple authorities only accepted certain types of reliable coinage, so both money-changing and the sale of animals for sacrifice (v 14) were necessary to enable temple worship to continue. Nevertheless, Jesus reacted with such righteous anger (vs 15–16) that we may be a little shocked. Many reasons have been suggested for his anger. It could be *how* they were trading, exploiting the poor. It could be *where* they were trading, in the temple courts when they could have easily been outside the temple. Certainly, Jesus saw that they were polluting the worship of God and filling the Court of the Gentiles, where the nations came to seek God. Jesus always opposed sin where he saw it, but few things drew his anger as much as *preventing others* from coming to God.

God's 'temple' today is every Christian. Are there 'tables' in your life that need overturning to restore God's rightful place in your life?

The Bible in a year: Genesis 3–4; Matthew 2

JANUARY 1–6

DAY 3

New life

As a schoolboy, I had handwriting that could be described generously as 'careless' (my wife says I still do!). I'll never forget having to stay indoors one lunchtime redoing an essay because it was illegible. What was most humiliating about starting again was accepting that my first try wasn't good enough.

John 3:1–8

Nicodemus acknowledged Jesus as a man sent from God, but didn't seem to want the embarrassment of acknowledging that belief publicly by coming during daylight hours (vs 1–2). I believe that Jesus sized him up immediately as someone who found it difficult to admit that he needed anything, but who deep down was genuinely hungry for God. He was a learned teacher himself, but he came to Jesus to be taught. He was an influential man, but he came to someone with no earthly credentials. Clearly his hunger for God was battling to overcome his pride, so Jesus cut right to the heart of things (v 3). We come to Jesus not to be enlightened, enabled or educated but to receive a totally new life that marks a fresh start. That means accepting that the old life was, in some respects, deficient. Nicodemus' response (v 4) indicates that he didn't really believe such a new start to be possible. Jesus' reply asserts that not only (with God's help) is it possible, but it is also essential (vs 5–8). We don't 'evolve' into salvation: God alone can save us.

Like me, you may not be able to name the date or time when you became a Christian. More important is knowing that Jesus is changing you now. Confess any pride or self-sufficiency that makes receiving difficult, and ask him today to help you live this new life.

The Bible in a year: Genesis 5–6; Matthew 3

JANUARY 1–6

DAY 4

Eternal life

What big decisions have you made in your life so far? Big or small, ask God to help you make the right choices today.

John 3:9–21

In yesterday's reading Nicodemus struggled to grasp that entering God's kingdom requires God's intervention. This passage shows that what is required of us is trust in Jesus (vs 15–16, 18). The idea of us lifting ourselves up to heaven is ludicrous – Jesus came down from heaven to do what we couldn't. Verses 14–16 point us to the cross, where he gave himself for us. There's always a danger of being overly familiar with Jesus' death and missing its significance. Remember just who it was who died (vs 16–18). If he, of all people, 'must be lifted up' on the cross (v 14), then his love must be incredible and our need must be great.

Jesus explained it to Nicodemus using the Old Testament story of Moses' bronze serpent-statue that the Israelites looked to for healing when under God's judgement (see Numbers 21:8–9). If the statue meant the difference between life and death for the rebellious Israelites, what does Jesus' death mean for us? Just as it may be difficult to accept the need for change generally, we might find it difficult to expose particular areas of our lives to God's inspection (vs 19–21). However, verse 16 seems to imply that the choice is 'eternal life' or life that simply 'perishes'.

Do you think of following Jesus as a 'lifestyle' choice or a 'life or death' decision? The answer we give to that question has enormous implications for our sense of gratitude in worship and for the importance we place on sharing our faith. Try to reflect upon verse 16 throughout today, responding practically to whatever God shows you.

The Bible in a year: Genesis 7–8; Psalm 1–2

JANUARY 1–6

DAY 5

Life from above

'The Son is the radiance of God's glory and the exact representation of his being' (Hebrews 1:3). Most people in our society would probably describe Jesus as nothing more than an inspired teacher. What reasons would you give for believing him to be more? Before you turn to today's reading, allow those thoughts to lead you into worship.

John 3:22–36

John the Baptist and Jesus came preaching essentially the same message about the kingdom of God, so no doubt people compared their ministries just as they compare preachers today. Underlying the comments of John's disciples (v 26) might well be a sense of competition or insecurity, but John himself was clear that his role was to be the forerunner (vs 27–30). John simply couldn't fulfil Jesus' ministry because he (John) came from the earth. Like all God's servants, he only knew part of the truth and could only point the way to heaven. Jesus' coming meant that heaven was breaking into our world – he came speaking the very words and truth of heaven (vs 32–34a), full of the things of heaven (vs 34b–35), bringing the life of heaven (v 36). 'Eternal life' means 'everlasting life', but it can also be translated 'the life of eternity'. It's the life that God always wanted us to enjoy and that only Jesus can give (v 36).

The twelve disciples' turning point would come when many others stopped following Jesus. He asked them whether they would leave also. Peter answered, 'Lord, to whom shall we go? You have the words of eternal life. We believe and know that you are the Holy One of God' (6:68–69). If you really want the life of heaven, have you prayed something similar?

Meeting Jesus: John 5:39–40

The Bible in a year: Genesis 9–11; Matthew 4

JANUARY 1–6

Going deeper …

Recently, my church held a large outreach to local schools to mark the millennium. As people came into the exhibition, the first thing they saw was almost one hundred images of Jesus, drawn from classical and contemporary art, as well as from around the world. It was fascinating to note the variety of ways in which people had painted Jesus, often with the artists' own racial features. We had Jesus as an African bushman, as Navajo Indian, plus plenty of 'Scandinavian' blue-eyed, fair-haired images. Very few pictures featured the face of a first-century Jewish male, perhaps because each artist instinctively painted Jesus as 'like me' – knowing that Jesus is 'my Saviour' for each of us who trusts in him. There was one picture in our exhibition however that many people, both Christians and non-Christians, found difficult. Called 'The Angry Christ', it showed Jesus' face during the overturning of the tables in the temple. The painting comes from the Philippines during a time of particular oppression and injustice. For the artist, a 'Jesus' who couldn't become angry wasn't good news.

We've seen lots of images of Jesus in these chapters of John. What struck you most? His generosity and grace at the wedding; his jealousy for that special place where people could meet with God? His insistence on a new start for us all? His unbounded love and compassion that makes new life possible? Or his unique ability to give us that life? It's important that, reading the Gospels, we let them challenge and shape our own understanding and image of Jesus. Visualise Jesus, as you imagine him. Then ask yourself, 'Could this Jesus laugh at a wedding? Could he wield a whip? Would he be good news for all the world?'

Signs and wonders

Conclusion

Although our readings this week only include the very first of the seven miracles of Jesus that John chose to highlight, these events set the pattern for the rest of John's Gospel. Jesus, 'thus revealed his glory, and his disciples put their faith in him' (2:11). It's easy for us to envy the disciples for their great privilege in seeing such signs and wonders. We probably all think that if only we could see such mighty works in our church or town then our faith would be so much stronger and many non-believers would be drawn in wonder to Jesus. That could easily happen, but it's clear from the Gospels that merely seeing miracles doesn't necessarily lead to faith.

The crowds who witnessed Jesus performing wonderful works of mercy and grace often went away to continue their lives in much the same way as before. It's the same today – I have prayed for many people who have experienced something undeniably supernatural (through those prayer-times) yet have failed to follow Jesus in response. Signs and wonders can lead people to life-changing belief (10:38); they can greatly aid the preaching of the gospel (see Romans 15:18–9); but they need to be received by open hearts (12:37–40).

The Bible in a year: Genesis 12–15; Psalm 3–4; Matthew 5

JANUARY 7–13

Friendship

Romans 15; Acts 4, 9, 11, 15, 19, 27; 2 Samuel 15–20

Can you imagine what it would be like if anybody who wanted to learn to drive was free to take a car onto the road, mess around with the controls and learn to drive by trial and error (without a learner's licence). Car accidents are a great danger to life and limb, so to prevent them as far as possible, aspiring motorists have to be taught to drive and pass a test before being let loose on the road.

The wreckages of broken friendships can be just as devastating to our well-being as those of crashed cars. We need friends, really *close friends*, 'a friend that sticks closer than a brother' (Proverbs 18:24). When I was starting out in the ministry, an old minister told me, 'Son, the ministry is a lonely road!' I suppose he meant to warn me that there would be few people to confide in. But my experience is that I need friends. As a matter of fact, I have many friends.

Some quote the idiom, 'Familiarity breeds contempt,' and give this as the reason for not having friends and trusting others. Dale Carnegie once said, 'You can make more friends in two months by becoming genuinely interested in other people, than you can in two years by trying to get others interested in you.' The Bible has much to say concerning friendship. 'A friend loves at all times' (Proverbs 17:17). 'Wounds from a friend can be trusted' (Proverbs 27:6). And Jesus told his disciples, 'You are my *friends* …' Come with me on a journey this week to discover more of what the Scriptures have to say.

Alfie Fabe is the Founder and Director of Kingdom Ministries International. After twenty-five years of pastoring, he now has an international ministry nurturing pastors.

JANUARY 7–13

DAY 1

Being a good friend

The early church exploded with growth because the Christians stayed together in fellowship. They were united because they knew the concept of friendship (see Acts 1:14; 2:1; 4:32).

Romans 15:1–13

If we are to develop friendships, we need to practice three things. Firstly, we need to *tolerate* one another (v 1). Friends have different temperaments, hence the tendency to irritate one another. In Acts 9:26–27 the disciples would at first not accept Paul, but Barnabas introduced him and vouched for his conversion. They eventually accepted him as genuine. If we cannot tolerate one another, how can we win the world?

Secondly, we need to *please* one another (v 2). The Amplified Bible says: 'Let each one of us make it a practice to please his neighbour for *his good* and for his true welfare, to edify him' (to build him up spiritually). How then can I please my friends? By building them up spiritually and encouraging them with the Scriptures (v 4).

Thirdly, we need to *accept* one another (v 7). The Amplified Bible says, 'Welcome and receive one another.' The latter part of verse 7 tells us how to do this, 'as Christ accepted you' (see also Philippians 2:3–5). We should accept each other despite our weaknesses and faults so that we can refine each other.

God is glorified when we accept each other (v 7b). Pray for someone you find difficult to accept, then ask God to grant you the strength to tolerate, please and accept him/her. Experience God's joy and peace (v 13) as you walk in his love.

The Bible in a year: Genesis 16–17; Matthew 6

JANUARY 7–13

DAY 2

Profile of a good friend

Paul said that Priscilla and Aquila risked their lives for him (Romans 16:3–4). He said that Onesiphorous was not ashamed of his chains (2 Timothy 1:16–17). As our profile of a good friend I have chosen Barnabas. We will look at various incidents in his life.

Acts 4:36–37, 9:26–27, 11:19–24, 15:36–41

The first thing we see in Barnabas' life is *generosity* (4:37). He sold his property and gave the money to his friends (the other believers). Good was not merely something he did, it was something he was. Good had got a hold of him. We should live to give, not to get. Become a 'load lifter' like Barnabas.

A good friend is also *forgiving*. If there had not been a Barnabas, there might not have been a Paul! He had the capacity to accept and forgive when the other believers could not (9:26). A good friend is also a *bridge builder*, just as Barnabas was between Saul and the apostles (v 27). When Barnabas arrived in Antioch he encouraged them in the faith (11:23). A good friend is an e*ncourager*. Throughout the book of Acts we notice that it was Barnabas who encouraged the believers. So much so that he earned the nickname, Son of Encouragement – Barnabas (4:36). In Acts 15:36–41 we encounter him as a 'failure fixer'. Whereas Paul rejected Mark (v 38), Barnabas saw potential in him, encouraged him and took Mark with him on his next missionary journey (v 39).

Why not write a letter of encouragement to a friend today, or pick up the telephone and encourage a friend through Scripture.

The Bible in a year: Genesis 18–19; Matthew 7

JANUARY 7–13

DAY 3

True friends will …

In 1 Chronicles 27:25–33 we have a list of David's trusted people, but only Hushai was referred to as the *king's friend* (v 33). Are you blessed with someone like him?

2 Samuel 15:32–37, 16:15–19, 17:1–16

In chapter 15 we see that *friends will serve you*. Without hesitation Hushai set off to go 'under cover' for David in Absalom's camp (v 37). Good friends will work with you to fulfil God's purpose for your life. 'Two are better than one because they have a good return for their work' (Ecclesiastes 4:9).

Friends will take risks for you (16:15–19). Hushai was right in Jerusalem masquerading as an Absalom fan. The situation was extremely dangerous, but he was prepared to work with David to thwart the conspiracy. A genuine friend will cover your back when danger lurks.

Friends will put you first (16:15–22). Hushai risked his reputation to protect David. He was willing to be regarded as a traitor to save David (v 17). Sadly, there are too many Absaloms and too few Hushais in the body of Christ!

Friends will protect you (17:1–16). Hushai purposely gave Absalom bad advice to protect David (vs 7–13), and then smuggled out an urgent message to warn him of danger (v 16). A friend's commitment is not governed by convenience.

'Though one may be overpowered, two can defend themselves. A cord of three strands is not quickly broken' (Ecclesiastes 4:12). How deep are your friendships? Have you shown appreciation for sacrificial friendship?

The Bible in a year: Genesis 20–21; Matthew 8

JANUARY 7–13

DAY 4

Three kinds of friends

The key factor in the kingdom of God is *relationships*. Jesus said, 'The kingdom of God is within you' (Luke 17:21). In other words, 'Demonstrate it!'

Acts 19:28–41; 27:1–2, 13–18

Today we will look at three kinds of friends. Firstly, *friends who cleave*. Aristarchus was such a friend. In Acts 19 Demetrius, the silversmith, caused problems for Paul by starting a mass protest (vs 28–29) against his preaching. Aristarchus stood by Paul in this time of danger. We need to assign top priority to our relationships.

In Acts 27 Aristarchus survived a storm with Paul (vs 42–44). As friends we need to survive the storms like financial crises and sickness together. We need 'a friend who sticks closer than a brother' (Proverbs 18:24). At one stage Aristarchus was even in jail with Paul (Colossians 4:10–11). True friendship means suffering with our friends.

Secondly, there are *friends who intercede*. According to Colossians 4:12, Epaphras interceded spontaneously ('he is *always* …'); he interceded seriously ('he is always *wrestling* …'); he interceded specifically ('for *you*'). We need friends who will make praying for us a priority.

Thirdly, there are *friends who leave*. Demas was a fellow worker with Paul in Rome, and part of the missionary team (Colossians 4:14), but in 2 Timothy 4:10 we read that he gave up his friendship – he deserted Paul.

What kind of friend are you? Do you cleave and intercede, or leave when the pressure is on?

The Bible in a year: Genesis 22–23; Psalms 5–6

JANUARY 7–13

DAY 5

Demonstrating friendship

David and Jonathan demonstrated a remarkable friendship from which we can learn many lessons. May we learn to 'demonstrate friendships' as a way of life.

1 Samuel 18:1–4; 19:1–2; 20:12–17, 30–34

The first lesson we learn from the relationship between David and Jonathan is to accept our friends in the way God accepts them. Jonathan loved David as he loved himself (18:3). He loved him warts and all! Romans 15:7 says: 'Accept one another just as Christ accepted you.' We need to accept one another with our faults and flaws.

Secondly, we need to 'cover our friends without covering up'. Saul told his son Jonathan to kill David (19:1), but Jonathan warned David (v 2) and defended him (vs 4–5). We are required to cover (protect) our friends without excusing their weaknesses.

Thirdly, in demonstrating friendship, we should *put our interests on the line for our friends*. In chapter 20 Jonathan risked his life (v 33) through his friendship with David. Remarkably, he was prepared for David to accede to the throne that was rightfully his (23:17); something his father could not stomach (20:31). David and Jonathan made a covenant with each other (20:12–17), a binding covenant that was witnessed by the Lord (v 42), and was honoured by David even after Jonathan's death.

'Jonathan went to David … and helped him to find strength in God' (23:16). Friendship is more than being friendly to others, it is a demonstration of love, God's love, to another. Let's demonstrate love today.

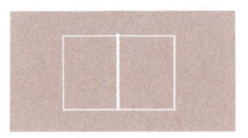

A covenant friend: 2 Samuel 9:1–13
Preserving our friendships: 2 Chronicles 13:4–10

The Bible in a year: Genesis 24–25; Matthew 9

JANUARY 7–13

Going deeper …

We were made for fellowship with God and one another. The early Christians devoted themselves to fellowship (Acts 2:42). 'Koinonia' (fellowship) was a term used in the legal contracts of marriages in those days. I believe Christian fellowship, like marriage, is designed to meet the deepest needs and desires of our hearts. It is here that we can find help. Friendship is all about carrying each other's burdens (Galatians 6:2). What does this involve?

- When we have failed as friends, we need to be forgiven.
- When we have stumbled, we need to be supported.
- When we have been hurt by others, we need healing words from our friends.
- When we have lost our way, our friends need to give direction.
- When we have been rejected by others, we need to be accepted by our friends.
- When we have been hated, we need to be loved.

Are you this sort of friend? We need to support each other emotionally as well as materially and physically. In an age in which loneliness is one of our greatest sicknesses, we need to reach out sacrificially to our friends.

Choose your friends well

Conclusion

The topic that we've looked at this week is not often mentioned or preached on. This could be because true friendship requires commitment to others. The Old Testament speaks of being good neighbours or companions. In the New Testament the Greek word for friendship is 'philos', suggesting a more affectionate relationship.

The Bible abounds with concrete examples of friendships. Notable among these is Abraham's relationship with God that was so intimate that he was called 'the friend of God' (James 2:23). Then there was Moses, 'The Lord would speak to Moses face to face, as a man speaks with his friend' (Exodus 33:11). How wonderful to have this sort of relationship with God! On a human level, Ruth's friendship with Naomi is a lesson in devotion (Ruth 1:16–18). Jesus and his disciples illustrate the way a master – servant relationship develops into friendship (John 15:14–15).

We turn to classical literature for a superb example of trust and devotion. Plutarch records the story of Damon and Pythias during the rule of Dionysius. Pythias had been condemned to death, but desired to see his family before he died. Damon offered himself as a substitute in case he did not return in time for the execution. When he returned in time, both were released by Dionysius who asked to be let into the secret of such great friendship.

We are blessed indeed if we enjoy friendships like that between Pythias and Damon. Jesus said, 'Greater love has no man than this, that he lay down his life for his friends' (John 15:13). Are you that sort of friend? Jesus himself set us the example!

The Bible in a year: Genesis 26–29; Psalm 7–8; Matthew 10

JANUARY 14–20

Lord, my faith is wobbly

Genesis 12–16

In the next two weeks we will follow the story of Abraham and his family as we read Genesis 12 to 22. Who was Abraham? He was a cultured, civilised man who lived 4 000 years ago in Ur of Chaldees. In those days Ur was a wealthy trading city with a population of a quarter of a million. A fifty-metre-high ziggurat served as a temple to the moon god. A wealthy man, Abraham would have lived in comfort in this pagan city.

Why did God choose Abraham to be the father of the Jewish nation? Did God choose him because he was cultured or rich? Was Abraham superhuman with a rock-like faith? Do we need such faith to be the seed of Abraham?

We will find that Abraham was far from superhuman. We will see ourselves in many of his frailties. He was not chosen for his riches. He carried them lightly and left them behind in Ur. He seemed, however, to have the knack of getting rich again quickly. He was not chosen for his culture. He left Ur, and later Haran, depending on his cattle to support him. His faith in the beginning was erratic: sometimes strong and sometimes wobbly. When crises came, fear overcame him.

Why then did God choose him? I believe it was because he was humble; he listened to God and was teachable. He made mistakes and repeated some of them, but as he grew closer to God, his faith grew and gave him the victory.

As we trace the steps of Abraham, may we too draw closer to God and grow in faith.

Fiona Watson retired in 1997 after being headmistress of Sans Souci Girls' High School in Cape Town for nineteen years. She is on the Pastorate of St John's Anglican Church, Wynberg.

JANUARY 14–20

DAY 1

Faith or fear?

Do you find it easy to trust God in some circumstances, but are crippled with fear in others?

Genesis 12:1–20

God told Abram to leave his country, people and father's wealthy household and go to the land which he would show him (v 1). It demanded great faith from Abram to leave the comfortable security of the known for the unknown, especially as he was already seventy-five years old.

This security, however, was man-made. God now offered him a spiritual security with blessings which reach even us. See Galatians 3:6–9. Abram, a childless man, would become the father of a great nation (vs 2–3).

Abram, in faith, left Haran (v 4). Are you where God wants you to be? Are you prepared to let go of the security you have built up for yourself and trust God even if he leads you into new paths? En route, Abram called on the name of the Lord (v 8) and God encouraged him (v 7).

Then trouble struck. A famine hit Canaan (v 10) and Abram continued to Egypt where his faith wobbled and he feared for his life. He took his eyes off God and looked in fear at Pharaoh. He looked at his beautiful wife, Sarah, and used her to speak and live a lie to ensure his safety (vs 10–13).

Abram might have taken his eyes off God and sinned but God did not take his eyes off Abram. He used Pharaoh, a pagan, to admonish him and send him back to where he should have been (v 20).

Ask God to help you to look at difficult situations through eyes of faith, not fear.

The Bible in a year: Genesis 30–31; Matthew 11

JANUARY 14–20

DAY 2

How do I choose?

When you choose a new home, you are advised to choose: neighbourhood … neighbourhood … neighbourhood.

Genesis 13:1–18

Pharaoh's generosity had enabled Abram to leave Egypt a rich man (12:16–20).

He and Lot returned to Bethel, where he built an altar to God and called on his name (12:8). Abram had been told to leave his father's household, which should have included Lot. Perhaps Lot had insisted on accompanying Abram, and Abram had given in to him. Abram would rue the day, as Lot caused him endless headaches.

At Bethel there was insufficient grazing for both Abram's and Lot's cattle, which led to clashes between their herdsmen (vs 6–7). The parting of the ways was at hand. Abram magnanimously gave Lot first choice of the land around them (vs 8–9). How did Lot go about making a choice (vs 10–11)? He did not ask God's will. He did not consider what would be best for his uncle Abram, his mentor and protector. He thought only of grabbing what seemed best for himself. He saw the fertile land but ignored Sodom, a city of great wickedness, nearby (v 13). He chose short-term gain but ignored long-term consequences. Abram was left with far less fertile land, but it was blessed by God, and he was promised innumerable descendants to inhabit it (vs 14–17).

Things seen through our eyes are not always what they seem to be. Pray that the Lord will give you spiritual insight to know *his* choice.

The Bible in a year: Genesis 32–33; Matthew 12

JANUARY 14–20

DAY 3

Giving and receiving

Whom do you love? What do you enjoy giving them? If you are offered something, do you consider the source of the gift and the motive of the donor?

Genesis 14:11–24

Verses 1–13 of this chapter describe how four city-state kings from Mesopotamia waged battle against five city-state Dead Sea kings. They defeated them, including the king of Sodom, and carried away the people and their possessions. Lot was among the captives.

Blood is thicker than water. Abram still loved Lot, in spite of his selfishness and foolishness, and called together his 'army' of 318 trained men (v 14). Abram defeated the kings despite their superior army (v 15). He rescued Lot, the men and women, and recovered their possessions (v 16). What cost was Abram prepared to pay for Lot?

Melchizedek, king of Jerusalem, came to meet Abram (vs 18–20). Melchizedek, both king and priest, foreshadowed Jesus, also King and Priest. Like Jesus, he is a priest forever (see Hebrews 7:15–17). He came with a double blessing for Abram (vs 19–20) and a reminder that it was God who gave him the military victory. Abram responded with a love gift to God.

The grateful king of Sodom wanted his people back, but offered Abram the possessions he had recovered. Why do you think Abram declined the offer (v 23)? Has Matthew 4:8–10 any relevance?

Do you love God? How much of yourself do you give him? How many of your possessions do you offer him?

The Bible in a year: Genesis 34–36; Matthew 13

JANUARY 14–20

DAY 4

Fears and questions answered

Do you feel free to share your doubts and questionings with God, or only general, non-personal matters?

Genesis 15:1–21

God knew that Abram still had fear and questions. 'Don't be afraid,' he reassured Abram. 'I will protect you; I will give you a great reward' (v 1). So Abram, the military hero, felt free to share his anxiety, 'How can I gain the reward of the promised land without offspring? My servant-son is my only heir' (vs 2–3).

God responded with specific assurances: 'You will have a blood son. Your descendants will be as numerous as the stars' (vs 4–5). How patient God is in reassuring us when we share our wobbly faith with him.

Abram's next question concerned the promised land. 'How can I know that it will be mine?' (v 8). Don't we sometimes want proof that our prayers will be answered? To strengthen Abram's faith, God reminded him of a promise already fulfilled (v 7). He also told Abram to prepare a sacrifice (v 9). The cutting of the animals (v 10) involved shedding of blood, while the fire passing between them (v 17) represented God's presence. We are reminded of Jesus' blood, the basis of God's covenant with us.

Bad news came with dreadful darkness while Abram slept. The promise would be fulfilled, but only after 400 years of slavery in Egypt (vs 13–14), although Abram himself would die at a ripe old age in the promised land (v 15).

Do you have pressing anxieties and questions? Bring them to the Lord. Be prepared for his perfect timing for his perfect answer.

The Bible in a year: Genesis 37–38; Psalm 9

JANUARY 14–20

DAY 5

Waiting for God

Is there anyone important to you who tempts you to lose your total trust in God by compromising?

Genesis 16:1–15

Sarai, Abram's wife, did not share his faith that she would have a child (15:6, 16:2a). Accepting only the humanly possible, she suggested a culturally acceptable solution. He could have a child by her maidservant, Hagar (v 2).

Abram had believed, but years had passed and still Sarai had not fallen pregnant. So he agreed to Sarai's suggestion (vs 2–4). Did he decide to help God by using a compromise? Have you ever had to wait a long time for the fulfilment of a prophecy given to you? Were you tempted to take matters into your own hands? There is a difference between co-operating with God and endeavouring to take over from him.

This passage describes the consequences of the compromise. The pregnant Hagar mocked Sarai (v 4). Sarai, rather unfairly, blamed Abram (v 5). Abram passed the buck back to Sarai, who ill-treated Hagar till she fled (vs 6–7). Seeing Hagar's misery, God mercifully intervened in this family crisis. Hagar must return to Sarai, and she is promised that she will have numerous descendants (vs 7–10).

There would, however, be evidence of the sins of the parents being visited on the children. Ishmael would be fiercely independent (as a wild donkey) and live in hostility with his yet to be born half-brother, as would his descendants, the Arabs, with the Jews (vs 11–12). The problem is still with us today! Compromise with God's ways always leads to human suffering.

Resolve to stand firm against temptations to manipulate God's plans for you.

Occupation 400 years later: Joshua 1:1–9
Wait patiently for him: Psalm 37:1–11

The Bible in a year: Genesis 39–40; Matthew 14

Going deeper ...

The Lord God said: 'It is not good for man to be alone. I will make a helper suitable for him' (Genesis 2:18). We are not made to be hermits. God has put us in families with a need to form deep, meaningful relationships. These can be loving and supportive or destructive. Abram's relationships were not perfect. Nor are ours. Like us, he had to learn that good relationships stem from a trusting relationship with God.

Relationships are two-way. Abram was afraid to reveal too much of himself to God, although God sees everything (16:13). God spoke to him and he obeyed, although not always perfectly. As he learned to open himself to God with his fears and questions, his relationship with God took a step forward (15).

People are not always easy, but as we share with God, he leads us into better relationships with those around us. Love isn't a possession. Abram's father had to let him go when God called him (12:1). As children mature, parents have to let them go. Abram's nephew, Lot, chose to accompany him. He was not an easy young man – selfish, self-willed, unwise and not always lovable. Abram, however, never failed in his love. Having given him first choice of the land, he let him go, but was ready to pick up the pieces when he failed (14:13–16). Abram's wife, Sarai, did not support him in his faith and led to his undoing with Hagar.

Are you in close relationship with God? Are your relationships loving and supportive? Do you build up others' faith, or allow their doubts to pull you down?

A firmer faith

In these chapters we have gained insight into the strengths and weaknesses of Abram, and have also shared his steps of faith. What have we learned?

We need to keep our eyes on God, to seek his face. When life is straightforward we think we can cope on our own. When crises arise, however, it is so easy to give way to fear and panic. We seek ways of escaping a fearful situation no matter what it takes. But if we are where God wants us to be, he will give us the courage, wisdom and strength we need, provided we face it with him. We saw Abram's failure in Egypt but his military success in Canaan.

God is a holy God but he is not remote. We need to share our every thought with him, even doubts and questions about what is happening to us. We need also to listen to him. A relationship can only grow if there is open communication. Abram's sharing of his questions and fears with God was a milestone in his walk with him.

We also need loving human relationships. Is our love as real as Abram's for Lot? We need to be aware of how relationships with family and friends can influence us. We dare not let their doubts weaken our faith. God blessed Abram and he gave a tenth of everything to God's representative, the priest Melchizedek. Have you experienced God's blessings? Are you giving to God's work?

The Bible in a year: Genesis 41–44; Matthew 15

JANUARY 21–27

Times of testing

Genesis 17–22

Think back to tests and examinations you have written. Wasn't it a wonderful feeling to achieve good results? All the hard studying was worthwhile. Have you failed an examination? Did you blame the teacher or did you pick yourself up and keep trying until you succeeded? Did you ask God to give you marks or did you ask him to help you do justice to the work you had done?

Life is full of tests, not just school, college, professional examinations or driving licence tests. Friends and family can test our faith. Knowingly or unknowingly they can challenge our beliefs, tempt us to compromise with God or try our patience. Non-Christians can tempt us into sin or can show us up by kindness and generosity which dwarfs our own.

God allows us to be tested, but not beyond what we are able to withstand (1 Corinthians 10:13). As we face and succeed in smaller tests, we become stronger and able to face more difficult ones. Strength of faith and character cannot come without testing.

As we continue with Abraham we will see that he too was tested. He passed a test in his love for Lot. Sarai, unknowingly, tempted him to compromise. He failed. With Abimelech he failed a test for the second time, but God helped him to get up again.

The graduation examination God put him through was a test most of us would fail. Incredibly God used a pagan practice of the Canaanites, child sacrifice. How did Abraham do? This week will reveal Abraham's response.

Fiona Watson retired in 1997 after being headmistress of Sans Souci Girls' High School in Cape Town for nineteen years. She is on the Pastorate of St John's Anglican Church, Wynberg.

JANUARY 21–27

DAY 1

Confirmation, covenant, circumcision

Have you ever broken a promise? Have others let you down? Does God break his covenant?

Genesis 17:1–21; 18:1, 10–14

Abram was ninety-nine years old and still had no son, other than Ishmael. But God had not forgotten him: he came and reconfirmed his covenant with Abram (17:1–2). A covenant is always initiated by God (v 2): he is the giver and man the recipient.

God's covenant promise to Abram was the fatherhood of many nations (v 5), with Canaan as their promised land (v 8). His name would in future be Abraham, 'father of many'. The outward sign of the covenant would be circumcision (17:9–14). Abraham signified his eager acceptance of God's covenant by getting the job done immediately (v 26). Abraham collapsed on the ground laughing when he heard that his ninety-year-old wife would bear a son (v 17). What do you think the tone of his laughter was? Was it similar to the way Sarah (her new name) laughed when she heard the same news (18:10–15)? She seemed to wonder whether the angelic visitors were so heavenly minded that they were ignorant of the facts of life!

Through Jesus, God has made a new covenant with us, gentile as well as Jew. He is our God and we his people (1 Peter 2:9), if we meet his condition – not circumcision or good works, but faith in Jesus.

'Is anything too hard for the Lord'? (18:14). How would you have responded if you were Abraham or Sarah?

The Bible in a year: Genesis 45–46; Matthew 16

JANUARY 21–27

DAY 2

Family problems

Do you plead with God for family members who do not know him?

Genesis 18:20–33; 19:15–29

One of the visitors told Abraham how the public outcry against Sodom and Gomorrah's sin had reached God's ears. He was about to act. Do you just watch passively as evil is perpetrated around us, or cry out to God and seek his will for action?

Abraham pleaded with God to spare Sodom if there were fifty righteous inhabitants, and then boldly decreased the number step by step to ten. He pleaded for God's justice towards the innocent righteous. Aware that he was talking to God Almighty, Judge of the world, he begged, 'May the Lord not be angry'. Each time the Lord graciously promised to grant his request (vs 23–32). Abraham did not mention Lot, but he was obviously uppermost in his mind.

The two angels persuaded Lot, his wife and two daughters to flee Sodom and led them out, leaving their disbelieving husbands behind (19:14). They were told not to look back, but Lot's wife did, and the volcanic eruptions accompanying the destruction of Sodom killed her as she inhaled the air and was covered with ash (19:26). In following God we need to look forward in faith and obedience, not backward to life's old pleasures. Note how the Lord understood Abraham's unspoken prayer for Lot. He answered his prayer, but not in the way he had expected. God hears even our unspoken prayers.

Recognising God's holiness, power, justice and mercy, pray for the protection of your loved ones from the evil around us. Look for God's answers in unexpected ways.

The Bible in a year: Genesis 47–48; Matthew 17

JANUARY 21–27

DAY 3

Not again!

How often have you strongly resolved never to repeat a particular action only to find yourself sinning yet again?

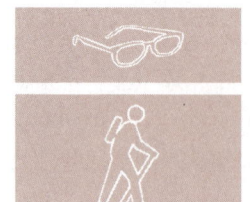

Genesis 20:1–17; 21:1–7

Did Abraham, walking with God and growing in faith, go back to square one when he lied about Sarah yet again (20:2)? This lie to Abimelech was one of deceit, for Sarah was indeed his half-sister (20:12). Do we make the excuse that it is only a 'white lie'?

Abraham again acted out of fear (20:11), and did not think of the consequences. What if Sarah had fallen pregnant by Abimelech when God had promised that she would bear Abraham's son within a year (18:10)? Often our lies, intended to get us out of trouble, escalate and later bring us bigger problems.

Without God, the result could have been disastrous. He kept Abimelech from sinning against Sarah (20:6) by revealing in a dream that she was married (20:3). God provided inner healing for all involved. He attributed innocence to Abimelech (20:6). He recognised Abraham's stature as a prophet (20:7) and provided public proof of it when Abraham's prayer for Abimelech brought physical healing to the whole family (20:17–18). Abimelech vindicated Sarah (20:16), rebuked Abraham (20:9–10) and actively forgave him (20:14–15). God's covenant remained intact. Sarah fell pregnant and gave birth to Isaac (21:1–3). 'Isaac' means 'he laughs'. At last Sarah could laugh with joy. A wife, who had frequently sacrificed herself in mind-boggling ways for her husband, now took a giant step forward in faith (21:6–7).

Confess those repeated sins that continually get you down. Trust God for forgiveness and healing.

The Bible in a year: Genesis 49–50; Matthew 18

JANUARY 21–27

DAY 4

Weeping, wells and water

Can tears be a prayer to God?

Genesis 21:8–33

Abraham was father of Ishmael by Hagar, and of Isaac by Sarah. He loved both sons and was torn between his firstborn son and the long-promised son of the covenant. Worse, their mothers did not get on (16:4) and Ishmael taunted Isaac at his weaning feast (vs 8–9). Things came to a head and Sarah insisted that Abraham send Hagar and Ishmael away. There seemed to be no solution to the problem.

God came to the rescue. His plans for them would still be fulfilled. Again he reassured Abraham that Isaac was the son of the covenant, but he would form a nation from Ishmael (vs 12–13). 'Listen to Sarah,' advised God (v 12). 'Send them away,' demanded Sarah (v 10). And Abraham reluctantly drove them into the desert.

God answered their physical needs with a well (v 19), and their deeper spiritual need with the reassurance that Ishmael would be the father of a great nation (v 18). His answer was ongoing, 'God was with the boy as he grew up' (v 20).

Another well brought Abraham and King Abimelech together again. Abimelech realised by then that God would always be involved in Abraham's dealings, 'God is with you in everything you do,' he admitted to Abraham (v 22). He knew that an oath before God was binding (v 23). So God was witness to the treaty whereby Abraham established his right to the well he had dug (vs 27–31).

Entrust yourself, your physical and spiritual needs to God. It's okay to cry. God hears.

The Bible in a year: Exodus 1–2; Psalm 11–12

JANUARY 21–27

DAY 5

Surely not, God

God so loved the world that he gave his only son. Abraham so loved God that …

Genesis 22:1–19

Abraham would have known how the Canaanites offered child sacrifices to Molech. God's ultimate test for him was, 'Offer Isaac as a sacrifice to me. Prove that your devotion to me is greater than that of the Canaanites to Molech.'

Abraham, with Isaac, started off for Moriah. He must have been perplexed and distraught. He and Sarah loved Isaac, their son promised twenty-five years earlier. Had God given him only to take him away? How could he father a nation if Isaac died? Surely God would not break his covenant! But Abraham loved and trusted God.

While they walked, thirty-year-old Isaac, carrying the wood, asked the dreaded question, 'We have the wood, but where's the lamb?' (v 7). In faith, Abraham responded, 'God himself will provide' (v 8). God provided, not a lamb, but a ram (v 13), and Abraham called the site 'The Lord will provide' (v 14). God also provided when Jesus carried his wooden cross in Jerusalem and became the sacrificial lamb of God.

Abraham passed this test of trust and obedience with flying colours. God also taught him that the sacrifice of sons was not his will. He blessed Abraham (v 17) and promised that all nations, including ours, would be blessed through his descendants (v 18).

God asked no more of Abraham than he did of himself when he gave his son to die for us. Can you trust God even when you cannot understand his plan for you? He will not ask anything of you which goes against his holy and loving will.

Jesus, the Lamb of God: Matthew 27:32–46
Help my unbelief: Mark 9:14–29

The Bible in a year: Exodus 3–4; Matthew 19

Going deeper …

God never breaks the covenants he makes with man, but man can break them by refusing to accept them. God's covenant blessings to Abraham were the promises of a multitude of descendants, Canaan as their land, and God as their God. The covenant was sealed with the blood of an animal sacrifice (15:9–10). The obligation for acceptance was the circumcision of all male babies (17:12–13). God's later covenant with Israel, through Moses, fulfilled these promises. The covenant blessings were: 'You will be my own people … my chosen people … a holy nation' (Exodus 19:5–6).

God's new, eternal covenant with his people includes us. We 'are a chosen people, a royal priesthood, a holy nation, a people belonging to God', with the obligation to 'declare the praises of him who called you out of darkness into his wonderful light' (1 Peter 2:9). The covenant was sealed with the blood of Jesus who, at the last supper, offered his disciples the cup, saying: 'This is my blood of the covenant which is poured out for the forgiveness of sins' (Matthew 26:27). God's covenant blessing continues to include the broader 'seed of Abraham'. For gentiles the obligation of physical circumcision has fallen away (1 Corinthians 7:18–19). God requires circumcision of the heart (Romans 2:29), symbolised by baptism – a dying to sin and rising to new life. Let us accept with joy God's new covenant, and keep his covenant by walking with him in faith and obedience.

Faith triumphant

Conclusion

We have finished the story of Abraham and his triumph of faith. Like Abraham, we do not have to drum up faith from our own resources but to recognise God's absolute faithfulness and take him at his word. Abraham's faith suffered glitches. He tried to help God by providing a son through Hagar. He had to learn that for God nothing is impossible.

He twice failed God through deception, firstly of Pharaoh and then Abimelech. His sin was not so much one of commission (as Sarah was his half-sister) but of omission. He kept quiet about her being his wife. He was not, facing an enemy against whom he needed to use deceit. God had promised him descendants. Therefore his life could not be in danger. He acted out of fear rather than faith. All of us are tempted to lie to get out of a tight corner. Are you prepared to trust God and tell the truth whatever the cost? God set Abraham on his feet each time. We have a merciful God who is willing to forgive us – even when we repeat a failure – and help us get started again.

In life we all make mistakes and get things wrong. A person who has made no mistakes is either Jesus or one who has done absolutely nothing, which in itself is a mistake! Let us not fear failure but step out in faith using our inborn talents and the gifts that the Holy Spirit has given us. We can and must learn from our mistakes.

The Bible in a year: Exodus 5–8; Psalm 13–14; Matthew 19–20

JANUARY 28– FEBRUARY 3

Power for all the people

Acts 1–2

Some months ago, early on a Sunday morning, I stood in the deserted Stellenbosch market square, waiting for the street people to emerge from their cardboard carton beds for our open-air worship service. Quietly enjoying the light beginning to play with the shade on the brick paving and white walls, I became aware of an approaching drumbeat. Soon a triumphal procession came into view. The leader carried a wooden cross in one hand, and operated a rattle with the other. The second in line had a huge bass drum strapped to his back. The third, a woman, walked behind him, banging out the rhythm to which they marched and sang. As they passed I caught their refrain: 'Jesus is my lover, Jesus is my lover …'

To Western ears schooled in the Queen's English, and trained from an early age to sing 'Jesus loves me this I know …' this little interlude demanded some major processing! The connotation of the words sung by these three Christians was, to me, very different to the experience they were expressing. The incident made me reflect on how we understand some of the events in the Bible, and the extent to which we accurately get in touch with the New Testament writers' understanding of Jesus Christ's earthly life.

The first two chapters of the Acts of the Apostles (some have suggested the Acts of the Holy Spirit would be more appropriate) give us the opportunity of exploring some of these issues. If we do this prayerfully we will emerge with a fresh understanding of what God is saying to us in the twenty-first century through these ancient writings.

David Evans is a clinical psychologist who is currently studying theology at the kweekskool in Stellenbosch. He is an elder at the Stellenbosch United Church, and is an accomplished potter.

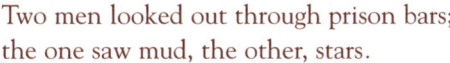

DAY 1

Two scrolls – one book

Two men looked out through prison bars;
the one saw mud, the other, stars.

Acts 1:1–11

Scholars have pointed out that Luke's Gospel and Acts, being the two longest compilations of the New Testament, would have fitted neatly onto thirty-five feet and thirty-two feet respectively of a standard papyrus roll, which had a forty-foot maximum length. On one level these constraints could explain Luke's statement in verse 1: 'I wrote about all that Jesus *began* to do and to teach.' But we should look deeper.

The passage goes on to contrast two kingdoms: the kingdom of God that Jesus had come to establish (v 3), and the kingdom of Israel with which the disciples were preoccupied (v 6). God's new kingdom was in its infancy; Jesus' work had just begun; and Acts records how it rapidly spread throughout the known world.

Today's passage ends with the disciples 'gazing upward toward heaven' (v 10, NRSV). Not a bad posture to assume, especially when we recall the author of Hebrews telling us to 'fix our eyes on Jesus' (Hebrews 12:2). But listen to God's two unnamed messengers: 'This same Jesus, who has been taken up from you into heaven, will come back in the same way you have seen him go into heaven' (v 11). The disciples were soon to discover that Jesus was still with them through his Spirit (v 8). Could *we* be looking for Jesus in the wrong place?

Ask God to help you to experience his presence in your mundane, everyday world, and to see Jesus in those around you today.

The Bible in a year: Exodus 9–10; Matthew 21

JANUARY 28–FEBRUARY 3

DAY 2

Waiting obediently

The Gospel accounts leave us in no doubt that the crucifixion had a shattering and scattering effect on Jesus' followers. The downcast apostles were found by the risen Christ in twos and threes in various places. Jesus instructed them to regroup in Jerusalem … and wait.

Acts 1:12–26

Luke, the physician, makes an excellent chronicler – he is punctilious about detail. It is hard to imagine, considering his vocational training and the shortage and cost of 'paper', that he would have reported any unnecessary or irrelevant detail. Why then, 'a Sabbath day's walk' (v 12), and the room 'upstairs' (v 13) where the eleven apostles met with the other believers? Space prevents us from pursuing these fascinating questions. We will confine ourselves to the overarching theme in the passage: the role of faithful obedience in the formation of the church.

In the Old Testament the word frequently translated as 'wait' (for or upon the Lord) implies expectancy, not passivity. The scattered followers of Jesus were not passive: they heeded his call to regroup, and they met together to pray! The result was that Peter was empowered to take up the leadership role to which Jesus had previously delegated him (see Matthew 16:18), and provided direction for the replacement of Judas (vs 15–22). In this way the apostolic body was restored to its full complement, and the stage was set for the next dramatic divine intervention.

The 'room upstairs' was a place of fellowship, and when this took the form of communal prayer, amazing things began to happen. If you are not participating in a prayer group, think about joining one.

The Bible in a year: Exodus 11–12; Matthew 22

JANUARY 28–FEBRUARY 3

DAY 3

The acts of the Holy Spirit

Many Christians look askance at what they consider extravagant forms of worship. Rarely nowadays are there charges of inebriation, merely references to mass hysteria, or just plain 'happy-clappies'.

Acts 2:1–13

For the Jews, Pentecost had a twofold significance: firstly, it was a harvest festival, a celebration of first fruits. Secondly, it commemorated Moses receiving the Ten Commandments on Mount Sinai. Both were good reasons for all to be 'together in one place' (v 1).

The happening described by Luke was unexpected, swift and dramatic, and filled with a sense of mighty power at work (vs 1–4). In the Hebrew Bible 'wind' and 'spirit' are the same word, and fire was prominently associated with powerful manifestations of God – think for example of Elijah's challenge to the prophets of Baal on Mount Carmel (1 Kings 18:16–40).

Not since the tower of Babel had such a diversity of languages been heard in one place (vs 9–11). This time God's intention was not to confuse, but to empower. Luke's inclusive listing of all the nationalities of the near eastern world endorses God's choosing of Israel to be the means of salvation to all nations. Christ's church, consisting of those whom he has empowered, transcends the divides of language and culture and ethnicity.

Luke identifies two reactions to the outpouring of the Holy Spirit: some people were amazed and perplexed (v 12). Others sneered (v 13). May God graciously open our minds to the work of his Spirit. May he preserve us from falling into the cynical second group.

The Bible in a year: Exodus 13–14; Matthew 23

JANUARY 28–FEBRUARY 3

DAY 4

The mystery of God

Augustine said: 'If you understand it, it is not God.' Some of us still struggle to grasp and understand the mysteries of God.

Acts 2:14–36

The events on the day of Pentecost are difficult to comprehend. For the past two centuries the West has been convinced that understanding is through rational thinking. Fortunately, we are beginning to discover that profound meaning can sometimes occur independently of logical reasoning.

Peter helps us understand these events with a powerful address. For the second time he takes the platform, this time addressing a large, curious Jewish audience. It is clear that Peter has the bit between his teeth. Using the Hebrew Scriptures he sets out to show that what they are witnessing to is not a new-fangled Hellenistic religion. It is precisely what the prophets spoke of (vs 16–17). The promises of the Lord have been realised: to Abraham, that the nation he fathered would lead all the nations to salvation (cf v 21 with Genesis 18:18); to David, that his offspring would occupy the throne for ever (v 30).

Jesus is indeed the Messiah (Hebrew) or Christ (Greek), and Lord (v 36). Having perfectly completed the work of redemption, Jesus returned to the Father and sent the promised Spirit (v 33) to indwell and empower the believers. The filling of the Spirit was Jesus' act of recreation. This was the Spirit that Jesus promised would come after he was glorified; who would provide 'streams of living water' (John 7:37–39).

Thank God for the wonderful gift of the Holy Spirit, the Counsellor who 'will teach you all things' (John 14:26).

The Bible in a year: Exodus 15–16; Psalm 15–16

JANUARY 28–FEBRUARY 3

DAY 5

The church is born

When conviction comes, responsive action becomes urgent.

Acts 2:37–47

In the final chapter of his Gospel, Luke records that 'Jesus himself stood among them' after his resurrection. Amongst other things, he said to them, 'This is what I told you while I was still with you: Everything must be fulfilled that is written about me in the Law of Moses, the Prophets and the Psalms' (Luke 24:36, 44).

This was the theme of the newly initiated church's inaugural message to the world through Peter's preaching. It provoked an immediate response. The group of believers numbering about 120 in Acts 1:15 swelled by 3 000 in one day (v 41), with daily additions thereafter (v 47). What exciting times these must have been! But should we be impressed by numbers today? Is the modern mega-church conducive to getting closer to God in our complex lives?

Careful reading of this chapter suggests that the gospel preached was Jesus Christ crucified, raised and ascended; and the Spirit descended, in fulfilment of the Scriptures (v 38). The response was devotion to an incredibly close (but not closed), caring community (vs 44–45); and fellowship with teaching, the breaking of bread and prayer. There is a wonderful sense of joy, freedom and spontaneity in Luke's account. To what extent have we retained this in today's 'institutionalised church'?

Are all of our attempts to get closer to God guided by the Spirit, promised to all whom our Lord has called? Are you prescribing the way you want God to work in your life and the life of your church or fellowship?

Pentecost promised: Ezekiel 37:1–14
True worship: John 4:21–24

The Bible in a year: Exodus 17–18; Matthew 24

Going deeper ...

The fourth Gospel ends with the statement: 'Jesus did many other things as well. If every one of them were written down, I suppose that even the whole world would not have room for the books that would be written' (John 21:25).

Perhaps this is hyperbole, but it is an effective statement of the historian's dilemma. What is told in historical narrative is a selected fraction of the whole. The question then arises: What criteria did the author use for his particular selection and rejection of material? And furthermore, what determines our particular selectivity in reading, interpreting and 'understanding'? Our tendency as humans is to concentrate on what 'makes sense', and reject or ignore the rest. As one writer put it, 'History is about the ways we create meaning from the scattered debris of the past.'

Are the writings of Luke accurate and reliable? Sir William Ramsay states: 'Luke's history is unsurpassed in respect of its trustworthiness ... Luke is an historian of the first rank.' Luke wrote with a purpose in mind. Surely more than twenty centuries later, that particular purpose can hardly still be applicable – or can it? There is no way we can put the clock back and recreate the first-century church. We can, however, look at it carefully through Luke's eyes to see how and why it succeeded, and contextualise those principles into today's many and varied social structures. This is an awesome challenge – and includes being clear about what and whom we're really witnessing to.

The church is continually reborn

The account of the day of Pentecost in Acts arises from Luke's commitment to historical detail. An accurate calendar, fifty days counted from the feast of Passover, plays a significant role. But if we become too attached to this calendar-keeping and get fixated on historic detail, there is a danger that the events proclaimed will only be commemorated and not encountered and experienced. We could run the serious risk of trivialising Pentecost, and lose out on its profound significance.

The wonderful message of Acts is that by the presence and power of the Spirit in the church, the *particular* story recounted in the Gospel of Luke, is now *universally* available in the world. This Spirit is none other than that promised through the prophets, notably Joel. The Spirit came in such a way that the Jewish feast which celebrated the giving of the Law to Israel on Sinai, fifty days after the feast commemorating Passover and liberation from slavery, was transformed into the sending of the Gospel to all nations and people everywhere.

We need to recognise that the congregation of Pentecost Day of AD 34, like the Emmaus gathering (Luke 24:13–35), can be understood as a prototype or symbol of every assembly of the church. The charge to proclaim the gospel – in whatever language of the world – comes to all of our gatherings. The Spirit poured out on our assemblies is continually giving birth to the church of Jesus Christ.

The Bible in a year: Exodus 19–22; Psalm 17; Matthew 25

FEBRUARY 4–10

Forgiveness

Hebrews 10; Romans 3; Mark 2; 1 John 1; Matthew 18

If we were to ask a cross-section of people what they believed to be the central human dilemma, we would get a range of answers: lack of education, poverty, unemployment, etc. The Bible highlights something rather different: the dilemma of human sin together with the universal need to have our sins forgiven and our hearts changed.

As we look at this subject, open your heart to God's scrutiny and surgery. No matter how much an offender has done right, it only takes one crime to make him a criminal. In like manner, it only takes one sin to make a sinner. Have you committed one sin? Maybe one a day? If we are honest, we have to admit that we boast a record which befits an habitual criminal, in spiritual terms! So, we need forgiveness.

Jesus told a parable of two men who went to the temple to pray. One, a Pharisee, commended himself to God on the basis of his good works. Jesus humorously described him as praying with himself. God does not hear self-congratulatory prayer! In fact, no religious ritual has any merit before we approach God like the second man in the parable. He would not even lift his face to heaven, but beat on his breast in anguish and pleaded: 'God, be merciful to me a sinner' (Luke 18:9–14). This is the prayer that must precede every prayer. It is the humility that frees God to act on our behalf. It is the broken and contrite heart that he will not despise. Come to him afresh in humble recognition of your need for forgiveness. He is near such humility.

After pastoring churches for many years, Costa Mitchell is now the Regional Overseer of the Association of Vineyard Churches in South Africa. He is based in Cape Town.

FEBRUARY 4–10

DAY 1

What is forgiveness?

Only in the Christian gospel is there a guarantee of forgiveness (Acts 4:12). No other religion even offers it. God says, 'I will meet you at the cross.' Are you aware of your need for forgiveness? You have come to the right place!

Hebrews 10:1–18

The old English word 'forgive' literally means, 'to give on behalf of'. It means to pay someone else's debt on their behalf, or to write off the debt. We enter the kingdom of God by being 'poor in spirit' (Matthew 5:3). The physically poor in the Bible had incurred so much debt that even if they worked for the rest of their lives for their creditor, they would not be able to pay it off. The poor in spirit acknowledge indebtedness to God, not only for time but also for eternity. We can never do enough good to 'pay the debt' of our sinfulness.

In the Old Testament the blood of atoning sacrifices *covered* sin, without removing it (vs 1–4, 11). In the New Testament, an incredible thing happened: the blood of Jesus Christ does not merely cover our sins – it removes them (vs 9–10)! The new covenant is radically different, because through it God can finally remove our sins from us and remember them no more (v 17).

Thank the Lord, that 'if we confess our sins, he is faithful and just, and will forgive our sins and purify us from all unrighteousness' (1 John 1:9). Remember that when God throws your sins into the 'sea of his forgetfulness' there is NO FISHING allowed!

The Bible in a year: Exodus 23–24; Matthew 26

FEBRUARY 4–10

DAY 2

Why I need forgiveness

Human beings have two things in common: we are all made in the image of God, and we have all sinned. We have used the first fact to empower the second. The genius of humanity is capable of great acts of creativity and mercy, but also of holocausts and unspeakable cruelty. Herein is our spiritual poverty. Confess your brokenness before God, with the following passage as your focus.

Romans 3:9–26

The Greek word for 'sin' was borrowed from archery contests. An archer who aimed for the bull's eye but missed it, was told, 'You have missed the mark.' The fact that he had tried to hit the target did not minimise the fact that he had failed. It is the same with all of us in our quest for righteousness – we have all missed the mark; or, in Paul's words, 'fallen short' of God's standard (v 23). We have allowed the image of God to become distorted and weak in us.

In addition to this basic lack of perfection, we have also developed a *habit* of sin. We have chosen responses to life situations that relieve us of stress, eliminate obstacles and make us feel better. So, sin is not only a *condition* we have, it is a *lifestyle* we choose – note Paul's catalogue of evil in verses 10–18. This puts us all in the same boat – we desperately need forgiveness!

Bring to the Lord both your sinful condition and lifestyle. Ask him to deal with them through Jesus. Praise him that he 'justifies those who have faith in Jesus' (v 26).

The Bible in a year: Exodus 25–26; Matthew 27

FEBRUARY 4–10

DAY 3

Forgiveness – Christ's purpose

Psalm 130:4 says of God: 'But with you there is forgiveness.' The central purpose of God in sending Jesus was the forgiveness of our sin. Come near to God today, celebrating the fact that with him, and with him alone ('with you') there is forgiveness.

Mark 2:1–12

Notice Jesus' purpose in his dealings with this man. He said to the paralytic, 'Son, your sins are forgiven' (v 5). Jesus' reply to the offended religious leaders further illustrates his purpose: 'That you may know that the Son of Man has authority on earth to forgive sins,' he said to the paralytic, 'I tell you, get up, take up your mat and go home' (vs 10–11). Jesus' miracles were done to draw people into a relationship with him through forgiveness. The miracle is the sign; Jesus is the destination; and forgiveness is the result.

You can experience as many miracles as you like, but until you experience his purpose for coming, namely the forgiveness of your sins, the miracles have not achieved their purpose. Paul, the apostle, said this in similar words, 'Here is a trustworthy saying that deserves full acceptance: Christ Jesus came into the world to save sinners' (1 Timothy 1:15).

Jesus is the sinner's friend. Thank him for this. He befriended sinners for a purpose. He went to a cross for the same purpose – our forgiveness. He is worthy of our humble faith. In response to that faith, he will fulfil his purpose of forgiving our sins.

The Bible in a year: Exodus 27–28; Matthew 28

DAY 4

Finding forgiveness

When a product advertises a 'lifetime guarantee', I wonder 'whose lifetime'? Our gospel is based on the most reliable words ever spoken, by the most reliable witness who ever lived. As you come to God's Word today, thank him that you have been given 'better promises' (Hebrews 8:6) on which to base your faith, and the guarantee of forgiveness.

1 John 1:1–2:2

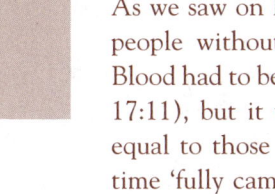

As we saw on Day 1, animal sacrifices 'covered' the sins of God's people without removing them, until a perfect sacrifice came. Blood had to be shed for sin (compare Hebrews 9:22 with Leviticus 17:11), but it would take the perfect blood of a perfect person, equal to those who needed forgiving, finally to remove sin. The time 'fully came' when Jesus came (Galatians 4:4–5). He had no sin against his own name. He was a human being, not an animal. His blood is eternal, because he is an eternal person (v 2). Only he has the credentials to be able to deal with our sin. It is the reason why we can have confidence before God. Our sin has been removed once and for all by the shedding of Christ's blood (v 7).

What do you have to do to appropriate forgiveness? Believe that the cross was where your sin was paid for, and that the blood of Jesus Christ is able to cleanse you. Confess your sins believing that the Lord has forgiven and cleansed you (v 9). Then, 'walk in the light' of this, and 'the blood of Jesus Christ will (continually) cleanse you from all sin' (v 7).

The Bible in a year: Exodus 29–30; Psalm 18

FEBRUARY 4–10

DAY 5

The proof of forgiveness

One of the marks of a real Christian is gratitude. A person who knows the desperate need for forgiveness, and who is forgiven, is a grateful person. Let your initial worship of God today reflect the gratitude that is due to him for his wonderful mercy (Luke 7:36–50).

Matthew 18:21–35

Peter begins this important dialogue by asking a quantitative question: 'How many times shall I forgive my brother?' Jesus' reply in the form of a parable amounts to a qualitative question, namely: 'How can you see the kingdom of God in a life?' or 'How can you tell who is a forgiven person?' The answer is that a forgiven person can be known by his or her forgiving nature.

The corollary of this appears in rather troubling form in Matthew 6:15 which says: 'If you do not forgive men their sins, your Father will not forgive your sins.' The fate of the unforgiving servant in today's parable bears this out (vs 34–35). Does this mean that we need to work to earn forgiveness? That would contradict the entire Gospel. It is, however, true that a forgiven person proves that he or she is forgiven by forgiving others. We must search our hearts to see if we are reflecting the love that has shone upon us. We are to forgive one another as Christ forgave us (Ephesians 4:32).

Thank the Lord for his forgiveness. Confess your lack of forgiveness to others. Ask for his grace to forgive from the heart, and to live out your forgiveness.

In the dock: Revelation 7:9–17
An anthem to the forgiving God: Psalm 103:1–13

The Bible in a year: Exodus 31–32; Acts 1

FEBRUARY 4–10

Going deeper ...

A stable Christian life is one which rests in forgiveness guaranteed by grace. To visit our sins repeatedly is to invite a lack of confidence. This is true vertically (between you and God), and horizontally (between you and other people). Do you remember what we learned from our analysis of the word 'forgive'? It means that we must be prepared to pay for someone else's indebtedness to us. We pay in the currency in which we have been offended. Reflect on this before God; celebrate your liberation from all sin; and cancel from your heart the debt of others toward you.

Here are three examples of how to do this: 1. Has someone taken material goods from you without paying? Make a conscious decision to let them have the goods, rather than regarding them as thieves. 2. Have you suffered emotional injury? Release the emotion to God and set the person free from having to pay you back. 3. Have you been rejected when you tried to love? Go back into the relationship with arms and heart wide open to the possibility of new love, and even new hurt.

This is the essence of the cross. It is not only the place where our sin is paid for; it is the place where we lay down our need, or right, to exact payment for the sins of others. In so doing, you will experience release from the unbearable load of unforgiveness. Torment of soul and overwrought emotion are the fruits of refusal to cancel debt. Forgiveness, freely received and freely given, is your 'get out of jail free' card. Use it, and live in the joy and peace of grace.

Be happy, don't worry

Conclusion

Psalm 130:1–8 sums up much of the topic on which we have focused this week. It is a symphony, a lyrical duet, between the needy sinner and the God of all mercy. Sin, let it be remembered, is a serious thing. It condemns us to death (Ezekiel 18:4). Unless we can be saved from it, we are doomed. The realisation causes the psalmist to 'cry for mercy' (v 2). He approaches God with joyful fear (v 4). He waits in tremulous hope (vs 5–6). Notice how the repetition in these verses expresses the psalmist's feverish, fearful impatience. Then almost in anticipation of a final redemption which is still thousands of years in the future, he finally rejoices in the realisation that with God there is forgiveness; there is unfailing love; and there is redemption from all sins (v 7).

His immediate response is to evangelise his brothers: 'O Israel, put your hope in the Lord' (v 7). In Psalm 51 David, after confessing his sin and receiving forgiveness, also turns into an evangelist: 'Then I will teach transgressors your ways, and sinners will turn back to you' (v 13). Why this sudden desire to evangelise? The joy of true forgiveness is impossible to contain.

Have you been forgiven? Worship and praise God! And tell the world!

The Bible in a year: Exodus 33–36; Psalm 19; Acts 2

FEBRUARY 11–17

The love of God in Jesus Christ

John 4–5

Karl Barth, a theologian of the twentieth century, said: 'We believe in a civilisation of "things". Jesus believes in a civilisation of "persons" empowered by the Holy Spirit.' Jesus Christ was often found amongst the 'discards' of society – the 'left-out' ones. An interesting and challenging book was recently published by the Africa Inland Mission in South Africa. Its title is *The Left Out Ones*, and it is written by Lorna Eglin, who recently retired after over thirty years in Kenya working amongst the Maasai-speaking tribes – the 'left out ones'. As they left, crowds waved them goodbye with a mixture of tears and joy, calling out, 'We'll see you in heaven!' The 'left out ones' had met Jesus: they had been found.

Our readings this week take us to individual 'left out ones' who also met Jesus and had their lives dramatically transformed. They were no longer discarded, but totally transformed by 'the love of God in Jesus Christ'. Let me introduce them briefly.

- The Samaritan woman. She walked alone, and came to the well while nobody else was around. She was so tired of being hurt and condemned.
- The royal official whose son was desperately ill. Did he feel 'discarded' by God who was apparently deaf to his prayers?
- The paralysed man at the pool of Bethesda. Helpless and hopeless in his deformity, after thirty-eight years, he had lost all hope for healing.

Walk with me this week in the footsteps of Jesus and let him heal and bless us together.

Cynthia Richards lives in Cape Town. She is a retired Methodist minister who is a much sought-after 'across the board' preacher and speaker.

FEBRUARY 11–17

DAY 1

Gentle love

Jesus has a unique encounter with a Samaritan woman at Jacob's well. It is a delicate situation: Jews do not associate with Samaritans because of historical differences in the way they worship. But God has other plans for the day!

John 4:1–15

John the Baptist and Jesus are becoming a threat to the religious leaders in Judea; but the time for Jesus to face conflict in his ministry has not yet come. He therefore sets out to return to his ministry in Galilee. There is a 'time to be silent and a time to speak' (Ecclesiastes 3:7). This is the gentleness and prerogative of true love – and that is Jesus!

On his way through Samaria, Jesus takes a rest at Jacob's well. A Samaritan woman approaches to draw water, and to her surprise he, a Jewish man, speaks to her, asking for a drink. His gentle, non-threatening manner reflects his love for her – a very needy woman living in ignorance of the love of God. His offer of 'living water', however, baffles her completely; especially the statement that she will never thirst again; but have a 'spring' called 'eternal life' (v 14). A source all her own? Eagerly she accepts his offer (v 15)! Surprise is mingled with fascination. She does not understand, but is willing to be drawn into conversation with Jesus, who appears to offer no threat to her. Somehow she feels safe; that she can trust him. He certainly knows something.

The gentleness of his love must have dawned on her later, but meanwhile she remained to ask questions. Where do you stand today in relation to Jesus?

The Bible in a year: Exodus 37–38; Acts 3

FEBRUARY 11–17

DAY 2

Tough love

Jesus' next startling statement to the Samaritan woman is almost harsh in its directness. 'Go! Call your husband!' Had this been his opening remark, she might have missed his gentle love and probably been offended by what turned out to be a very skilful demonstration of his tough love. But she was now committed to this encounter.

John 4:16–30

With hindsight we know the enormous love behind this embarrassingly direct reference to a husband (v 16). He has put his finger on the root of the problem. In self-defence she steers the conversation to a 'safe' discussion on worship (vs 19–20). But she is talking about 'religion' and he is talking about 'relationship'! Her reference to the coming of the Messiah elicits a most amazing revelation. He himself is the Messiah (vs 25–26) 'I am' ('ego eimi' in Greek) is the name of God – the 'I am' (Exodus 3:14). He reveals this awesome fact to this woman! It is the only time Jesus reveals himself to anyone until his trial. Understandably she is awe-struck. Could this really be the Christ? Overwhelmed by this revelation she immediately rushes off to the village to tell her friends.

Tough love hurts in its dealing with painful truth. The woman had, however, unknowingly begun a relationship with this unique man, the Messiah himself, and wanted to share this with her friends. We need to ask ourselves, 'Is my present lifestyle pleasing to God? Have I allowed Jesus to put his finger on the problem areas? Where am I in my relationship with him?'

The Bible in a year: Exodus 39–40; Acts 4

FEBRUARY 11–17

DAY 3

Sovereign love

The disciples returned as Jesus was concluding his conversation with the woman. They were surprised, but did not ask him the questions that puzzled them, as they observed the excitement of her hasty departure. An unlikely harvest was about to be reaped as the approaching villagers became visible in the shimmering heat.

John 4:27–54

Many Samaritans believed because of her enthusiastic testimony (v 39), and many more believed as Jesus himself graciously spoke to them (vs 41–42). What a mission! And all because a 'nameless' woman had allowed Jesus to search her heart and life.

Then Jesus, his business accomplished in Samaria, moved on to Galilee where they remembered him as the miracle worker at the Cana wedding (v 46). In Capernaum, a royal official in Herod's service asked him to come and heal his dying son (v 49). Without travelling to see the son, Jesus spoke the words of healing and the father believed them (v 50). The boy was healed and the whole family came to faith! This was a sovereign move of a sovereign God to heal from a distance! Sovereign love indeed!

Herod's official came to faith without any knowledge of the teaching of God. The Samaritan woman respected the writings of the Pentateuch, but this 'respect' blocked her perception of the present, until Jesus led her to see who he was, skilfully using her attempted diversion as a tool (4:21). She listened with all her heart. That is the way to 'hear' Jesus and to know him.

Knowledge about Jesus is academic; personal knowledge of him is life changing.

The Bible in a year: Leviticus 1–3; Acts 5

FEBRUARY 11–17

DAY 4

Healing love

It often saddened Jesus that people sought physical cures and material benefits rather than the spiritual gifts he offered them. He said, 'You seek me for the loaves and fishes' (John 6:26). Yet the healing love of Jesus repeatedly took him to places of physical need. This time it was to a pool for the paralysed – to another outcast of society.

John 5:1–18

Jesus was back in Jerusalem. All the religious leaders had gathered in the temple, but Jesus was found with the helpless and hopeless at the pool of Bethesda. Characteristically he sought the most desperate case – a man paralysed for thirty-eight years! He readily talked to Jesus and a relationship was formed. His only hope lay in the supposed curative powers of the water, but he had no one to take him there. He was happy just to chat to Jesus, but suddenly Jesus' authoritative command motivated him to co-operate. The next minute he was standing on his own two feet! 'Don't just stand there,' says Jesus, 'pick up your mat and walk!' What a celebration!

Sadly, all the Jews saw was a mat being carried on the Sabbath Day, and therefore a Jewish law being broken! Their indignation and determination to destroy Jesus was gaining momentum. Jesus' response to the disturbed Jews was, 'My Father is always at his work to this very day, and I, too, am working' (v 16–17). The healing love of the Father was reaching out to them through Jesus, inviting them to believe and receive him (see John 1:11–12).

Have you responded to his call and received him into your life? That is healing love indeed!

The Bible in a year: Leviticus 4–5; Psalm 20–21

FEBRUARY 11–17

DAY 5

God's love

The Jews were planning to kill Jesus. They reckoned he had broken the rules by healing a man and telling him to carry his mat on the Sabbath. Also, he was making himself equal with God by calling God his Father! Let us examine Jesus' brilliant response to their accusations.

John 5:19–30

Jesus affirmed that he was the son of his Father, God (vs 19–20). This infuriated the Jews who would not accept Jesus as the Christ and refused to acknowledge the work of God in his miracles. Then Jesus claimed that everyone who heard his words and believed the Father would immediately cross over from a death to eternal life (v 24).

They were questioning Jesus' authority. So he claimed that the Father had 'given him authority to judge' (v 27). Jesus insisted that he was constantly guided by God alone (v 30). Later in this chapter Jesus used the testimonies of both John the Baptist (vs 33–35) and the scriptures (v 39) to confirm his authority. The cry from Jesus' heart was: 'Yet you refuse to come to me' (v 40). Powerfully, painfully and alarmingly their non-acceptance of him confronted the Messiah. There was both longing and sorrow in his observation. 'I know that you do not have the love of God in your hearts' (v 42).

Picture yourself in Jerusalem at that momentous time: surrounded by scoffers and ignorant people; disturbed by the godless and the worshippers of foreign gods. And there stands Jesus, the Jewish Messiah and his band of faithful followers, proclaiming the love of the Almighty God, the Father of Jesus. What would have persuaded you to believe?

Constant love: Isaiah 40:27–31
Is this your mindset?: Romans 8:28–39

The Bible in a year: Leviticus 6–7; Acts 6

Going deeper …

To the Samaritan woman Jesus said: 'If you knew the gift of God …' (4:10), and gave her the gift of eternal life (Romans 6:23) through revealing himself as the 'I am' (v 26). But the gift is to be received and shared; it's private and personal, and for public declaration. In putting his finger on the root of the woman's problem – sex and relationships – Jesus was using supernatural knowledge called discernment, one of the gifts of the Holy Spirit. Jesus promised the baptism of the Spirit before his ascension (Acts 1:5) and commanded his disciples to wait for it in Jerusalem. On the day of Pentecost 'they were all filled with the Holy Spirit' (Acts 2:4). Then they turned the world upside down! Have you asked for this fullness in your life?

The man healed at Bethesda ran into problems (5:10–15). Jesus found him in the temple, and encouraged him, but warned him to 'stop sinning' (5:14). How often sin has robbed a person of his healing. It leads to doubt about the power of the healer and a falling away from faith.

Later Paul, in writing to the believers in Ephesus, warned, 'Be very careful, then, how you live' (Ephesians 5:15). Finding Jesus in healing and deliverance is declaring war on Satan. From his hideous audacity in tempting Jesus himself, we learn to be ready to oppose him in the name of Jesus. Spiritual warfare requires us to 'put on the whole armour of God' (Ephesians 6:11), and stand our ground against the powers of darkness (v 13).

Amazing love

'Jesus, I am amazed at your enormous love for the outcasts of society, the discarded and left-out ones – and for me!' The amazing love of God prepared the Samaritan woman's heart to listen to Jesus. The amazing love of God caused the nobleman to ask Jesus to heal his son. The amazing love of God prepared the heart of the paralysed man to respond to Jesus' command.

In the Sermon on the Mount Jesus was not addressing the crowds, but rather the disciples who gathered round him. Those who had not responded to him as Messiah could not be expected to keep the standards of the sermon without the forgiveness of their sins and the transforming work of the Holy Spirit in their lives. At the very least, the words of Matthew 5:11–12 would be ridiculous. In my own strength I cannot 'rejoice and be glad' when evil is spoken or enacted against me. Merely remembering the persecution suffered by the prophets and others doesn't help me at all! The Sermon on the Mount only makes sense in terms of the transforming love of Jesus which we have been reading about this week. He is our role model, who not only shows us the way, but is the way: 'I am the truth and the life. No one comes to the Father except through me' (John 14:6).

'For the love of God is broader than the measures of man's mind. The heart of the eternal is most wonderfully kind.'

The Bible in a year: Leviticus 8–12; Psalm 22; Acts 7

FEBRUARY 18–24

Living proof

John 5–6

I once reported on a court case where the offender thought he was God. The wild-eyed man who stood before us in the dock wearing only a pair of ragged jeans had the previous night driven at high speed on a treacherous mountain road, without headlights. To his passenger (a man who will no doubt never hitchhike again) he continually shouted 'Fear not!' The unanimous verdict of everyone in that courtroom was that this man was not the Messiah, just mentally disturbed.

This week in John's Gospel, we will be confronted with another man who thinks he is God, and we will be asked to deliver our verdict. Jesus of Nazareth, the carpenter's son, will calmly and methodically present his case for divinity to his friends and opponents. He will present evidence from Israel's prophetic history, from Scripture, from his own actions, from creation and finally from God the Father himself.

This is one of the most exhilarating sections of the Bible. We see Jesus' scholarly command of Jewish theology and his fearlessness in facing down the religious leaders. We see his strong sense of purpose. We glimpse his awe-inspiring power over the natural world. And we begin to understand what his approaching death will mean for us.

At the end of this week we will have to make a choice. Is Jesus mentally deranged, a pathological liar, or Lord of the universe? This choice cannot be taken lightly. It will determine how we live our lives and where we spend eternity. And it can open up to us a whole new world of energising possibilities. Read with me and make up your own mind.

Belinda Pollard is a freelance journalist and editor based in Brisbane, Australia.
She writes news and feature articles for publications in Australia and the USA and has edited numerous books including Bible commentaries and biographies.

FEBRUARY 18–24

DAY 1

In the witness box

Ask God to help you understand his Word as you read it today.

John 5:30–47

In John 5:17–27, Jesus declared himself equal with God. Like a lawyer presenting his case in court, he now calls his witnesses to prove that outrageous claim. The religious leaders think he is the one who must defend himself, but he turns the tables and puts them in the dock.

The Jewish leaders were intrigued by John the Baptist for a time, and like empty-headed moths they danced happily around his flame (v 35), but never understood that his message pointed to Jesus. They have watched Jesus' works and miracles without recognising the mark of the Messiah (v 36). They have made the study of the Scriptures their life's work, but have never seen that they all pointed forward to Jesus (vs 39–40). Even Moses, the ancestor of whom they are so proud, is a witness against them, because he predicted Jesus' coming way in advance (vs 45–46). And most damning of all, they are defying the witness of the Father himself (vs 32, 36–37). They have worked out their own way of running religion, but it is not up to them to decide who God is and how he is to be worshipped. They love to talk about God, but don't love him (v 42). They will not accept a Messiah who doesn't fit their definition (v 43). Jesus convicts them of a criminal lack of perception and wisdom.

Did you understand something new from the Bible today, or were you reminded again of a familiar truth? Make a few notes about it on a slip of paper that you can take with you and look at during any quiet moments today.

The Bible in a year: Leviticus 13–14; Acts 8

FEBRUARY 18–24

DAY 2

King of the world

What do you think it means for Jesus to be King? You might like to write down a few things that come to mind, and consider them further as you read today's passage.

John 6:1–15

Signs and wonders will always draw a crowd (v 2). But the crowd doesn't always get the point. These people manage to lift their sights beyond lunch, but only as far as political power (v 15). Jesus is King, but he has a much bigger concern than the political aspirations of one group of people at one point in history.

The word 'sign' is very important in John's Gospel (vs 2, 14). A sign has little value in itself. The sign that tells us where to find Parliament House is just metal and paint. Its whole worth and purpose is tied up in what it points to. This picnic on the grass is not about food. And it is not about worldly power either (v 15). This is a Messiah miracle. Food is a symbol of God's blessing throughout the Bible. The Promised Land was to be a place of abundant food (Deuteronomy 8:9). Jesus will satisfy our spiritual hunger for a relationship with God, by surrendering his own life. And, like this meal, Jesus doesn't just provide enough to get by. His provision is overflowing in its abundance (vs 12–13).

People today still want 'bread and circuses', rather than the Kingdom of God; a health and wealth guru rather than a crucified Servant King. And Jesus is still King on his own terms.

Do you, like me, ever think of Jesus' job description as 'providing my needs'? If so, repent with me, and ask him to fill you with a bigger vision of the Lord who loves you.

The Bible in a year: Leviticus 15–16; Acts 9

FEBRUARY 18–24

DAY 3

Never fear

'The fear of the Lord is the beginning of wisdom' (Proverbs 9:10). What do you think this statement means?

John 6:16–24

The disciples have dealt with an enormous crowd, seen a remarkable miracle, and are having to absorb the fact that Jesus doesn't seem to want to be a king. To cap it all, a storm blows up as they sail home without their leader (v 17), and they have to struggle against it every inch of the journey (v 18). Imagine how they must feel when, out of the darkness, they see a man walking towards them across the storm-tossed waters (v 19).

They are right to be more afraid of the man than the storm. Jesus is the King of the world, Lord over the elements, more powerful than the raging sea. His statement to them from the water (v 20) means, 'Don't be afraid, it's only me'. But the very fact that he's standing on the surface of the lake when he speaks means he's also saying, 'Yes, it's me, the Lord of all, but don't be afraid.' Jesus is the living, breathing embodiment of why we need no longer be terrified of the Almighty. Because Jesus died in our place, we can now approach the Lord with reverent confidence (Hebrews 4:15–16).

Next day, the disciples are beginning to understand Jesus, but the crowd is still on the same old track. They are looking for someone who makes bread appear (vs 22–24), rather than the Creator of the world.

Do you ever feel as though your life is a bit of a cyclone? Think about what it means in those moments for Jesus to say to you, 'It's me, don't be afraid.' Respond to him in prayer.

The Bible in a year: Leviticus 17–18; Acts 10

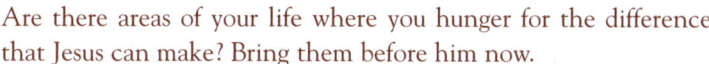

DAY 4

Spiritual hunger

Are there areas of your life where you hunger for the difference that Jesus can make? Bring them before him now.

John 6:25–40

This passage provides a classic case of people talking at cross purposes. The crowd begins by asking Jesus when he arrived (v 25), when surely the question should be 'How?' Their next question is how they can earn God's approval (v 28), when Jesus has just told them it is a free gift that he himself will give (v 27). And when he advises them that the only requirement is to believe in him (v 29), they immediately ask for proof (v 30), forgetting that it is Jesus' miracles that have brought them here in the first place.

They do not understand because they have been drawn to Jesus by their stomachs, not their souls. Finding bread for the table was a daily struggle for these people, which makes their obsession a little more understandable. But by focusing on the bread, they lose sight of the bread-giver (v 33) who is able to satisfy every hunger of the human heart (v 35). Jesus wants to raise their sights from their physical hunger to their spiritual needs. He knows that eternal life is what these people really need, and only he can give it (v 40).

Sometimes we can be a bit like that crowd, forgetting the eternal side of our lives amid the crush of daily pressures. It is reassuring to know that our eternal destiny depends not on our consistency, but on the strength of Jesus who holds us in his hands (v 39).

Write down the things that you plan to do today. Then ask Jesus to help you keep your eyes on him throughout each activity.

The Bible in a year: Leviticus 19–20; Psalms 23–24

FEBRUARY 18–24

DAY 5

The turning point

Once, I struggled against giving up a relationship that would not please God. It became a turning point for me. I discovered I had to follow Jesus on his terms, not mine.

John 6:41–71

The language of this passage sounds a little like a Communion service, but, fundamentally, Jesus is talking about his coming death. It will only be possible for people to receive eternal life through an act of the most appalling violence (v 51) – the murder of the life-giver.

This is the turning point of John's Gospel. It is time for people to decide who they think Jesus is. The religious leaders are sure they know, because they have seen him growing up, the son of the local carpenter. They are shocked by his pretensions (v 42). Many in his wider circle of disciples have believed him to be a miracle worker and political liberator. But the cross is not what they signed up for, so they turn away (vs 60, 66). In a similar way, many people today are happy to accept the harmless baby Jesus of Christmas, and even the good moral teacher, but the passionate, powerful and suffering Lord of Easter repels them.

Peter knows who Jesus is. Sometimes it seems like this impetuous and likeable disciple opens his mouth only to put his foot in it. But he also has moments of sheer brilliance, and this is one of them. Jesus is 'the Holy One of God' (vs 68–69). Peter may not always like what Jesus says, but where else would he go? Once you really know Jesus, you realise how empty all the other options are.

If you struggle to yield to Jesus, ask him to help you. Thank him for his unfailing love.

No doubt: John 20:24–29
Choose life: Joshua 24:14–18

The Bible in a year: Leviticus 21–22; Acts 11

FEBRUARY 18–24

Going deeper …

'If there is a God, I think he's loving. I won't believe in a God who wants to judge or punish people.' I didn't know how to answer my agnostic friend's complacent words. The big theological issue of how to balance God's love and justice faded into a minor point. What troubled me most deeply was my friend's assumption that she could tell God who or what he could be.

And yet in preparing this week's readings I have realised how many times I do the same thing. It sounds different, but it boils down to the same mistake. I love Jesus and want to serve him, but sometimes I fall into the trap of seeing him only as he relates to me. He is *my* Saviour, *my* Provider, *my* Healer, *my* God. I focus on the things I want him to do for me, as though he were my personal Santa Claus. I lose sight of the bigger picture of what Jesus wants to do with his people in his world.

When Moses, the famous ancestor of the Jews, met God in the wilderness, God told him his name: 'I am who I am' (Exodus 3:14). This is a Hebrew word that can also be translated: 'I will be what I will be.' These very same words, translated into Greek, are what Jesus said to his terrified disciples in the boat that stormy night (John 6:20): 'I am.' No one tells Jesus his job. No one tells Jesus who to be. No one.

The Jesus who loves you is also an almighty, majestic, self-defining God.

Words of eternal life

Conclusion

What is your verdict after reading Jesus' evidence? Throughout this week's readings we have seen two broad groups of people: those who believe Jesus and follow him, and those who reject him or miss the point. The crowds reject him because he is not the kind of Messiah they've been looking for. They want plentiful food (6:30–31) and an end to Roman oppression (6:15). They don't want a Messiah who will save them through dying, and even many who had been in his wider circle of disciples fall away when they begin to hear such teaching (6:60–66). Jesus already knows that one of the twelve closest to him will turn against him (6:70–71).

The religious leaders come in for heavy condemnation from Jesus. They have trivialised John the Baptist's testimony (5:35), failed to understand Scripture despite studying it for countless hours (5:39), and even rejected the testimony of Moses, for whom they profess great devotion (5:46). It was their job to be a guiding light to God's people, and yet they are too blind even to recognise the signs of the Messiah in their midst (5:36). They are flying in the face of God himself (5:37–38).

In contrast, the highlight of this week has come from among the twelve disciples. Frequently they seem to be as clueless as the crowds, but not this time. They will not fully understand who Jesus is until after his death and resurrection, but they are tantalisingly close to the truth. Peter declares, on their behalf, that Jesus is 'the Holy One of God' (6:69). Asked whether they will stick with Jesus, Peter correctly observes that there *is* nowhere else to go (6:68). Jesus holds the key to eternal life.

The Bible in a year: Leviticus 23–26; Psalm 25; Acts 12

FEBRUARY 25– MARCH 3

Of icebergs and Babylon

Ezekiel

The voyage of the famous ship, *Titanic*, built to gigantic specifications, was ended through human pride and an iceberg! The designers used the wrong materials and the captain demanded a higher speed than was safe under the current weather conditions. While they thought their skills had reached the peak of human potential, they were no match for the ice which they had chosen to ignore.

God showed the prophet Ezekiel that his chosen vehicle, Israel, had been lost in a similar way. The reason was 'pride'. Their faith in him was small while their confidence in their own way was too strong. So God deliberately turned the political tide against them.

Israel had become too secure as the 'chosen nation', and too confident of the international status of Jerusalem to bother remaining faithful to God. They explored other gods and idols, putting their spiritual well-being at stake. Individuals simply felt they didn't need to be 'godly'.

God takes a very personal interest in salvaging his truth and his way, and he wanted to save those who wished to be faithful to him, but he would only do it after they could no longer cling to the political state of Israel or the temple in Jerusalem.

The 'iceberg' God chose to sink Israel was the pagan nation of Babylon. God also chose to discipline those who had led the people astray and demanded that everyone take responsibility for following him (18:1–18; 14:13–14). He wanted a relationship with individuals based on their worship of him. Those who could find a heart for him would survive, but would still be sent into exile.

Trevor Hoek is a clinical psychologist. He and his family emigrated to England from East London in the middle of 2001.

FEBRUARY 25–MARCH 3

DAY 1

Ceremony, majesty and plain speaking

One of John Michael Talbot's beautiful songs contains the angelic line 'Glory to God in the highest and peace to his people on earth'. How wonderful majesty and peace of God are.

Ezekiel 1:1–9; 2:1–2, 9–10; 3:1–3

God, awesome and powerful, came to Ezekiel in the form of thunder and lightening (v 4) and announced the start of Ezekiel's visions. The next events speak as much about God's awesome nature as his faithfulness. The prophet, flattened by the visions (1:28), was raised to his feet so that God could 'talk to him' (2:1–2) and give him a scroll (2:9) of bitter judgements to eat, which tasted as sweet as honey to the righteous priest (3:3). Ezekiel realised how the anger of God was completely understandable under the circumstances. Ezekiel knew that, regardless of how perilous the situation seemed, God had become very involved personally and was fully in control. Those who had abandoned God would find themselves experiencing the full effects of the coming political storm against Jerusalem from Babylon without the comfort of their God.

Are we listening to God today? Is this a warning for us today, or is it just dry old history? God said to Ezekiel: 'Listen carefully to me and take to heart all my words. Go to your countrymen and speak to them' (3:10–11).

Lord, let me hear your voice speaking to me today, whether in majesty, thunder or plain speech. Let me hear your sweet message of concern. Be my good parent and correct me in love. Let me understand how your love and concern justifies everything you do.

The Bible in a year: Leviticus 27; Numbers 1; Acts 13

FEBRUARY 25–MARCH 3

DAY 2

Zooming ahead without God's direction

The *Titanic's* master foolishly ordered top speed in iceberg conditions. In contrast, God is a completely trustworthy captain. He wants you to be held together by titanium rivets of faith that will not rust, and to travel at his pace!

Ezekiel 1:10–21; 2:3–5

Ezekiel's first vision showed four creatures: part human, part animal and part spirit (vs 10–14). They rested in a square formation, with a wheel beside each of them (v 15). The *Good News Bible* gives the strong impression of a parked vehicle! The creatures then flew off and zoomed around wherever their spirits took them. God's word to Ezekiel points to a possible meaning of this: 'Son of man, I am sending you to … a rebellious nation … the people are obstinate and stubborn' (2:3–5).

Humans, represented by these creatures, are spiritual beings, which means they are able to choose, but they also have a rebellious 'animal' spirit. This means that we often do exactly what we please, choosing disloyalty to God.

Without God for direction we rush one way then another in a panic (v 14). One moment we are passive like an ox, next we roar like a bull or lion, and finally we try in vain to rise above the mess on wings of wax and feathers (v 10–12). How many times are you inconsistent, changing direction as your moods determine? Is it because you are not prepared to approach God humbly for direction? When the heat's on, which way do you choose, your own or God's?

Lord give me stability of mind. May I be 'quiet but determined' and be able to look ahead calmly to see the solutions you offer.

The Bible in a year: Numbers 2–3; Acts 14

FEBRUARY 25–MARCH 3

DAY 3

God leaves the building!

To what extent will God tolerate being our Provider, Parent and Servant (which he tells us he is) if we take him for granted? At what point will he down tools?

Ezekiel 10:18–19; 11:23–12:6

Ezekiel was instructed by God to act out a play for the citizens of Jerusalem, in which the prophet abandoned the city (12:3–6). This portrayed the departure of the glory of the Lord from the temple and the city, as he rode above the spectacular heavenly vehicles (10:18–19; 11:23).

Ezekiel's role play depicted the departure of God from his role as protector and provider for Israel, and announced the exile of his people from the pit they had dug for themselves. For God saw Israel as a place no longer worthy of his glory, and he regarded the nation as an insult to him. Had Israel not considered it painful to do what God required, it would still have had a special relationship with him.

Have you considered it possible in your own life that God could turn away from you? That he could actually say, 'If that's the way you want it, that's the way it will be?' Have you become too proud and self-assured in your inadequate relationship with him to hear him telling you that all is not well? Are you humble enough to take the risk of allowing God to show you how you are hurting yourself and him?

Go to the Lord as your loving parent, and ask him to give you 'time out' to review your weaknesses and mistakes. Ask him to help you to correct your ways. Trust him for strength and forgiveness.

The Bible in a year: Numbers 4–5; Acts 15

FEBRUARY 25–MARCH 3

DAY 4

Hot engines and whirling wheels!

When people obey God's direction with energy and determination, events unfold in a precious and amazing way.

Ezekiel 3:14; 9:11–10:22

Years ago drag-racing was popular. The cars had huge back wheels, exposed engines and could go very fast. In today's reading the creatures also have majestic, shining wheels and 'hotted-up engines'. We read that a man took coals from between the wheels driven by the creatures (vs 6–7) after being instructed to scatter them over the city (v 2).

There was a hum of activity in the courts of God. A blazing light rose up (v 4) and the wheels and powerful wings made a mighty roaring noise (v 5). Adequately 'fired up', the creatures in control spread their wings and flew up from the earth, but paused at the East Gate of the temple covered by the dazzling light of the glory of God (v 19).

Are you enthusiastically involved in serving God and actively exploring his truth? You could be like 'the man in white linen', scattering fire and reporting to God, 'I have carried out your orders' (9:11). Are you moving powerfully forward directed by his Spirit, or are you uncertain about where you ought to be? Ezekiel had felt himself being carried along by the Spirit, with the power of the Lord strongly upon him (3:14).

Ask God to lift you up and fill you with a spirit of fire, so that you will follow his instructions with energy and obedience.

The Bible in a year: Numbers 6–7; Psalm 26–27

FEBRUARY 25–MARCH 3

DAY 5

Loved, chosen and ungrateful!

Do you have regular meeting times with God, meetings which lead to a wonderful sense of his presence and well-being? What a gift! Justifiably you feel that God has chosen you personally.

Ezekiel 16:4–22; 20:4–13

Many of us only turned to God after being emotionally or physically wounded by the world (16:5). Are we grateful for the life of deep beauty and joy (16:7–14) he gives to those who love him?

Sadly we often respond to his care with an ungrateful heart (v 22). Instead of being faithful and fruitful and ensuring that our children come to God, we sacrifice our lives and theirs on the altar of the world (vs 20–21). We encourage pride in our children by modelling to them destructive and worldly life styles (v 23–26).

But the most evil of temptations is a 'spiritual' rebellion, favouring a life filled with idols such as material possessions, worldly status and knowledge, as sources of greater spiritual 'truths' than God can offer (20:8).

Are you perhaps obstinately withholding something from God? Do you have a special talent which is precious to God, but which you don't use for him? Talented people are more easily self-reliant and cold to God, 'flying off' under their own steam. How many times have you decided to do things your way, for your own interests?

Lord, remind me constantly of the times when I looked to you and only you and was rewarded by the peace of your presence.

Fire and salt: Genesis 19:16–28
God is a storyteller: Matthew 13:10–17

The Bible in a year: Numbers 8–9; Acts 16

Going deeper …

Ezekiel's visions, renowned for unusual symbols, led him to cry, 'Lord everyone is complaining that I always speak in riddles' (20:49). The pictures and riddles demand that we dig deeper, because riddles require an answer. And God wants us to know his will thoroughly.

Do they mirror God's majesty in being 'cosmic and eternally mysterious' and nothing more? I believe that with help from the Holy Spirit, we are able to mine some of the secrets of heaven directly from these pictures, stories and parables. Everything God reveals shows valuable insights into his will.

God does not beat about the bush in his messages to Israel. For example, he says to Ezekiel that the mistakes of Israel are to be demonstrated by Ezekiel cooking his food over human excrement, and that Ezekiel must pack his bags and push off – a mocking taunt to Israel about how they are going to go into exile. He notes that those who disobey him are continually putting 'the branch to their nose' (8:17), possibly the equivalent of an obscene gesture with the fingers. Only those who think Ezekiel made up these images himself will take them lightly! We should not trifle with God: he punishes those stupid enough to rebel deliberately against his power.

Should we not acknowledge our weaknesses and bring them to God? Or do we harbour twinges of pride, which say: 'God wouldn't do any of these things to me; I'm too upright and too protected by his eternal grace'?

Closer to God

Are we able to humble ourselves and listen to God's concerns as intently as Ezekiel did? Or would we rather live like the average Israelite in Ezekiel's day, not wanting to know God and doing our own thing. Do we cling to our church organisation merely because of its status and what it can do for us? Do we avoid a real and intimate relationship with God, because it is a little too demanding at times?

Ezekiel was privileged to have God's constant individual attention and to experience its awesome sweetness, but also its exhausting demands. God wants us to understand our special status in his eyes, and he wants our talents to be used for his honour, rather than for protecting our pride and advancing our own interests. At great cost, God has made it easy for us to be saved, but he demands the same loyalty as he did from Israel. He is not only the God of churchgoers and high priests: he is the Creator of the universe and requires every knee to bow.

After attending church or reading the Scriptures, are you able to relax and enjoy the gentleness of God' presence? Or are these feelings foreign to you? God longs to have a personal, intimate relationship with you, the sort of relationship he had with Ezekiel. Pray that the Lord will enable you to understand his complicated but wonderful love for you. Ask him for the grace to seek his face even when it feels uncomfortable and difficult, so that you will reap the ultimate reward of seeing him face to face.

The Bible in a year: Numbers 10–14; Psalm 28–29; Acts 17

MARCH 4–10

Christmas trees and shepherds

Ezekiel

Why Christmas trees and shepherds at this time of year? Well, it's always good to remember God's eternal hope, and his promise of new life and a fresh vision, which are an integral part of the Christmas message. The Christmas story also reminds us of God's powerfully creative imagination; that he plans our lives like poems, pictures and colourful stories.

What other eye could picture an eagle in flight grasping the tip of a tree and then planting it, to grow it into a shelter for the whole of creation? A wonderful picture of Christianity. Then he made the picture a reality by coming to our world as Jesus; to hang on a cross to enable man to attain joy and peace.

How glorious it is to stare down the corridor of time and see how the prophet Ezekiel, who lived so long ago, heard God's 'picture-story' of Jesus as the tender shoot that would offer new life to the great tree of Israel and usher in the Christian era. It really gives us hope.

There are three inescapable truths – guaranteed to distress proud people – about following God. Firstly, God is Lord of our lives in a way which will astound many in the world. Secondly, he expects us to be prepared to sacrifice and suffer for our faith, whether it is giving up 'the pleasures of sin' or giving up physical comforts and luxuries. Thirdly, in the end the joy of coming to know him intimately is nothing less than 'heaven on earth', regardless of the cost.

Trevor Hoek is a clinical psychologist. He and his family emigrated to England from East London in the middle of 2001.

MARCH 4–10

DAY 1

Hope and bright new beginnings

Hope lies in the certainty that good things *will* come about and that there *really is* a way in which this new life is possible.

Ezekiel 17:22–24

Hope is especially strong when you have someone that you can really rely on, who will definitely keep his promise. God makes a number of very clear promises in Ezekiel, and they have the ring about them of being utterly trustworthy. He says to Ezekiel, 'I will' four times in these verses, but his promises extend beyond Ezekiel, and encourage us to recognise and respond to God.

The way of the world and of God's opponents is to try to convince us that God does not live up to his promises: that God's 'I will' is not reliable. Yet the Lord is absolutely emphatic in verse 24, 'I the Lord have spoken, and I will do it.'

The word of the Lord has unlimited power. It was by his word that the world was created (Hebrews 11:3, KJV). Surely I can trust his word for my life.

Have you allowed yourself to doubt that God answers prayer and responds to your needs? Have you felt that his promise of a better life is not true? These doubts will stop you believing in him and open the way for the devil to win you over.

Lord, remind me that your plans for my life are bigger than I can imagine, and that even if I cannot see you at work, I must trust that you are indeed working to ensure the best outcome.

The Bible in a year: Numbers 15–16; Acts 18

MARCH 4–10

DAY 2

Tender sprouts on tree tops

I have the privilege of writing this piece in a home that overlooks a number of cedar trees. The youngest tip of each forms a perfect cross. Have a look the next time you see a cedar.

Ezekiel 17:22–24

We look at these verses once again today, as we continue with the theme of God's promises. They show us how much God enjoys making promises. God's enthusiasm just seems to ooze from his repeated 'I wills'. 'I the Lord have spoken, and I will do it,' he says emphatically (v 22).

We certainly have a good dollop of God's promises for a better future in these verses. He said that he would take the tender cross at the top of the cedar tree and grow it into a shelter for birds of 'every' kind (v 23). The promise is that Jesus will make a spiritual home for all the nations of the earth. He offers to give everyone protection and life in abundance.

The fact that God kept his promise of creating a secure spiritual home for the nations, is good reason not to doubt his goodness and his truth. God's plan is inclusive. All nations and races are offered his rich blessings. He wants to provide shelter for every community including your own: shelter from crime, poverty, corruption and HIV/Aids. How we need this in South Africa. If only we would turn to him!

The cross is the landmark for transforming families, communities and nations. Pray earnestly for a turning to Jesus in your city or town.

The Bible in a year: Numbers 17–19; Acts 19

MARCH 4–10

DAY 3

Sour grapes and kids' teeth

Are you feeling bitter against God? God hears our angry grumbling against him and understands that it harms us more than him.

Ezekiel 18:1–13, 21–25

God becomes hurt and concerned, like any good parent, when his children get the wrong end of the stick about him. What a thought: the great God of the universe worries about my opinion of him!

The Israelites' unhappiness with God is summed up in verse 25. 'The way of the Lord is not just,' they were complaining. They suffered under the illusion that the father's 'sour grapes' set the children's teeth on edge (v 2), i.e. that the children had to suffer for their parents' sins.

God's answer is clear and concise: 'The soul who sins is the one who will die' (v 4b). Only those who are worshipping other gods and acting in a way that is destroying the lives of others will be punished (vs 10–13). But there is hope even for the wicked. God has no desire to see them perish (v 23) and invites them to turn from their sin and receive forgiveness (vs 21–22).

Our God is a just God although, like the Israelites, we are sometimes persuaded otherwise by circumstances.

Have you allowed bitterness or anger at God to cloud your faith in him? There are no easy answers to the pain and injustice of life. Ask God to help you to keep looking to him in faith even though you are tempted to look elsewhere for answers.

The Bible in a year: Numbers 22–23; Psalm 30

MARCH 4–10

DAY 4

Loss without mourning

The requirements God places on us sometimes appear harsh, but the lesson we need to learn is to obey despite our questions. When we achieve this, his blessings are enormous.

Ezekiel 24:15–27

God does not want to attain his aims without the co-operation of people like you or me. And he will go 'to the ends of the earth' to gain our active co-operation. It is a startling thought that God relies on our co-operation to achieve his plans for humanity.

He sometimes needs to break our pride so that he can harness us and put us to work. We in turn need to know that the abilities we have for doing good, like the power of speech, come from him, and we need his wisdom to put them to the best use.

Ezekiel had to make a huge sacrifice. He would not only lose his wife (v 16), but he was not allowed to mourn her passing (v 17). His wife's death and his failure to follow the normal mourning practices served as an object lesson to the people (v 19).

To what extent are we able to contemplate loving God so much that we could sacrifice 'the delight of (our) eyes' (v 16)? Paul was able to say that he had been crucified with Christ (Galatians 2:20): self-interest had died in his determination to live only for his Lord.

This passage is hard to digest. How could God expect such a sacrifice? Ask the Lord to enable you humbly to accept that his plans for you are always for good and not evil (Jeremiah 29:11). Ask him to help you to obey them.

The Bible in a year: Numbers 17-19; Acts 19

MARCH 4–10

DAY 5

Gathered together

God's anger does not last forever. Its ultimate purpose is to cleanse not kill, to purify not destroy.

Ezekiel 22:17–22; 28:24–26

What a contrast there is between these two passages! Interestingly enough, in both passages (22:20; 28:25) the Lord declares that he will gather his people. But that is where the similarity ends. In chapter 22 God gathers his people in wrath in order to punish them (v 21), while in chapter 28 he promises to bring his people back to their land, to safety and fruitfulness (v 26).

God sees Israel as unrefined ore, but when they are smelted in the furnace, only dross remains (22:18) – copper, tin, iron and lead are the dross of silver. The image of smelting speaks of judgement, not refinement, in contrast to some other prophets, e.g. Zechariah 13:9. There seems to be no hope for Israel.

It's a relief to move on to our verses in chapter 28 which are all about restoration: restoration to the Promised Land; but more important, restoration as the people of God. 'They will know that I am the Lord their God' (v 26).

We need to see that, because God is God and he is eternally good, there 'must' in the end be hope 'after all'. There is restoration for the sinner: the refining process can indeed be purifying.

Imagine that you are in God's melting pot. What is emerging from the process: dross or refined silver?

True honour: John 8:49–55
'Do not be afraid': Revelation 2:10–11

The Bible in a year: Numbers 24–25; Acts 21

Going deeper …

We might be tempted to believe that God's people are the 'heroes' of God's great plans and that cruel non-believers are the 'enemy' or the 'anvil' on which we are tested. Perhaps, though, it is not flesh and blood that is the issue.

Last week we explored the fate of Israel, whose disobedience and pride brought the wrath of God upon them through defeat by Babylon. We pictured Israel and ourselves as being God's vehicle, and realised the danger of being 'written off' if we are not steady and true. Yet, if we use our talents to serve his purpose we will flourish.

We saw that Babylon served God's purposes by defeating Israel and bringing his spoiled nation back to its knees. We compared the wayward Israel with the Titanic which sank because of overconfidence in human technology and an arrogant disregard for the forces of nature. This week we realised, however, that God's overall wish for Israel was restoration. The 'enemy' that the Lord wished to destroy was not a particular national state or person, but the sins of 'pride' and 'arrogance'.

In his sovereignty God used an evil and proud nation like Babylon to achieve his purposes, but this did not mean that they were right with him. He would bring them to their knees under the same judgement as his own nation. Wherever there is pride God brings judgement, but he never fails to support the humble. 'God opposes the proud, but gives grace to the humble' (James 4:6).

Painful pruning

Getting to know God intimately is a wonderful experience, but it also involves pain. We believers have an amazing power for good in our lives. We enjoy an unbeatable sense of meaning, through the Holy Spirit indwelling our lives. But the Lord's work in our lives involves refining and pruning.

God wants the best for us and of us: he wants our spirit to be free; he wants us to be full of faith and hope; he wants our talents to be used only for good. In John 15 God the Father is portrayed as the Divine Gardener who devotes much time to the 'branches' (v 2) – the followers of Christ (v 5). He wants us to bear fruit, and so he needs to prune us.

The Father uses many methods of pruning. Often it is a painful process, but two facts should encourage us. Firstly, it is the branches that *are* bearing fruit (not those that are barren) that are pruned (v 2). Pruning is a sign of spiritual life. Secondly, it is the *Father* who is doing the pruning. He is motivated by love and will only give us 'good things'.

If we disregard God's work in our lives, we end up in a similar situation to those who have never come to know and love God: with a life half lived at best, with a life that cannot boast of joy and contentment despite circumstances.

There is always hope and the assurance of a brighter future, but the cost is obedience and surrender to God's purposes – more than many are prepared to pay.

The Bible in a year: Numbers 26–29; Psalm 31; Acts 22

MARCH 11–17

God's promises are 'Yes' and 'Amen'

Matthew 11; John 16; 1 John 5; Psalm 91; Hebrews 11

Throughout history man has been chasing after the proverbial pot of gold at the end of a rainbow: always looking for something that will bring him contentment. The problem is that many people die empty handed in pursuit of it. The older one gets, the greater the desire for satisfaction. Some call it identity crisis; some a desire to belong and be accepted. We are all looking for security, sometimes in the wrong places.

Today we are presented with so many options in life. The market offers us products that will instantly bring the results we have desired for so long. There are promises of quickly earning extra money from home; of losing weight in a few days without changing our lifestyle; the list goes on and on. Politicians add more colour to the picture by coming up with their own promises. 'If you vote for me, I will make sure that the quality of your (or is it 'my'?) life improves.' Often we are disappointed as people fail to deliver on their promises.

But with God things are different. What he has promised will come to pass. 'For no matter how many promises God has made, they are 'Yes' in Christ. And so through him the 'Amen' is spoken by us to the glory of God' (2 Corinthians 1:20). His word will never return to him void.

Don Phillips is the minister in charge of the Christian Centre in Umtata, South Africa. He is married to Nomsa and they have two children.

MARCH 11–17

DAY 1

Rest for your soul

Have you tried to improve your life, with minimal success? Instead you feel as though the whole world is resting on your shoulders. So many people have disappointed you that you find it difficult to trust anyone. Jesus is the only person you can really look up to.

Matthew 11:25–30

The angel instructed Joseph that the child Mary was to bear should be called Jesus 'because he will save his people from their sins' (Matthew 1:21). Jesus' mandate was to address the question of sin once and for all. He was God's perfect and final antidote for sin.

In our Scripture portion today Jesus addresses folk who are weighed down with sin. There is rest for your weary soul in Jesus (v 28). He understands your problems, be it loneliness or fatigue. He was born to rescue you. Your life can have meaning and purpose when you surrender to him. So stop trying by yourself and give everything to him. His yoke is easy and his burden is light (v 30). It is heartening to hear that he will be gentle in dealing with your situation (v 29).

No other religious leader made such promises and fulfilled them. If you have never handed the burden of your sin to Jesus, why don't you do so now? He is faithful and just to forgive all that you have done wrong. Jesus wants to give you rest and a future. Ask him to help you and give him every burden that you carry. If you are a child of God you nullify God's sacrifice when you remain in a burdened state. He promised and he will deliver!

The Bible in a year: Numbers 30–31; Acts 23

MARCH 11–17

DAY 2

My Counsellor

Jesus Christ was everything to his disciples. Imagine how they felt the day he called them together to announce his departure. They must have been devastated. He was their teacher and friend: no one could compare with him. And yet he said, 'It is for your good that I am going away' (v 7).

John 16:1–15

Jesus told the disciples that the Holy Spirit was going to bring a new dimension to their ministry. He would enrich their lives in many ways. They had not been able to assimilate everything Jesus taught them, and the Holy Spirit would remind them and teach them the deep truths of God.

Jesus called the Holy Spirit the 'Counsellor' (v 7). He is our aide when we are stuck, not knowing where to go and what to say. He guides us into all truth (v 13). He backs up our preaching and witness by convicting sinners of their sin (v 8), relieving us of the responsibility of bringing people to repentance.

Maybe you did not know that you have a senior partner in the Holy Spirit. You have tried to live your life through trial and error. It has been tedious trying to please God the Father. Realise today that the Holy Spirit is available to aid you in your Christian life. Stop striving and ask the Father to fill you with his Spirit (Luke 11:13).

The Bible in a year: Numbers 32–33; Acts 24

MARCH 11–17

DAY 3

Overcoming the world

Jesus knew that the world would not be kind to us. He never promised that life would be without challenges: in fact he considers us like sheep sent amongst wolves. There are battles to be won, but he promises us victory. Paul says we are more than conquerors through Christ who strengthens us.

1 John 5:1–5

We are living in a wicked world that hates God and those who follow him. The devil would like to see the church incapacitated and riddled with immorality and sin. But we thank God for the supernatural power with which he endows us. Power to overcome the world and live victoriously. But this power is dependent on our being 'born of God' through 'faith' (v 4). No one can mimic this. In Greek the word faith is 'pistis' which means: firm persuasion, trust and conviction based upon hearing. This faith in Jesus Christ the Son of God (v 5) is the weapon that defeats the allurements of the world. False religion sets up a list of things we must do or places to which we must go to overcome evil, but all we must do is believe in Jesus.

Are you overly concerned by what is happening in the world around you? Has your life become a dismal ritual of trying to live right? God's 'commandments are not burdensome' once we have been 'born of God' (v 3–4) through our faith in Jesus, his Son.

The Bible in a year: Numbers 34–35; Acts 25

MARCH 11–17

DAY 4

Protection against all harm

Security has become a major concern for most of us. We are threatened with armed robberies, car hijackings, rape, murder, and the list goes on. We are conditioned to be extremely conscious of our safety, even to the detriment of our own happiness.

Psalm 91:1–16

We serve a mighty God (v 1)! Nothing is too difficult for him. And he is at our side when danger lurks! The theme of this wonderful Psalm is that God is 'my refuge and my fortress' (v 2). He is there to save us in every conceivable situation (vs 3–13).

God's protection is with us night and day (v 5). He is never off duty! The Lord covers us with his wings (v 4), which suggests that we need to stay close to him all the time. Do not treat him like your security company. You only call them when an intruder activates your alarm, seldom making contact when there is no danger. Don't only turn to God in times of need. Be in daily communication with him.

I was walking with my wife one evening when a neighbour's vicious dogs charged at us. I decided to run, expecting her to follow. When I stopped to see where she was, she was walking slowly behind me. She told me that she had realised that we could not outrun the dogs. She thought of Psalm 91 and ordered them to stop in the name of Jesus, which they promptly did. The Lord protects from dogs as well as lions and cobras (v 13)!

'Because he loves me,' says the Lord, 'I will rescue him' (v 14). Trust him!

The Bible in a year: Numbers 36; Deuteronomy 1; Psalm 32

DAY 5 — The key of faith

Faith is a powerful force, under-utilized by most believers. Our minds and faith are constantly at war with each other. The mind cannot comprehend what faith sees. Yet Paul encourages us to 'live by faith, not by sight' (2 Corinthians 5:7).

Hebrews 11:1–6

Verse 1 gives us God's description of faith: 'Being sure of what we hope for and certain of what we do not see.' When we relate this description to our discussions this week, we can see that the key that unlocks God's promises is our faith. It is faith that moves God (v 2). Most people try to please God in one way or the other, but we must approach God on his terms. The way of faith is the God-pleasing way (v 6a). He rewards those who seek him by faith (v 6b), not religious works. Faith is not something that you desperately try to drum up: it is God's gift (Ephesians 2:8). Simply ask him for it.

Faith is not what I trusted God for *yesterday*: it is a reality *today*. Jesus taught us to pray for our *daily* bread. You need today's faith for today's challenges.

Paul tells us that 'faith comes from hearing the message, and the message is heard through the word of Christ' (Romans 10:17). Delving deep into God's word is a sure way of developing your faith. Grow and be strong in faith. Start by trusting him for small things and move on from there. Then you will surely be able to say, 'God's promises are "Yes" and "Amen".'

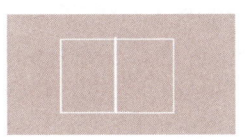

His thoughts, not mine: Isaiah 55:8–11
God has prepared a way: 1 Corinthians 2:6–16

The Bible in a year: Deuteronomy 2–3; Acts 26

Going deeper …

There are many examples in the Bible of people like you and me who inherited God's promises by faith. God is not a respecter of persons. He is moved only by our faith. Faith in God turned ordinary people into extraordinary heroes. What seems insignificant to man becomes a pillar of strength when presented to God. Take the little boy who gave his lunch to Jesus (Matthew 14:13–21). Nobody would have thought those five loaves and two fishes could be significant in the face of such need. But in the hands of Jesus they more than fed five thousand people.

Soon after I gave my life to the Lord, I heard teaching on faith at church. I went home, entered my bedroom, and prayed to God for a tie. Such a small thing, but to me at that time it was a mountain. A few minutes later my brother, who was not serving the Lord, called me to his room and gave me a beautiful tie that he had been given by our aunt. That to me was a miracle. From that day I began to trust God. Today I trust him not only for myself but for our congregation as well.

You must start to trust God somewhere. Do not allow Satan to steal from you. He will tell you that your need is insignificant before God. That is a lie: God cares about every detail of your life. Even the hairs on your head are numbered! Take your need to the Lord in faith.

Keeping the faith

When Paul was approaching the end of his road, he wrote these words to Timothy, 'I have fought the good fight, I have finished the race, I have kept the faith' (2 Timothy 4:7). Life had been a series of struggles and difficulties for Paul. Through it all he had learned to put his confidence in his God, and so at the end of his life he could honestly claim, 'I have kept my faith.'

We may lose everything else, but not our faith in God. Some people run their course; they fight a good fight; but along the way they lose their faith. Look at the ten spies that Moses sent to explore the promised land (Numbers 13:1–33). They saw the good land (v 27), they successfully avoided being captured by the enemy; they even brought back the fruit of the land (v 23). But they did not believe what God had said (v 1). The difficulties they faced in occupying the land seemed insurmountable (vs 28–29), and their faith faltered at the crucial hurdle. And so they came back and spread unbelief in the camp (vs 31–33). Only Caleb and Joshua kept their faith (v 30).

Beware of situations that will shake you just as badly as a Christian. Hold on to your faith. With time God will come through for you. His promises do not fail.

The Bible in a year: Deuteronomy 4–7; Psalm 33; Acts 27

MARCH 18–24

Worship – gaining perspective

Psalms

There are times when, to gain perspective, we need to be spoken to seriously. An honest outsider is needed to show us what is really going on within and around us. Hard as it is to admit error, a wise man will listen to a rebuke and change his ways.

The psalmist has a sound approach. Before someone else reads the riot act to him, he gives himself a good talking to. 'Praise the Lord,' he says to his soul (Psalm 103:1–2). He follows this with seventeen verses full of good reasons for acknowledging that the Lord is most excellent. At the end he repeats the command to himself. 'Praise the Lord, O my soul' (v 22). Although the psalm ends neatly at that point, you can be sure that the psalmist does not end there. So far we have had a command, sound reasons for obeying the command and a repeat of the command. I am sure that the psalmist goes on to obey the command.

I don't plan to define the word 'worship' too precisely this week, but worshipping is not simply saying: 'I worship, I worship, I worship,' however many times it is customary to repeat these words in your local fellowship. 'Praise the Lord!' bears repeating as does 'Hallelujah', which is the same thing in another language. 'Praise the Lord' is, however, a command to get on with the task. You would feel rather silly in a congregation that kept repeating: 'Tell God how excellent he is' ad nauseum, if they did not heed their own command, begin to talk to God and get very specific about just how excellent he is.

Sam Troost is a Business Analyst. His divergent pastimes are singing (opera) and orienteering. He is married to Cathy and has two daughters.

MARCH 18–24

DAY 1

No glory to us

Forget about yourself and your concerns! Don't you hate being told what to do? Jesus had the same end in mind, but with a far better understanding of human nature, phrased it differently. He taught 'Our Father … hallowed be your name.'

Psalm 115

Who is the psalmist talking to? Notice how he turns from one group of listeners to another. The Lord himself was obviously also at the meeting, as he is the first to be addressed (v 1).

It did not bother them that God could not be seen. At least he could hear, unlike the false gods who could not hear in spite of the fact that they had ears (v 6).

Watch the psalmist make comparisons (vs 3–7) and follow his example. Compare God to the computer or money, the TV, your employer or cars or a football star – whatever false god is worshipped in your community. How silly to rely on something that dies when you pull the plug from the socket. How ridiculous to build your life around a car that runs out of petrol. How about the soft drink that says '… is life!' An older generation may remember a financial institution that used to claim (but no longer does) that it was '… your anchor in life'.

We certainly need help and a shield (v 11). Blessing (v 13) and growth (v 14) will be most welcome. Notice that these are given to 'those that fear him' (v 11). Make a list of God's qualities (use this Psalm as a starting point) and it will become a lot easier to trust him.

The Bible in a year: Deuteronomy 8–9; Acts 28

MARCH 18–24

DAY 2

I will fulfil my vows

Perhaps one day I will love the Lord without ulterior motives. Until then I love the Lord because …

Psalm 116

Don't let the psalmist put words in your mouth. You might find yourself making big promises: 'I will call on him as long as I live' (v 2). Promises made must become promises kept. God won't forget, nor will he be fobbed off with a token payment.

If you are part of a congregation like mine, you will have been led to sing words (flashed on the overhead projector) that are promises, e.g. 'I will sing of the mercies of the Lord forever'. You should always read the fine print of any contract. Serious contracts like employment provide for at least a month's notice in case the conditions become too onerous. My marriage vows are a contract that is valid 'as long as I live', if my wife does not die before me. Those vows took months of negotiation and seeking God's will before we signed the deal.

Now, it is natural to want to repay God's goodness (v 12). But you can't. So don't try to by making foolish promises. An extravagant gift from God may, however, trigger an extravagant response. There is a place for making promises and the psalmist made several (vs 2, 13–14, 17–18).

If you are reluctant to make open-ended promises, you could promise God something like 'I will thank you publicly in church this Sunday for doing …' (v 17–19). He knows your weaknesses and won't look askance at your small offering. A small promise fulfilled is acceptable, while a large promise left unfulfilled is worse than nothing.

The Bible in a year: Deuteronomy 10–11; Romans 1

MARCH 18–24

DAY 3

Be specific

'The heart is deceitful above all things and beyond cure' (Jeremiah 17:9). A dismal but accurate evaluation of man. Confess that there is nothing in you that commends itself to God. 'Praise my soul the King of heaven!' does *not* mean that the King of heaven should praise *your* soul!

Psalm 104

The trouble with getting specific about God's accomplishments and character is that it makes us quake in our boots and want to hide in shame. It is easy to say, 'God made everything and everybody,' and then just walk away. But to say, 'God made plants for man to cultivate – bringing forth food' (v 14), and to continue, 'including the bitter, oversized Brussels sprouts on my plate right now,' means that you are faced with questions about your attitude to cultivation.

It is one thing to say, 'When you open your hand they are satisfied with good things' (v 28), but rather more difficult (but no less true) to acknowledge that 'when you take away their breath they die' (v 29). God is not controllable. He can't be bribed. No amount of nagging will get him to do what he does not want to do. He is the sovereign creator and we need to worship him as such. This psalm does not give man a privileged place in creation. We get a mention between the cattle (v 14) and the trees (v 16). We can come out after the lions have gone to sleep (vs 20–23)! Let it be the way it is.

Understand the greatness of God and the insignificance of man, and marvel that he chose us to worship him.

The Bible in a year: Deuteronomy 12–14; Romans 2

MARCH 18–24

DAY 4

Relent, O Lord!

No approach towards God in worship is likely to leave us unaware of our sin. Confess your reluctance to have everything you think and do inspected.

Psalm 90

Note that this prayer is accredited to Moses, a man of God. It is awesome that God, whose power and range of activities is so vast, should be interested in us. But why has he focused on our sin (v 8)? Follow Moses' example and shout, 'Get off my back!' (v 13). No need to be polite or use 'proper' language. You will know the sort of words to use if you have a spouse with exacting standards – desperate, passionate words! It's not that you don't want to be perfect. It's that you know you can't. You've tried and tried and tried. 'Let up! I can't take it any more.'

This kind of honesty is not impolite or impertinent. Moses had clearly admitted God's vast superiority over people (vs 3–5) and admitted that fear was due to him (v 11). He was willing to learn (v 12), but called for other aspects of God's personality to respond to him as well (vs 13–15). Instead of God sweeping them away (v 5) he asked for their work to be established (v 17). God's response was favourable, as this prayer itself is one of Moses' works that God established. Proof? We are reading it several millennia later.

If you find God frightening, but believe that he is compassionate, approach him and worship him.

The Bible in a year: Deuteronomy 15–16; Psalm 34

MARCH 18–24

DAY 5

Don't trust in mortals

Tell your soul to praise. It is not what you feel that counts, but what is true. When you least feel like worshipping you invariably most need to do so.

Psalm 146

I always find 'do not' commands difficult to obey. This is because doing the wrong thing is often motivated by a strong need. I desperately need a way out. I need someone strong and knowledgeable to take my side. If I obey the 'do not' command I am left isolated.

This psalm delivers a stern 'do not' (v 3), and gives a very good reason (v 4). Then we are pointed to a much better way in the remaining six verses.

Which of the categories of people highlighted in verses 7 to 9 do you fall into?

Which of these are you afraid you might eventually tumble into? Have you made arrangements to rely on mortal men?

Credit and investment portfolio managers build their careers around researching whether the person wanting the deal will be able to deliver on his promises. Recruitment specialists, company buyers and supply chain managers also spend much effort on discerning the other party's ability to deliver. Be as zealous as they are in checking out the credentials of the person you are going to entrust your life to!

'The Lord sets prisoners free' (v 7). In what areas of your life do you need freedom? Review God's abilities and willingness to help you, and do what is necessary.

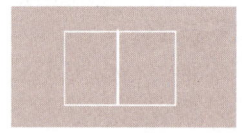

Worship arouses opposition: Revelation 13:1–10
Worship the Lamb: Isaiah 53:1–12

The Bible in a year: Deuteronomy 17–18; Romans 3

MARCH 18–24

Going deeper …

Times of worship can feel like a personal disaster. You may feel that everyone is really connecting with God except you. Alternatively you may feel that others are simply making a racket or not doing enough, and this hinders your worship.

Obviously how you feel is not the ultimate barometer of what is happening, but the discomfort must be dealt with. Jesus told the Samaritan woman that 'true worshippers will worship the Father in spirit and in *truth*'. John made it clear how you spot the untruthful worshipper: if you say, 'I love you, Lord,' yet hate your brother, you are a liar (1 John 4:20). If this describes you, rest assured that God never convicts without providing the power to change and overcome. Confession is the first step; sometimes this needs to happen in public (James 5:16).

Jesus was adamant that you cannot worship in the midst of disharmony: 'If you are offering your gift at the altar and there remember that your brother has something against you, leave your gift there in front of the altar. First go and be reconciled to your brother; then come and offer your gift' (Matthew 5:23–24). You will need courage to take this step (which may also need to happen in public), but 'perfect love drives out fear' (1 John 4:18) and prevents your worship from being a clanging cymbal (1 Corinthians 13:1).

Tell it like it is

Conclusion

We were made to praise God: to enjoy someone so trustworthy and powerful; someone so in love with us. He wants us to know him, and sent his Son who is an exact representation of his being. He knows our frailty and has provided purification for sins. He is unstoppable. One of my favourite images, from Revelation 1:18, is of a risen Jesus holding the keys of death and Hades which he purchased for me at immense cost.

He is so approachable. Friends of a crippled man could bring him to Jesus on a mat and jump the queue by lowering him through the roof. When Jesus saw their faith, he forgave the cripple's sins, even though nobody had dreamed of asking for so much (Mark 2:1–12).

God is Spirit, but that does not mean he is abstract. Even a cup of water given to a poor person is accepted as a gift to him (Matthew 10:42). Your few words of thanks, praise and worship may seem rather feeble. Think of them as small dots on a pointillist painting – small but integral parts of the beauty. Your testimony, your witness is vital. In our sub-culture we think of testimony and witness as the impassioned twenty-minute story of our dramatic conversion. Going back to telling what we've seen and heard (1 John 1:1) is what it is all about. *Stick to the facts and stick up for the facts!* See Revelation 12:11 for the effect your evidence has.

The Bible in a year: Deuteronomy 19–22; Psalm 35; Romans 4

MARCH 25–31

The cross

John 3, 19–20; Hebrews 9; Luke 23; Matthew 27

The death of Jesus is a very significant event in history. Jesus clearly lived as though his death was the most important event in his life. His birth was just the gateway to Calvary. Almost one third of the Gospels is devoted to the events around Jesus' death and resurrection. The early chapters scan his life and ministry, and then the narrative moves from fast forward into slow motion, as the final events of his life are described. Even the Apostles' Creed moves from 'born of the Virgin Mary' to 'suffered under Pontius Pilate' without even a mention of his life and ministry. Jesus himself asked us to remember him through a meal of bread and wine signifying his death on the cross. Seems a bit bizarre, asking to be remembered by the way that he died! Imagine if we built a little shrine around a wrecked motor car, because someone we loved had been killed in it, and we wanted to remember them by it! Even more bizarre is the fact that the cross was a very cruel means of execution, yet we have it displayed in our churches and hang it around our necks. Imagine walking into a place of worship where a hangman's noose or a guillotine was prominently displayed as a sacred effigy.

Well, the cross of Jesus is significant, because on it the Son of God died to redeem us from sin, defeat the forces of darkness, and free us from the great enemies of death and hell. During this week we will look at some of the events surrounding Calvary, and the response of some of the people.

As this is Holy week, I have provided seven days of notes instead of the usual five, plus a 'Going deeper' column.

Donovan Coetzee is the Chairman of Assemblies of God in South Africa. He is based in Cape Town.

MARCH 25–31

DAY 1   The Ray Ban believer

Have you ever visited a church where they asked visitors to raise their hands or stand and you hoped no one would notice you?

John 3:1–15; 19:38–42

Nicodemus is a very interesting character. One who lived in the shadows. He lived, as it were, with dark glasses on. He was the Ray Ban believer; the man who moved at night. He was too brave for cowardice, but too hesitant for heroism. He was a member of the Jewish ruling council, the Sanhedrin, a group opposed to Jesus. However, Jesus' teaching and ministry intrigued him.

So he came under cover of night to ask questions about miracles (v 2), and instead received teaching on being born again (vs 3–8). He stood within an inch of the Kingdom, but it seems that the price was too great: he'd have to face the Sanhedrin and turn his back on tradition. He got another opportunity in John 7:50–51. He came to Jesus' defence. But again appears to back off. So near yet so far!

Three heads drop on three spent breasts: Jesus and the thieves are dead. Joseph and Nicodemus claim Jesus' body (vs 38–39). At last Nicodemus has come out of the closet and, together with Joseph, buries Jesus. Maybe it was the boldness of Joseph that helped him. Was it too little, too late – like roses at a funeral? Does he cry, 'If only I could turn the clock back'?

Are you battling to stand as a disciple of Jesus? What is the price you are struggling to pay? Don't wait until it's too late. Seize the moment; don't let it slip away. Stand! Ask God to help you today.

The Bible in a year: Deuteronomy 23–24; Romans 5

MARCH 25–31

DAY 2

Honest doubt

Ever failed or made a bad mistake? Have you struggled to shake off the stigma of that mistake? How often we label people according to the mistakes they make. Thomas doubted once, and for 2 000 years we've used him to label others!

John 20:19–31

Thomas missed one meeting (v 24). It was the meeting at which the resurrected Jesus turned up. Why was he not there? I think it was because his faith had been shattered. He had followed Jesus for three years, believing that he was going to destroy the oppressor, Rome, and usher in the new Messianic order. He had been loyal and totally committed. He once even said, 'Let us also go, that we may die with him' (John 11:16).

When Jesus surrendered without a fight, he was (I believe) disillusioned and gave up. So when he heard that Jesus was alive, he retorted that unless he saw and touched he could not believe (v 25). I believe that he meant it with all his heart. There is more faith in honest doubt than in most of the creeds! Jesus knew he meant it and turned up once more – just for Thomas. He invited Thomas to do what no one else had done: touch his wounds (v 27). What an awesome privilege! Just a thought – the only fingerprints in heaven belong to Thomas. Not a bad privilege for a doubter!

Is there something you are struggling to believe about Jesus? He sees your heart. Call on him and ask him to reveal himself to you in a special way. You are just as precious to Jesus as Thomas.

The Bible in a year: Deuteronomy 25–26; Romans 6

MARCH 25–31

DAY 3

'Sinner, come in'

The other day I shook hands with Nelson Mandela. I was amazed at how personable he was. Truly great people are always accessible and welcome you into their presence. Have you ever been in the presence of someone truly great?

Hebrews 9:1–14; Luke 23:44–46

A curtain separated the Holy Place from the Holy of Holies in the temple (9:2–3). This was where the glory of God was manifest. No one was allowed beyond this curtain except the High Priest, once a year on the Day of Atonement when he offered a sacrifice for the sins of the nation (9:7). Even then he did so in fear, not knowing whether God would accept his sacrifice. He had pomegranates and bells on the hem of his garment. When he walked they made a noise and the people outside knew that he was still alive. He also had a rope tied around his leg in case he was not accepted and died. They would be able to pull him out without having to go in and face death. This curtain had invisible words on it, 'Sinners keep out'.

When Jesus died, he – as High Priest – offered his own blood (9:12). No more sacrifices were needed: the ultimate sacrifice had been offered through which sinners were able to approach God (9:14). And so the curtain was torn from top to bottom by God (23:45), and blazoned across the entrance to the presence of God were the invisible words, 'Sinner, come in.'

Have you grasped the enormity of what Jesus did? Do you take access to God for granted? How much time do you spend in his presence?

The Bible in a year: Deuteronomy 27–28; Romans 7

MARCH 25–31

DAY 4

Following the crowd

Have you ever been in a group that was voicing an important opinion which was different from yours, and you were afraid to say anything?

Matthew 27:32–44, 54–56

There were crowds of people in Jerusalem for the Passover. Many of them passed by the cross, commenting on Jesus as he hung there. I am convinced that there must have been some who had been healed by him; others who had heard him teach or been fed when he multiplied the loaves and fishes. Yet as he hung there, they were swept along by the crowd; they became victims of 'mob mentality'.

Among them were learned people – teachers of the Law (v 41); hard, robust people – soldiers; gentler types – the women for instance; and even robbers (v 38). They all seemed to have lost their sense of proportion and many abused Jesus (vs 39–44), except the Centurion who exclaimed: 'Surely he was the Son of God' (v 54). He had been at many executions, but had never before witnessed a dying man saying: 'Forgive them, for they do not know what they are doing' (Luke 23:34). He'd never seen someone who, instead of fighting and resisting, was 'led like a lamb to the slaughter' (Isaiah 53:7). Or someone who noticed his mother in the crowd and asked a friend to look after her (John 19:25–27). But most importantly, he saw the eclipse and heard the quake (v 54).

Are you easily influenced to abandon an opinion based on the word of God? Ask God to help you to be faithful to his word and to take a stand for it.

The Bible in a year: Deuteronomy 29–30; Psalm 36

MARCH 25–31

DAY 5

Good Friday
Too sad to shine!

I recall, as a little boy, watching the eclipse of the sun through a photo negative. I remember people up and down the street looking at the heavens, and how we all reacted in amazement to this phenomenon.

Matthew 27:45–54

One of the most astonishing occurrences at Jesus' crucifixion was the darkening of the sun. This took place at three in the afternoon and lasted for three hours (v 45). Amazing! Why did this happen? There could be many answers, but I have a few suggestions for us to contemplate.

We are told that God hid his face from Jesus. Jesus cried out: 'My God, my God, why have you forsaken me?' (v 46). The eclipse of the sun represented this. Also I believe that every demon of hell was there waging war against Jesus. After all, the future of every human ever born was being fought for on the cross. This was a battle royale. The darkness of hell covered the face of the earth. Another possibility is that God did not want mankind to look on his Son dying in such a humiliating way. Perhaps we should just say that it was a sad day, and the sun refused to shine!

Jesus dying on the cross meant that God hid his face from him, so that God can gaze upon us with acceptance. Try to grasp this incredible truth. The forces of darkness were defeated on our behalf so that we can live a life of victory over sin.

Thank God for going to such great lengths that even the sun had to respond. He did this all for you!

The Bible in a year: Deuteronomy 31–32; Romans 8

MARCH 25–31

DAY 6

Lady in red?

How easy it is to typecast people. We judge by culture, accent, suburb, school, and so on. We also hold people in the prison of their past, and even see it as worse than it really was. How many of us are imprisoned by other people's opinions?

Luke 8:1–3; Matthew 27:55–56; John 20:1–18

Mary Magdalene is an interesting woman. One often hears that she was a prostitute, but nowhere in the Bible does it say this. What we do know is that she had seven demons cast out of her (Luke 8:2). She obviously had a very dark past. But that all changed when she met Jesus. For once, she met someone who did not condemn her, but simply liberated her from her past. He did for her what no one else could do. As a result she followed him and his disciples from that day forward and ministered to their needs (Luke 8:3). Hers was grateful, committed, sacrificial love.

She was most distraught when Jesus was arrested and killed. She was one of the few at the cross after the others had fled, and seems to have followed him all the way to his tomb (Luke 23:55–56). She was the first at the tomb after the Sabbath to anoint his body. What a shock it was to find the stone rolled away (John 20:1), and to think that grave robbers had been at work (v 2). But her joy was unspeakable when her risen Lord appeared to her in the garden (vs 14–17).

She followed Jesus to the end and was rewarded by seeing him alive first (Mark 16:9). Does your devotion match Mary Magdalene's?

The Bible in a year: Deuteronomy 33–34; Joshua 1–3; Psalm 37; Romans 9

MARCH 25–31

DAY 7

Easter Sunday
Mission impossible

What would it take to keep Jesus in the tomb? If we think the nails kept him on the cross, then maybe the seal on the tomb would secure him (v 66)! Think of the enormity of the resurrection of Jesus before reading today's portion.

Matthew 27:62–28:15

'Take a Guard. Go, make the tomb as secure as you know how' (v 65). Mission impossible! Jesus was not killed, but 'gave up his spirit' (27:50). He entered into death and the grave to defeat sin, death and hell. His resurrection was simply part of his march back to the Father to report: 'Mission accomplished!' Nothing could stop him from emerging from that tomb.

A fable tells of how the devil, before taking a three-day holiday, told death to hold Jesus so that Corruption could corrupt him. On returning, the devil found Hades in total chaos. Prison doors were open and captives had been released. He was told that Jesus had caused the chaos. He demanded to know from Corruption why he had not corrupted the body of Jesus. Corruption replied that, as Death could not hold him, he was unable to corrupt him.

When Jesus said he would rise again (Matthew 20:19), he meant it and nothing could prevent it. Therefore if he says to you: 'Never will I leave you; never will I forsake you' (Hebrews 13:5), and: 'I will come back and take you to be with me' (John 14:3), he means these words as well.

Thank Jesus for defeating your real enemies – sin, death and hell. Thank him also for being with you and that he will one day return to take you to him.

MARCH 25–31

Going deeper ...

After being raised from the dead, Jesus appears to his disciples on a number of occasions. Why did he do this? I believe to show that even though he was not visible, he was nevertheless present. He had promised that he would never leave them nor forsake them. And he was there when they spoke about him, or when they discussed their futures. He knew that they would be afraid, so when they locked themselves in the upper room for fear of the Jews, he came to them and showed himself to them. 'Don't be afraid: I am with you,' is what he was communicating. He wanted them to be sure of the fact that he was no longer dead, and that he was going to prepare a place for them – as he had told them, and that he was coming back for them.

In order to convince them thoroughly, he appeared to them at various times over forty days (Acts 1:3–4). He did not just rise from the dead, appear once and then disappear. He wanted to convince them that he was alive, that he had conquered death and that his mission was still on track. Then in order to underline this fact, he made sure they all saw him when he ascended. He wanted them to know that he had finished making his appearances, but that he was not leaving for good. Of course the ascension astounded them, but he sent two angels to explain exactly what was going on (Acts 1:10–11).

He is alive! He will return! Let us respond by representing him with passion and integrity.

APRIL 1–7

The gospel from scratch

Romans 1–3

There seem to be two different ways in which people learn to use computers. Some sit down at the keyboard and start experimenting; they pick things up as they go along and phone a friend if they get really stuck. Others only start when they have a how-to guide to hand. They love the step-by-step logic of the manual which starts with the basics and gradually explains how the whole system works.

Paul's letter to the Romans is the nearest thing we have in the New Testament to a step-by-step guide to Christian doctrine. In it he gives us a careful explanation of Christian belief, from the starting point of our human problem through to the wonderful realities of God's grace, the gift of salvation in Jesus and the work of the Holy Spirit. He argues logically from one step to the next and pauses to consider potential objections along the way. Perhaps not surprisingly, Romans is the longest of Paul's letters. His other letters were written to churches he knew well and his agenda was set by their pastoral needs. This letter was written to a church he had never visited, so he sets out to introduce himself by making a plain statement of the message he preaches.

From the outset he emphasises that his message is the gospel (literally 'good news'). Before he can explain the good news of salvation, however, he has to show what we need to be saved *from*. This week's readings explore the problem of human sinfulness. They show that if we reject God's will we cannot shrug it off as unimportant or treat it as someone else's problem. Sin changes the whole nature of our relationship with God. It is the deepest problem we face – and a problem which God alone can sort out.

Martin Hodson is the minister of the Red Hill Baptist Church, Worcester, England. He and his wife, Becky, have three boys and live in a house full of toys, music and visitors.

APRIL 1–7

DAY 1

Hello everyone, it's me!

When you meet someone new, what do you tell them about yourself? Perhaps like me you mention where you live, who you live with and what you do. But what are the most important things about you that you would really like other people to know? Come into God's all-knowing presence using Psalm 139:1: 'O Lord, you have searched me …'

Romans 1:1–17

Last week I answered the phone and an unfamiliar voice said, 'You won't know me, but I'm from …' She went on to describe the Christian organisation she works for. Her brief introduction reassured me that we share the same goals and left me feeling excited by her commitment to serving God.

In Romans, the apostle Paul is writing to Christians who mostly do not know him personally. He introduces himself by telling them of his goal and his commitment. He has been 'set apart for the gospel of God' (v 1) and his goal is to fulfil that calling. His commitment is transparent. He is serving with his whole heart (v 9), he is eager to preach (v 15) and he is not ashamed of the gospel but utterly convinced of its power for the salvation of everyone who believes (v 16). You can imagine the Roman Christians responding to his infectious enthusiasm for the gospel.

Paul does not focus entirely on his own ministry. He is careful also to encourage his readers. They too are called and loved by God (vs 6–7); their faith is widely reported (v 8) and Paul longs to see them, not only so that he can pray for them to receive more spiritual gifts but so that they can encourage him (vs 11–12).

Pray for someone to be affected this week by your enthusiasm for Jesus and your encouragement.

The Bible in a year: Joshua 4–5; Romans 10

APRIL 1–7

DAY 2

Holy hostility

'Holy, holy, holy is the Lord God Almighty.' Repeat these words a few times and sense God's awesome and perfect presence.

Romans 1:18–32

Before Paul explains the good news of the gospel he sets out the bad news. God is angry because people ignore him and fail to keep his commands (v 18). This idea was hardly more palatable in the ancient world than it is to modern Western society, which is steadily losing its confidence in moral right and wrong.

God's wrath is not like a human fit of anger where someone flies off the handle about something. It is his holy hostility towards evil which justly deserves punishment (v 32). Paul describes, in all its ugliness, the sin which arouses God's anger. It arises out of ignoring what is plain – that a creation must have a Creator and that a universe with a physical order also has a moral order (v 20). Because we are made to be worshippers, ignoring God results in worship of created things instead of the Creator – be it bowing down to images of false gods or the more subtle idolatry of materialism (v 25). Such worship has no moral constraints. Sinful desires have free rein (v 24) and in turn lead to sinful deeds (v 26). Although the illustrations of sin are at first drawn from sexual immorality (vs 24–27), it is made clear in verses 29–31 that all other sins of thought, word and deed are part of the same rebellion.

Living in a sin-soaked world, I sometimes find that I stop noticing sin, both around me and within me. I have to ask the Holy Spirit to give me a holy hostility towards all that offends God. In the light of this passage, let's do that today.

The Bible in a year: Joshua 6–7; Romans 11

APRIL 1–7

DAY 3

Bringing it home

Jesus is the sinless friend of sinners. Hear him calling to you as a friend. Say your name a few times aloud, then as you hear the 'echo', in your imagination think of Jesus calling you as his friend, to come and be at his side.

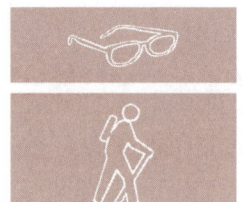

Romans 2:1–16

The faults we see most clearly in others are often the ones we are most blind to in ourselves. We have a subtle impulse to project our failings onto others, perhaps in the hope that it will make us feel better. Here Paul makes it clear that we cannot excuse ourselves by accusing others (vs 1–3). We can't avoid God's judgement by disguising our wrongs. Our only hope comes from recognising God's kindness which leads us to honest repentance (v 4).

Some people think they will avoid God's judgement because they live a good life. It is true that God gives to everyone according to what they have done (v 6) and that eternal life would be the reward for anyone who perfectly persisted in doing good (v 7). But what is obvious to every honest reader is that none of us live that perfect life; we have to admit our complicity in evil one way or another (v 9). We can't hide behind the fact that we simply *know* God's commands (v 13); God's requirement is that we obey them. Our problem is not ignorance but disobedience. And even those who might claim ignorance nevertheless have the Maker's stamp on them in the form of their conscience, alerting them to the fact that they too do things that are both right and wrong (v 15).

Is there anyone you have a critical attitude towards? Check that you're not seeing your own faults in them. Pray that God will teach you something through them.

The Bible in a year: Joshua 8–9; Romans 12

DAY 4

True belonging

God has 'anointed us, set his seal of ownership on us, and put his Spirit in our hearts' (2 Corinthians 1:21–22). Ask God's Spirit to speak into your heart and remind you that before any other claims are made on your life, you belong to Jesus.

Romans 2:17–29

When I studied theology at university I was astonished by the sheer number of books in the faculty library. I was relieved when I discovered that it was not necessary to read them all in order to graduate! I continue to be an avid reader of Christian books and have a regular teaching ministry in our church, but I'm strongly aware of the caution in this passage: knowledge alone is not the way to a living relationship with God. Knowing and approving God's will (v 18) are vital but not an end in themselves; guiding and instructing others is important (vs 19, 20) but it can also be a way of ignoring our own need of God's grace (v 23).

Jewish men generally assumed the outward mark of circumcision automatically meant they belonged to God's people. Here Paul says this is not the case (vs 25–27). It is when the Spirit of God is at work in our hearts (v 29) that we are marked as truly belonging to God. We cannot win a place in God's family by our knowledge or our outward acts; it is only when his Spirit comes to dwell in us that we know we are God's children (see 8:16).

Think of anyone you help to guide or instruct in Christian living. Pray for wisdom to share with them and for integrity to live by the principles you teach others.

The Bible in a year: Joshua 10–11; Psalm 38

DAY 5

Feeble excuses

Jesus is Lord! Think of ways in which his lordship is being worked out in your life and give him thanks for each one.

Romans 3:1–8

Imagine taking an exam. The examiner has made the questions incredibly difficult. No one in the whole country passes the exam. There is an outcry against the examiner. A few desperate students, however, make a last ditch attempt to impress him by saying that their inability to answer the questions actually highlights the examiner's brilliance and proves that his intellect is incomparably greater than theirs. He ought to recognise that their failure is actually a compliment to him and reward them accordingly. Their logic is absurd, but it is the logic of the argument Paul is resisting here (vs 5–8).

It is absurd firstly because the standards set are 'the very words of God' (v 2). The law of God is not open to negotiation. It stands in stark contrast to the do-it-yourself approach to morality which says people should just do what 'feels right for them'. At times we too may be tempted to justify our actions by clever words or mental gymnastics when we know in our heart of hearts that we are not sincerely obeying the words of God.

Furthermore, since God is the righteous judge of the whole world (v 6), it is ridiculous to envisage him seeing a positive aspect to unrighteousness! We have misunderstood the purity and holiness of God if we think there are loopholes in his law that exempt us from full obedience.

God has shown me times when I've used foolish arguments to justify doing what I wanted instead of obeying his word. Ask him to show you if you are doing this in some way.

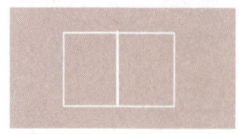

Be holy: 1 Peter 1:13–25
Purify my heart: Psalm 51

The Bible in a year: Joshua 12–15; Romans 13

Going deeper …

Romans 1:28–31 is perhaps the most disturbingly comprehensive list of sins in the New Testament. The good news is that through the cross our status has changed from 'condemned sinner' to 'beloved child of God'. We need to enter more and more deeply into the forgiving grace of God. We invite the Holy Spirit to search our hearts, convicting us of attitudes, words or deeds which offend against God's righteousness. Unlike Satan, who condemns us for our sins and tries to make us feel like helpless failures, the Spirit of Jesus highlights our sins so that we can bring them to the cross and receive there the forgiveness of God.

One way of experiencing this is to offer a particular aspect of our lives to God and ask him to point out where sin has a foothold. You may choose for example the previous day or the last week, or perhaps your work, friendships, marriage or ministry in the church. With an openness to the Spirit's prompting and a pen and paper to hand, note down anything he brings to mind. Then go through the list, naming each sin before God, resolving to turn your back on it and letting the grace of his forgiveness flow into your life as you go. Ripping up the list when you have finished is a powerful way of saying that those sins are now done away with. There may be times when we find forgiveness hard to receive and need to take our list to a close friend or pastoral leader and (following the command to confess our sins to one another in James 5:16) ask them to pray with us and declare God's forgiveness to us.

So what?

Everyone agrees that there is something wrong with the world. It's not all we want it to be. It's not all we sense it *should* be. But, what needs to be changed? Some people believe the solution lies in better political policies. Others are sure that better education would solve our problems, and still others think that creating the best environment will bring out the best in people. All these changes may be good, but none of them addresses the root of the problem. We have seen this week that the basic human problem is a dislocation in our relationship with God. Everyone has rebelled against God and fallen short of their full God-given potential. The result is that everyone must face God's just judgement. No one can escape from this by pointing the finger at others who seem worse than themselves. Everyone is implicated.

The gospel which Paul expounded shows how faith in Jesus is the only way to be saved from this. God in his loving kindness has reached out to offer us the gift of forgiveness and the power of his Spirit to set us free from the hold of sin.

Every day we see evidence of sin, whether it is on the scale of a selfish thought or an international conflict. As we seek to live close to God's heart, we begin to share the grief he experiences at the spoiling of his creation. This causes us to pray with new fervour: 'Your kingdom come, your will be done on earth as it is in heaven,' and inspires us with new zeal to share the good news of salvation.

The Bible in a year: Joshua 16–22; Psalm 39; Romans 14

APRIL 8–14

Righteousness from God

Romans 3–5

A hush comes over the courtroom as the judge prepares to deliver his verdict. Everyone present is convinced the accused is guilty, including the accused himself. It is to their great astonishment therefore that the judge declares, 'I find this person not guilty.' The accused has been acquitted of the crime. A judgement has been passed upon him and in relation to the law he has been deemed righteous.

The central theme of our readings this week is 'justification'. This is the heavy-duty word Paul uses for God's decision to declare us righteous. We have all clearly sinned by breaking God's law at many points; this became amply clear in last week's readings. But now God has made a way to declare that we are not liable to the penalty for sin and are entitled to all the privileges due to those who have kept the law (5:1–5).

How can he do this? He has revealed his own righteousness to us in Jesus Christ, who perfectly met the demands of the law and died as a sacrifice for the sins of everyone who had broken the law. When we put our faith in Jesus, God credits his righteousness to us as a gift and we change from being the objects of his wrath to the objects of his blessing.

As we get down to the basics of our faith in this week's readings, be prepared to rejoice in everything that God has done for you. You may be very busy doing things for God, but remember that what matters above all is what he has done for you. Be ready to rediscover the central truth that salvation comes not by our good works but by God's grace alone.

Martin Hodson is the minister of the Red Hill Baptist Church, Worcester, England. He and his wife, Becky, have three boys and live in a house full of toys, music and visitors.

APRIL 8–14

DAY 1   Holy dissatisfaction

A new hospital is being built near my home. As the vast new building rises, it occurs to me how strong the foundations must be to support all this. Whatever is built now and in the future depends on those foundations. Ask God to strengthen the foundations of your faith this week.

Romans 3:9–20

We naturally enjoy celebrating our achievements and those of our friends. If someone gets promoted or wins a contract, or if the sports team they play for excels, we are quick to congratulate them. If it were a competition to prove our righteous achievements to God, however, there would be no winners. Everyone would be on the losing side, even those who practised hardest and paid most attention to the rules. The status of being righteous in God's sight is something we cannot achieve by our own efforts (v 20).

Without Jesus there is one thing we all have in common: we are 'under sin' (v 9). We are under its power to destroy our relationship with God and exclude us from the joy of living in his presence. This is not some new idea Paul devised when he was having a bad day and feeling pessimistic. The clear teaching of the Old Testament is that people fall far short of God's perfect ideal for us. Paul provides a battery of quotations from Psalms and Isaiah to prove the point (vs 10–18). In some way we all carry within us the dissatisfaction that we are not all that God made us to be.

Face that holy dissatisfaction in yourself. Give thanks to God that he is not waiting for you to become perfect before you can know him but has sent his perfect Son to satisfy his righteous demands in your place.

The Bible in a year: Joshua 23–24; Romans 15

APRIL 8–14

DAY 2

The gift

With open hands pray, 'Lord, I have nothing to bring to you except myself. By faith I receive your love, your mercy and your grace in my life.'

Romans 3:21–31

My young son dreamed of having a new bicycle but quickly worked out there was no way his pocket money would amount to enough for him to buy one. I can still see the look of delight on his face on Christmas morning when he saw the gleaming mountain bike that had his name on it. What he could never afford himself, he had been given as a gift. This passage sums up the essence of the good news: the righteousness in God's sight which we could never earn by our good works, God himself has given us as a gift.

Twice Paul emphasises that this righteousness is 'from God' (vs 21–22). It is by grace (v 24) – not the result of our success but of God's lavish generosity to people who don't deserve it. The initiative is all God's. He declares that we are acquitted of our sin (the meaning of 'justified', v 24). He presents the sacrifice for our sin (v 25). He demonstrates his own justice by justly punishing sin (v 26). There is no suggestion that we contribute in any way to our own righteous status before God. We can only recognise our desperate situation (v 23) and depend utterly on God for rescue by putting our faith in Jesus (v 28). If we are tempted to boast of how 'spiritual' we are, this passage reminds us that no part of our salvation is our own achievement – it's all God's (v 27).

Think of a generous gift someone has given you. What was your response to their kindness? How does that compare with your response to God today?

The Bible in a year: Judges 1–2; Romans 16

APRIL 8–14

DAY 3

Faith or works?

Think about some inspiring Christians you know or have read about. Remember that every one of them was saved by faith – not by their impressive deeds. And so are you.

Romans 4

A well-known TV presenter recently resigned from the BBC. The newspapers reported that by some administrative oversight he had continued to receive his (very generous) salary for some time after he left. They declared this a scandal and were pleased to inform us that he had returned the overpayment. They could take it for granted that everyone agrees that a person should not be paid for work they have not done. In Romans 4, Paul is addressing the sense of scandal we might feel at the gospel, which says God grants to us his righteousness without us having to work for it (v 5). He defends this conviction by saying that this is how it has always been with God. Going back to the early chapters of the Bible, he shows that Abraham was credited with righteousness when he believed God (v 3). This step of faith took place before his own memorable act of obedience (v 10).

God had given Abraham a promise that all peoples on earth would be blessed through him (Genesis 12:3). This promise has been fulfilled in Jesus. Anyone can now enter God's blessing (the alternative to God's judgement) through faith in him (v 16). But we learn from Abraham that faith is not a superficial 'yes' to a list of beliefs. Faith means trusting God's promise in Jesus for our future, our reputation and our righteousness (vs 23–24), come what may.

What motivates you to work for God? Are you attempting the impossible and trying to earn something from him, or is your motivation sheer gratitude?

The Bible in a year: Judges 3–4; Mark 1

APRIL 8–14

DAY 4

The benefits

Imagine God enthroned in splendour. Jesus takes you by the hand and leads you into his presence. You draw near to him. You stand before him. He reaches out and puts his hand on your head. 'You are my child,' he says.

Romans 5:1–11

People who have lived through a war know the relief that comes from hearing the words, 'Peace has been declared'. Hostilities are ended and there is hope for a better future. Here Paul says the outcome of God's free gift of righteousness is that we have peace with God (v 1).

We are no longer God's enemies or objects of his wrath. This is not because we have negotiated a settlement with God, but because he has taken the initiative and reconciled us to himself through the death of Jesus (vs 9–10). His simple motive for this is love (v 8). If we need a reason to rejoice in God, this is surely it (v 11)!

Now we receive all the benefits of being God's friends. Jesus gives us access into his presence (v 2). There is never a 'no entry' sign on his door. We have the freedom of children to come to our Father. Furthermore, our future is safe with God. Whatever our immediate circumstances, we know that our ultimate experience will be living in God's glorious presence, finally transformed into the likeness of his glory (vs 2–4). Here and now the Holy Spirit makes real our experience of God's love for us. He doesn't just give us a few drops of it but generously pours out God's love into the deepest parts of our being (v 5).

Ask the Holy Spirit to give you some words now that express God's love for you. Write them down and put them somewhere you'll notice later.

The Bible in a year: Judges 5–6; Psalms 40–41

DAY 5

The great reversal

Remember the moment or period in your life when you first received God's grace by faith and came to know Jesus personally. Thank God for taking hold of you. Recall the change he made, the new ambitions he gave you and the way you felt.

Romans 5:12–21

The coming of Jesus is the turning point of history. The Western calendar recognises this by dividing the years of human history into BC and AD. The first period is defined by the sin of Adam, through which death entered the world (v 12). The second period is defined by the righteousness of Jesus, through whom God's grace overflows to the world (v 15).

This is not a simple tit-for-tat reversal. What Jesus has done is not the equal-and-opposite of what Adam did, but is something far more wonderful than that. Adam's sin resulted in the bleakness of death; Jesus' righteousness resulted in the joyful gift of God's grace (v 15). From Adam came the hopelessness of condemnation; from Jesus comes the only hope of justification (v 16). In Adam, death gained the power to reign over us; in Jesus we gain the power to reign with him through grace (vs 17, 21). To reign like that means living in the confidence that sin does not rule over our destiny, our relationships or our potential. Jesus has overcome the power of sin and as we live through him we know that we are on the winning side.

Pray for God's grace to reign in your life. Ask first for it to reign over any guilt that troubles you with regard to sins you have honestly confessed to him. Then ask for his grace to reign in your relationships with others, enabling you to forgive as you have been forgiven.

Paul's story: Philippians 3:1–11
A cry for mercy: Luke 18:9–14

The Bible in a year: Judges 7–8; Mark 2

Going deeper …

'God has poured out his love into our hearts by the Holy Spirit, whom he has given us' (Romans 5:5). Whatever we may know about God, we can understand nothing unless we first know he loves us. Whatever sacrifice we may have to make to obey him, we will never make it willingly unless we first know he loves us. In 1 Corinthians 13 Paul explains that the whole of Spirit-filled living is animated by the receiving and sharing of God's love.

It is not surprising that God has provided a special means of infusing his love into our hearts. His Holy Spirit is the bringer of the Father's love. When the Spirit comes upon us, he always draws us closer to the Father's heart. Whether he comes with healing or with spiritual gifts, whether he comes to convict us of sin or to teach us God's truth, it is always with the reassurance that we are loved by the Father. Nothing less than the eternal self-sacrificing love of God flows into the centre of our being. His love is poured out in us. This is far more than the measured operation of pouring a dash of milk into a cup of tea! It is a liberal outpouring – the kind John the Baptist envisaged coming with the drenching force of a baptism (Mark 1:8).

Perhaps the Spirit will fill you next time you worship in your church, or when someone prays with you, or as you quietly wait on God alone, even now. As he does so, hear him say, 'I love you, my child.'

The heart of the matter

So we have a new status before God. He has forgiven our sins and credited the righteousness of Jesus to us. But what difference does this make?

Our identity. We now know that our relationship with God depends not on our weak and changeable efforts but on the trustworthy and unchanging work of God through Jesus, whose love is confirmed in our hearts by the Holy Spirit. When we are tempted to crumble under a sense of failure because we have let God down, or when Satan whispers to us that we are condemned for our sin, we can hold onto the fact that we are God's children only because of *his* perfect work, not because of the quality of our good works.

Our actions. We can't pretend that because we have been justified in God's sight we have become morally perfect. Justification is an event that happens when we put our faith in Jesus. Becoming righteous in practice (sometimes called 'sanctification') is a process that then begins as God's Spirit works in us to make us more like Jesus. Being already justified gives us the best reason to grow in practical righteousness: to become what God has already made us to be. Our challenge is not to save ourselves from sin (God has already done that). God has declared us holy and our challenge is to live up to that.

Our future. God has brought our final judgement forward into the present and given his verdict on us which will never be reversed. When we meet him face to face we will not encounter his wrath but experience the completion of his good work in us.

The Bible in a year: Judges 9–10; Mark 3

APRIL 15–21

Mud, mud, glorious mud

Exodus 1–4

Gazing out into the fields through a window, God challenged my perception. In front of me was a mighty oak, but I felt God saying, 'Look at that acorn.' Why that acorn grew and not any other is beyond me, but God knows, and through it demonstrates the glorious potential of humble beginnings.

Egypt was a fertile, fruitful land – usually. The people were not used to famine, those seven years when Joseph was prime minister had been exceptional. The Nile provided for their needs, and the Egyptians worshipped gods such as Hapi, the flood god, for annually bringing both water and fertile mud to the nation. Without the Nile, Egypt would be as much of a desert as her neighbours.

The economy flourished, culture flourished, and a small minority group with a strong sense of identity could also flourish. This group knew their presence in Egypt was the result of the failure of the Nile back in Joseph's day, and the faithfulness of their God. They knew the God of Abraham, Isaac and Jacob was the provider of all this. The Nile's goodness was merely a pointer to the source of all goodness. Egypt, luxuriating in self-sufficient pride, became a defensive and then oppressive power. They worshipped the created instead of the Creator.

In this situation the children of Israel were a threat to be removed. Indeed, God's plan was to remove them. They would be a people called and delivered according to God's promises, so that they could worship the Creator in spirit and truth (John 4:24), and that glory would go only to God (Isaiah 42:8). Exodus, so famous for the opening chapters of deliverance, ends with the glory of the Lord revealed in the place and practice of worship.

Colin Veysey is the full-time pastor of a church plant in the Chilterns, where he has lived for the past four years with his wife Joan and two daughters. He first trained in medical laboratory science, before going on to London Bible College. His interests include playing the guitar, song writing and running.

APRIL 15–21

DAY 1

God's incubator

Only after a period of incubation does an egg hatch, or the symptoms of an infection become apparent. What are you anticipating being 'hatched' by God in your life or church? What are the symptoms of the kingdom of God that you would like to see break out in your neighbourhood or nation?

Exodus 1

'Be fruitful and multiply' God said (Genesis 9:7, RSV), and the Israelites in Egypt were certainly obedient to that command (v 7). But such thriving produced not only the seeds of growth, but of confrontation. Egypt felt threatened, and like a cornered animal began to fight back (v 10). Strangely, it is not warriors who take centre stage, but childless women who worship and fear God (v 17), and won't let themselves feel threatened. Why midwives? Because the writer is preparing us for the entrance of other *deliverers*: Moses, Jesus, you and I. Each, after long periods of barrenness, is destined for blessing and fruitfulness worked through obedience (v 21). This is what Pharaoh fears, and so he turns to his god, the Nile, for help (v 22). His god, worshipped as the giver of life to Egypt, will take on the God of the midwives. The stage is set for a heavenly battle, a mighty deliverance – but not yet, the incubation period has only just begun.

You may never have thought of yourself as a midwife, but God has placed each of us in a position to pray for this and the next generation to be saved from the evil oppression of sin. We stand, in prayer, between those in this world who would rob them of life, and God, who has the power to give life. Jesus taught us to pray, 'Our Father … your kingdom come, your will be done on earth …'

The Bible in a year: Judges 13–14; Mark 4

APRIL 15–21

DAY 2

Special delivery

'Owing to circumstances beyond our control …' When we hear this, we know something must have gone wrong – lost television transmission, late flight arrival. Consider what might seem out of control, and thank God that we can still pray, 'Thank you, Father, that you are with me in every circumstance.'

Exodus 2:1–10

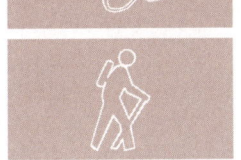

Not a good time to become pregnant, when an angry ruler is set upon ethnic cleansing by infanticide. Imagine what effect and grief the loss of such innocent lives must have had on the whole community (1:22). One family, looking back to their history, chose to trust God. They knew that an ark had been the means of salvation from a flood, so their firstborn was cast into the Nile in another 'ark' (v 3). Ironically, it was this 'obedience' to Pharaoh, and through the help of Pharaoh's own family, that the 'one that got away' would achieve the outcome Pharaoh feared most. Maybe Pharaoh's daughter could not agree to her father's policies, but what could she do (vs 6–8)? The sight and sounds of the basket and its contents moved the young Egyptian princess to compassion, action, even civil disobedience. She could do something, and through her, Egypt unwittingly harboured and provided for Israel's deliverer. The echo of this irony would again ring out when another child, the Deliverer, would find refuge from an angry king in Egypt (see Matthew 2:13–15).

We rejoice that God saved this one baby, but why so much innocent blood? How much are our hearts moved by the callousness that caused the death of so many innocents? Today is also a day for mixed emotion. Praise God for the privilege of receiving his grace in our lives, but let us pray for the multitudes of children suffering today.

The Bible in a year: Judges 15–16; Mark 5

APRIL 15–21

DAY 3

The hand of the shepherd

I used to have a skeleton in my cupboard – the result of being married to a physiotherapist! God knows every hidden act, which would be scary if forgiveness and restoration were not the hallmark of God's character. Praise God that, through the spirit of prophecy and restoration, even a load of dry bones can be restored to a mighty army (Ezekiel 37:3–6, 10).

Exodus 2:11–25

Moses had everything – he was a prince with privilege and a problem. His roots were beginning to show (v 11)! It was probably time for him to choose a wife, one of the Egyptian beauties from high society. Torn between the beautiful life and his suffering family, what could he do? Suddenly, compassion broke the chains of Egyptian control, passion raged through his veins. In a moment he was a murderer, his hands stained with blood (v 12). He probably felt a mixture of liberated solidarity and fear, till the awful realisation that the secret was out. No longer acceptable to either side (v 14), he ran, lost and alone like a frightened sheep; yet guided by the hand of the Good Shepherd (v 15). Guided to a well, and to another flock, to raise his hand again, this time in a brave act of deliverance (vs 16–19). And the result: he won the hand of a shepherdess (v 21). Just as the patriarchs before him, he found himself learning the ways of the Father in a foreign land (see Genesis 24, 29). Meanwhile, the Lord watched with compassion, waiting for the right time to demonstrate covenant love and faithfulness (vs 23–25).

Be angry, but do not sin. When we see injustice and are stirred to anger, it may be an indication of God's hand at work in our lives. Consider what stimulates that passion and ask the Good Shepherd to purify you and guide you.

The Bible in a year: Judges 17–18; Mark 6

APRIL 15–21

DAY 4 The drawing of the fire

Do you find that wallpaper becomes invisible in time, just part of the surroundings? Take a moment to look at what is around you. Maybe you are in a special quiet place with significant items present, maybe a very ordinary place. God can use the common place to rekindle the Holy Spirit's fire and speak afresh of love and calling.

Exodus 3

To those poor, oppressed, praying Israelites it must have seemed as though the heavens were as unyielding as brass. But their cries did not fall on deaf ears. The response was not to them, but to a distant, ageing peasant whose dreams had all but died. Still he felt drawn towards God's mountain (v 1). He had learnt Midianite desert farming and family ways, so was he just torturing himself to think there may be more? 'Drawn out of the water', he was in the driest place conceivable, where bushes are burnt to ash in minutes. But, the fire God kindles does not consume the messenger (v 2). It was not a holy bush, but a holy meeting called by the Holy God (vs 5–6). No wonder Moses hid, and needed assurance. Egyptians didn't do deals with shepherds (Genesis 46:34), particularly fugitive, murdering ones (vs 10–11). God's grace towards him was wonderful, the name on God's calling card (v 14), the words to share (vs 15–18), the prophetic promise of success (vs 19–20). Moses was challenged and charged with a 'mission impossible', humanly speaking.

God transforms the present to enable the future. What is 'I AM's' aim for you? Close your eyes and ask God to reveal to you the purpose of your life. Then open them, look around and thank God for the love he has for you and the potential he sees in you.

The Bible in a year: Judges 19–20; Psalm 44

APRIL 15–21

DAY 5

Life signs

Near my home is a pub that was once called The Office. From there people would sometimes phone home to say they were at the office. This was true, but misleading. Nearly opposite the pub there is a signpost at a T-junction pointing across the fields, in the opposite direction to where the village actually is! Our lives have a purpose, and should point towards God. 'Lord, let us not mislead people.'

Exodus 4:1–17

Moses, understandably, felt that the Israelites might not believe his story (v 1). Neither his CV, nor his communication skills (v 10) would inspire confidence. God generously gave Moses three signs to authenticate his testimony. They pointed Moses back through his life. In the wilderness he was only a Midianite shepherd, but his staff indicated something different (vs 2–5). The hand that had killed the Egyptian, God could restore (vs 6–7). The Nile, that should have killed him as a baby, would become blood (v 9)! It seems common in Old Testament times that when prophets were called they felt unable to speak (see for example Jeremiah 1:6), and Moses was no exception. God understood and graciously reassures (v 12). However, when the assurance of his creator was not sufficient, Moses embarked on the dangerous strategy – 'Lord, here I am, send someone else.' Yet even for this situation God has already provided. Aaron had been among the Israelites all this time, he was eloquent, he would receive his call, but he did not have Moses' qualifications in deliverance, passion and shepherding. He would mislead the flock (Exodus 32). The staff of authority was to stay with Moses.

If you revisit your life journey, do you see the signs that demonstrate God's presence? Ask God to authenticate your testimony and give you the power to raise faith in others.

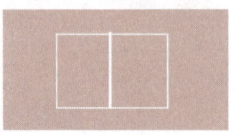

Mine: Matthew 13:44–46
I know a man who can!: Psalm 69:13–18; Galatians 1:3–5

The Bible in a year: Judges 21; Mark 7

APRIL 15–21

Going deeper …

Consider the things upon which you depend: the supermarket, insurance, electricity, career, income, house, etc. Write at the top of a piece of paper, 'God, the Father of my Lord Jesus Christ, provides for me, and then list the things, services and people on which you depend. Read Job 1:9–20. If the things you listed were removed from you, God would still protect and provide – but would your response be worship? With just one or two of the items on your list, talk to God about what would be different, and how you would manage. How would you manage if the Bible were removed from you? Moses grew up with Egyptian culture, with their reliance on the Nile and the worship of all their gods. Suddenly he found himself in Midian, his dependence on Egypt broken. He was not drawn out of Egypt into a vacuum. God knew his needs and provided a different environment in which to learn. He was unaware that he needed to know Egyptian ways and worship to defeat Pharaoh. He also needed to spend forty years learning desert family shepherding ways to be equipped to lead God's people out of Egypt. We may be more like the Israelites in Egypt than Moses in Midian. We will probably not be extracted from our culture. We must be 'in the world, not of it'. Jesus is praying for us that we will be kept from the evil one (John 17:15). Let's pray with him that we would come to depend on God's kingdom and love, and learn to see everything else as God's overflowing grace.

Prayer and worship

Conclusion

Nothing's happened … yet! A seed is planted, but there's no shoot. A cry to God ascends, but no apparent answer. From the Israelite perspective, the continuing trauma of slavery was unbroken, and God seemed deaf to their prayers. But God was at work and, as in a great theatre, the scenery and actors were in place for the curtain to rise on one of the greatest dramas of history. As Moses turned his face from the burning bush towards Israel, he knew that very significant changes lay just beyond the horizon. The eighty years in Midian probably seemed wasted, but God had been teaching, preparing and equipping him. A decorator tells me that the preparation work is always the longest and hardest part, and this is true of God's work too. It is so easy to get frustrated, disappointed or to give up. Jesus told the disciples a parable to show that they should pray and not give up (Luke 18:1). If you are in need of a deliverer, keep crying out, and rest assured that in your circumstances God is with you for good. Once rescued, the Israelites were never to forget their time of slavery. They were to treat aliens and strangers well, and enjoy the regular Sabbath rest that the Egyptians never afforded them. God is not only preparing to deliver you, but also working towards making you like Moses – and Jesus – that you will become a deliverer, to comfort others with the comfort God has given you (2 Corinthians 1:3–6). God is calling you to take up your cross and follow Jesus, bringing freedom to captives in his name, and giving worship and glory to him.

The Bible in a year: Ruth 1–4; Psalm 45; Mark 8

APRIL 22–28

A bigger Jesus!

John 7–8

Clio Turner is married to Vince, who has also written for *Closer to God*. As well as being on the leadership team of Ichthus, Pimlico, she works as a part-time writer and video producer. She and Vince have two children.

The world does not need more answers. We've all had more answers than hot dinners and the answers don't seem to be working. In many nations, the gap between rich and poor is steadily getting larger. The rich are dissatisfied, the poor are hungry. The rich live without meaning, but the poor often live without hope. We do not need more theories, more 'solutions' or more speculations as to what would make the world a better place. Instead we need to admit defeat and start crying out 'Help!' And what we need more than anything else is a saviour, who is capable of lifting us out of the mess. This is exactly the sort of hero figure that John's Gospel presents us with. Unlike the synoptics (Matthew, Mark and Luke), John concentrates his attention not so much on what Jesus did, but on who Jesus was. From the end of chapter 1, John focuses on Jesus' claims to be God. Each of the famous 'I am …' statements that ring out through these verses reflects a crucial aspect of Jesus' identity. And we need every one. We need to know Jesus as our sustaining bread. We need to know Jesus as our defining light. We need to know Jesus as our empowering resurrection. We need him as our way, we need him as our truth, we need him as our life. As Christians we need a bigger Jesus! It's no good just having a set of ideas that will one day take us into heaven. In John 7, we will meet a person with a personality who will start sorting us out now …

APRIL 22–28

DAY 1

Waiting on God

How rich is your inner life? If all your daily activities were stripped away, how much would there be left? Imagine for a moment that you are physically very restricted (say by a stroke, or some other disabling illness). Would the strength of your secret life with God be enough to hold you?

John 7:1–13

Jesus never let the world around him squeeze him into its own mould. But the world tried its hardest to do just that. By this time Jesus has already lost many of his disciples (John 6:66) because of his unpopular teaching. Now his would-be spin doctors urge him to take the limelight at the Feast of Tabernacles. Notice that, because they only see the outer miracles and have no sense of the inner life, Jesus' brothers completely misunderstand his motivation (vs 3–4). He wasn't wanting to impress the world, but to save it.

Jesus could keep in step with God even when the pressure was mounting because he waited on God, studiously obeyed God and withdrew to spend time with God. Only if we have a clear idea of what God is saying can we risk being obedient rather than being popular.

Trying to meet other people's expectations can be a debilitating disease. Spend a few moments writing down how you think other people see you, and what they want of you. (It is important to include key figures such as parents and spouses in this exercise.) Now spend time 'clearing the decks'. Ask God how he sees you and if there is something special he wants you to do for him. Remember, God's agenda for us will always flow out of who we really are.

The Bible in a year: 1 Samuel 1–3; Mark 9

APRIL 22–28

DAY 2

Speaking for God

How 'surrendered' is your life? If God says 'go', do you go? If God says 'speak', do you speak? If you are not sure that you hear God that clearly, don't let it stop you saying 'yes' whenever you think God is asking you to do something. The worst that can happen is that you get it wrong! God's voice becomes clearer as we obey him.

John 7:14–24

Jesus lived to do his Father's will. But he was not an automaton. He did all that he did, by submitting to God. 'The Son can do nothing by himself; he can do only what he sees his Father doing' (5:19). It is because he was so surrendered, that he was so effective. The inner life gives the outer life its fruit.

Jesus arrives at the feast late by his brothers' estimation, but bang on cue for God. He speaks only what God wants him to say, so his words come 'hot off the press' from the Father (v 16). They shock (v 15). They even horrify (v 20). But they have an uncompromising purity and power that will not be diverted. It is because Jesus' only agenda is to fulfil God's agenda that he has such authority.

Rather dauntingly, the church, as Christ's body, is supposed to speak with similar authority today. We are God's mouthpiece to a broken, hurting world. Often the mouth is gagged by fear, complacency or simply not recognising the calling on our lives. But we do not have to wait for God to give us a special message for his world. The Holy Spirit is already causing us to respond with God's heart to what's around us. Decide now to speak up next time you see unfairness, unkindness or contempt for God's ways.

The Bible in a year: 1 Samuel 4–6; Mark 10

DAY 3

Talking like God

If there is one debilitating condition that is dogging the lives of Christians today, it is poor self-image. Most of us carry on as if we have to apologise for breathing the air of planet earth rather than behaving as if we're sons and daughters of its King. But we've got to remember that however successful the rest of the world might appear, we're the ones who really know what life's about.

John 7:25–36

Although Jesus came to the feast discreetly, he is now shouting out in the temple courts. Jesus knew who he was because he knew the Father, and he knew what the Father had told him to do (v 29).

People who dispute that Jesus ever claimed to be God, ignore the fact that if Jesus was not God, he was incredibly big-headed! Jesus draws attention to himself again and again and claims an authority that would make any other holy man blush. In this passage he uses the famous 'I am' epithet for God five times! He is not wanting people to focus on his ideas, he is wanting them to focus on *him*.

Let's work on our battered self-images. Remember that if we know Jesus, he is our key to the goodness of God. Read aloud these blessings based on Deuteronomy 28. 'God intends me to be the head and not the tail! God wants to bless my family. God wants to bless my work. He wants to bless my home. Opposition that rises against me, God wants to turn back. God is pleased with me. I know his favour. Why should my life not be an example to others of what it is to live in the approval of God?'

The Bible in a year: 1 Samuel 7–9; Mark 11

APRIL 22–28

DAY 4

Behaving as God

How desperate are we for the presence of the living God? Often we get so good at carrying on under our own steam that we can 'do' church whether God turns up or not. Think back over the last few months of your Christian life. If it's been a bit 'business as usual', ask God for a fresh touch.

John 7:37–52

Jesus is making no bones about it now. He is taking centre-stage and seeking our attention, speaking as 'no one ever spoke' (v 46), claiming the sort of power that only God could have. Jesus takes the imagery of the feast's last day (when water from the pool of Siloam was offered up to God) and reinterprets it. He says that it is only his presence that can revive our lives. He alone is the bubbling spring that can refresh the human condition. He alone has the power to reconnect us to eternity. He demands that we look at him (v 37). He demands that we respond (v 38).

To get really thirsty for God, we have to stop satisfying ourselves with any God-substitutes. Relationships, success and money are not wrong in themselves but if they start filling the space that is meant for God, we will never know how dry we've become. Stones of complacency block up the spring inside us.

Repent of all the things in your life that may have taken the place of God. Ask God to make you thirsty again. Now stay in his presence. Worship him. Wait until he comes. Remember Jesus promises that if we come to him we will drink (v 37).

The Bible in a year: 1 Samuel 10–11; Psalms 46–47

APRIL 22–28

DAY 5

Forgiveness from God

Luke's Gospel records how Jesus talked about two men who had debts cancelled (Luke 7:41–43). The one who was released from the larger amount is bound to be the most grateful. He will love the master more. Think about this. The extent to which we have received Jesus' forgiveness is the extent to which we will love him.

John 7:53–8:11

Most people agree that this story is 'tacked-on' to the narrative and may not really belong here. Few however doubt its authenticity.

Jesus has been teaching publicly (8:2). The Pharisees are jealous and they try to catch him out (8:3–6). If Jesus agrees to stone the woman, he will be in trouble with the Romans; if he does not, he will be breaking the law of Moses. With brilliant lateral thinking Jesus springs the trap, turning the censure back on the Pharisees (8:7). Their consciences will not let them throw a stone. Ironically, Jesus is the only one who has the right to, and he declines.

For the Pharisees, the woman is just a piece of bait. For Jesus, she's a person. Imagine what a state she was in, dragged out in public, having been caught in the very act of adultery! Imagine the way Jesus might have looked at her as he let her go free.

'Neither do I condemn you', Jesus says (8:11). Time and time again Jesus chooses not to press charges against guilty humanity (see Luke 23:34). That's the sort of God we've got! Why don't we live, believing it? Christians can be some of the most falsely condemned people in the world, and yet we're supposed to be the ones who know we've been let off the hook! Spend time now thanking the Father for forgiving you.

Infectious life: John 4:7–14
Generous love: Luke 7:44–50

The Bible in a year: 1 Samuel 12–13; Mark 12

APRIL 22–28

Going deeper …

'If anyone is thirsty, let him come to me and drink' (John 7:37). Imagine that it's a very hot day. You are walking along a dusty track in the middle of nowhere and you haven't had anything to drink for several hours. The sky is like brass. The monotonous landscape feels unwelcoming and your journey seems a burden. The only thing that keeps you going is the thought of water at the end of it. Your throat feels tight. Perhaps it is sore. How are you feeling emotionally? Are you scared? Are you numb? You force your legs to keep going. The panic is rising. Your body aches. You can't keep this up much longer … Then all of a sudden, you turn a corner and it's over. Other people are standing by the side of the road and they're all drinking water. Someone rushes up and offers you a cup. You drink. It's cold. How does it feel as the water goes down your throat? What does it taste like? You sit. Your head is spinning. You drink, trying not to drink too fast. Slowly it dawns on you that you are safe …

Jesus is like that: water to our parched souls. We are dry and cracked without him. Everything in our being is designed to thirst for Jesus. He is the only one who replenishes and refreshes. Each cell of our body and every impulse of our mind is designed to be lubricated by him. Spiritual dehydration sets in the moment we turn aside and do things our way. We are desperate for his presence. We are dependent on his touch. Spend time consciously rehydrating. Drink in the Lord Jesus. You may want to worship. You may just want to 'be' with him …

A life laid down

Conclusion

In John 7, Jesus chooses to walk into the epicentre of Jewish antagonism. He mounts the most dangerous platform in the world, the temple steps, and declares publicly that only he can meet the people's need. The Pharisees must have been seething. He was on their home turf, apparently flouting them at their own front door! But Jesus was in his Father's house (Luke 2:49). The temple was built in his honour. It was the natural place for his glory to be revealed. Jesus was able to go right into the danger zone because he was totally submitted to God. Because he always kept in step with the Spirit, the Spirit could lead him out into the wilderness of temptation (Luke 4:1–2) or into the stronghold of worldly opposition. Jesus' life was laid down. He had no will other than to do the will of Father. But in case you think that Jesus was a one-off, Paul and Peter reached that same position. Paul said: 'I have been crucified with Christ and I no longer live, but Christ lives in me. The life I live in the body, I live by faith in the Son of God' (Galatians 2:20). Peter told his followers to live 'as aliens and strangers in the world' (1 Peter 2:11). How are we doing? Only we ourselves can answer this question honestly. Do we aim to serve God in everything? Or do we behave as if this world is all there is, holding on to as much of it as possible? How surrendered is my heart? Spend some time, thinking about this question and ask God to renew your heart.

The Bible in a year: 1 Samuel 14–17; Psalm 48; Mark 13

APRIL 29– MAY 5

Sheila Pritchard is self-employed after twenty years lecturing in spiritual formation at the Bible College of New Zealand. She enjoys encouraging others in their spiritual journey through teaching, writing and personal mentoring. She also enjoys walking the beaches and bush tracks in beautiful New Zealand.

Stark choices

John 8–9

When you are face to face with Jesus it's not the time for procrastinating! This man provokes reaction. He's not a vague, kindly preacher whose views you can digest over lunch and then forget. No. When you are right there seeing him, hearing him, being challenged by him, a choice has to be made. What's more, these choices affect the direction of your whole life from here on. Scary? Exhilarating? It depends on who you think Jesus is!

Somehow it's a lot easier to sit back and discuss theological questions than it is to make active choices. I have a suspicion that many apparently learned discussions are a convenient smokescreen for avoiding commitment. A genuine search for understanding is one thing. Hiding behind intellectual rationalisation is another. Jesus is very good at seeing the difference! In this week's readings there are a lot of things that the original hearers found hard to understand but the choice to step out and trust Jesus was clear. It is probably the same for you. Most of us have plenty of unanswered questions and a few things in the 'too hard' basket. The most important question of all is: will I take the next step forward in trust? Yes or no? That's the choice.

As you begin this week's adventure with Jesus, remind yourself again that God is love. A child can leap off a high wall into the arms of a strong, loving father because she trusts her dad, not because she understands the law of gravity and the power of his muscles to support her weight!

APRIL 29–MAY 5

DAY 1

Who are you, Jesus?

If Jesus was sitting down beside you, what questions would you want to ask him? There may be several! Before you read, focus on what you want to find out about Jesus himself.

John 8:12–30

I have to say that I'm not surprised the Pharisees were rather confused about Jesus. From their perspective he was making some strange and outrageous claims. Put yourself in the position of a scholarly, religious leader and see how you would react to this unconventional teacher who doesn't fit the orthodox 'box'.

Now listen again to what Jesus says. This time let yourself be curious and attracted by who he is and what he says. Even if there's still a lot you don't understand, notice what does draw you in. You might want to jot down those things.

It is clear that the people listening to Jesus on this occasion had a mixture of reactions. Some wanted to argue, others to throw him out. Yet in the end 'many put their faith in him' (v 30).

As we read this account today we have the advantage of understanding more of what Jesus was talking about because we have the perspective of history. But we have the disadvantage of not seeing the person of Jesus, hearing his voice, catching the light in his eye, the enthusiasm in his invitation to believe.

Sit quietly with what has most touched you in this time and make a choice about your response. Will it be to challenge, to 'throw out' or to put your faith in who Jesus is? How will that choice affect your life today?

The Bible in a year: 1 Samuel 18–19; Mark 14

APRIL 29–MAY 5

DAY 2

Truth sets you free

Begin today by asking the Spirit of God to open up to you some new truth that will be freeing and life-giving.

John 8:31–47

Expanding our understanding of what faith in Jesus really means is an ongoing process. Jesus is talking here to those Jews who had believed in him following the animated discussion recorded earlier in the chapter (vs 31–32). Yet it seems they still had a lot of unlearning and relearning to do. They thought they were already free, so were rather affronted by Jesus implying they needed to be set free (v 33)! Can you identify with this? Are there times when something you read or hear challenges your comfortable image of how neat and tidy your faith is? When it does, how do you feel?

It's natural enough, I think, to find it a bit of a shock to discover the framework of our faith is too small. At first it feels more like an attack on something very sacred and secure than an invitation to freedom. I'm glad Jesus can handle the to-and-fro discussion as we, like the Jews in this passage, need to ask questions, chew it over and decide what to do with a new truth. Is there something you are needing to engage with in this way? It may be a new truth about yourself and how God can set you free from things that hold you back. It may be a new truth about God, or the Bible, or prayer, or the work of the Spirit, or …

Pause and be open to receiving a new truth that will expand your understanding and freedom. Remember this is what you asked for as you began today.

The Bible in a year: 1 Samuel 20–22; Mark 15

APRIL 29–MAY 5

DAY 3

Demonic or divine?

Discernment is needed in our contemporary culture where so many 'spiritual' options are on offer. Ask God to sharpen your ability to discern what is truly of him.

John 8:48–59

Calling someone demon-possessed (v 48) is a pretty serious charge. The Jews who accused Jesus in this way seemed to be making their judgement because he was saying things they couldn't understand; things that threatened and frightened them. The claims Jesus was making didn't fit their theological framework so they attributed them to a demonic source. We may judge them as being small-minded, stubborn and just plain wrong! But let's be careful – 'demonising' things which are threatening may be what we do too.

Jesus refutes their accusation with two key statements. He says, 'I honour my Father … I am not seeking glory for myself' (vs 49–50). These are the marks of his authenticity. I can imagine Jesus standing quite vulnerably in the face of their attack on his character and saying simply: 'This is who I am. This is why I came.' They couldn't comprehend the things he was trying to explain, so Jesus asks them to look at his character. But this group of people couldn't get past their intellectual questions and tried to stone the one they had demonised (vs 58–59).

When a person honours God and gives glory to him and not themselves it is important to listen carefully however much their words may stretch us. God often doesn't fit our boxes!

Prayerfully hold the two marks of authenticity alongside any situation where you need discernment. Does it honour God? Is glory given to him?

The Bible in a year: 1 Samuel 23–24; Mark 16

APRIL 29–MAY 5

DAY 4

Mud, spit and mystery

Spend a few quiet moments opening yourself to the mystery of a God who constantly surprises us. Approach God's Word today with an expectant heart.

John 9:1–12

When tragedies happen the question 'Why?' is natural enough (vs 1–2). Unfortunately, it usually doesn't have a satisfying answer. Several people I know are asking, 'Is this awful event somehow my fault? If not, why did God let this happen to me?' The answer Jesus gives the questioners in this story is a total surprise. He changes the perspective from finding someone to blame, to finding an opportunity to see God at work (v 3). 'This isn't about sin and punishment,' Jesus says. 'It's a chance for you to see God's mercy and power.'

The second surprise is what the 'work of God' in this situation looked like. Making mud by spitting in the dust sounds pretty basic (v 6). Perhaps the onlookers would have been more easily convinced by a more ostentatious approach. Yet the blind man's co-operation with the simple instructions of Jesus brought undreamed-of results (v 7).

A friend of mine, who is currently experiencing deep tragedy, said recently, through her tears, 'You know, it is amazing but life has become so much simpler. I have only God to hold onto and I'm experiencing his love in ways I've never done before. It's a mystery!' Co-operation with God in the midst of dark times may be as basic as 'mud, spit and trust' with no easy answers. The mystery is that this is when Jesus brings light into even the deepest darkness.

Pray for yourself, or others you know, to receive God's wonderful and mysterious light in the darkness.

The Bible in a year: 1 Samuel 25–26; Psalm 49

APRIL 29–MAY 5

DAY 5

Who's blind now?

Think back over your life and recall times when you have personally experienced the goodness or power of God. Give thanks for those experiences.

John 9:13–41

Which comes first, experience or belief? Perhaps that's just as hard to answer as the 'chicken and egg' question! In this story though, it is clear that the blind man who is healed believes in Jesus much more readily than those who only look on and talk about him.

Experiencing God's goodness and power opens up our spiritual eyes to see things we may otherwise reason away. The Pharisees had their view (their inner 'vision') of who Jesus was and saw everything else through that filter. Their view was that Jesus was a sinner and definitely far from God (vs 16, 24). This filtered vision completely blinded them to the truth. The 'blind' man, on the other hand, knew from personal experience that whoever Jesus was he had done something profoundly good and healing. From that vantage point he was open to find out more and to believe with new understanding (vs 35–38).

However, in Mark's Gospel, Jesus points out how limited he is to influence the lives of those who refuse to believe (Mark 6:4–6). It seems that faith and experience go together. Maybe the order in which they come varies. Believing in Jesus can widen our vision to expect and receive his personal touch. And an unexpected experience of God's power in our lives can open our inner eyes to new levels of faith.

Ask God to reveal to you any filters which may be blinding you to what he longs to do in your life. Open yourself to experience his grace.

Be full of light!: Matthew 6:19–24
Be free!: Galatians 5:1

The Bible in a year: 1 Samuel 27–28; 1 Corinthians 1

APRIL 29–MAY 5

Going deeper …

In this meditation I invite you to enter into what blindness might mean. Imagine that you cannot see. Keeping your eyes closed, move around the room. Notice how blindness changes the way you walk, the way you feel, your confidence, the choices open to you … Without opening your eyes, sit still and think about all the ways your life would change without sight. Take time to imagine a normal day at work, at home, going shopping, transport, recreation … Imagine Jesus coming close and touching you. Hear him saying he has a way of restoring your sight. Notice your feelings – excitement, scepticism, fear that it's too good to be true and you'll be disappointed … Hear Jesus spit on the ground, feel the sticky mud on your eyes, allow someone to lead you to the water. Notice at every stage what you are thinking and feeling. Bend down and wash your eyes. Now open them. What is your reaction? What do you say and do and feel? How do you want to respond to Jesus?

Now sit quietly and ask the Holy Spirit to interpret this experience to your inner life. Where are the blind spots? Where do you need to see more clearly? Take time to recognise that spiritual blindness affects our life with God just as profoundly as physical blindness. Replay the meditation in your imagination, this time focusing on spiritual blindness. With your eyes closed raise your face towards Jesus. Listen to his instructions and carry them out so that you may have clear sight restored.

Your turn to choose!

Conclusion

Life is filled with choices. We choose what to eat, what to wear, what to say, what to buy, whether to smile or frown. We decide who to talk to, who to trust, what priorities to act on, how to respond to a challenge, whether to say yes or no to a child's request. We make faith choices all day too. We choose to trust – or not trust. We choose to see God as loving – or judgemental. We choose to acknowledge our dependence on God – or to be fiercely independent. We choose to believe that Jesus is who he says he is – or to treat him as a storybook character.

As you live your life in your family, workplace, church and neighbourhood, your choices will powerfully shape your influence in these communities. We have seen people make choices for truth and freedom or for doubt and limitation. We have seen someone who chose to trust and receive new sight and others who chose to stay blind. What would it mean to choose truth, freedom and clear-sightedness?

I find it helpful to have a brief phrase or motto as a compass pointing me in the right direction. In the busyness of the day and its many demands, this can keep me on track in making clear-sighted choices. Some possibilities are: 'The truth will set me free.' 'What would love do here?' 'Let me see this with your eyes, Lord.' 'Choose life!' Ask the Holy Spirit for the prayer phrase that is right for you. Then use it often to make life-giving choices!

The Bible in a year: 1 Samuel 29–31; 2 Samuel 1–2; Psalm 50; Corinthians 2

MAY 6–12

A matter of life and death

John 10–11

Have you ever been in a 'life and death' situation? I have. It was a very strange feeling to be wheeled into surgery knowing it was just as likely I'd wake up in heaven as on earth. As a matter of fact I didn't know which I would prefer! I felt rather like Paul saying, 'For to me, to live is Christ and to die is gain' (Philippians 1:21).

There's something even worse than physical death though and that is being alive and yet not really living. Sadly, I think that might describe how it is for many of us at times. There's that 'something missing' feeling; a wistful desire to find the key to living life to the full. If you've ever felt like that, this week is for you! Jesus is adamant that following him is the key to living life 'to the max'. He calls it abundant life. Why waste your life feeling half dead when abundance is on offer?

It's a serious choice though. Choosing life means not choosing the things that lead to death. Strange as it may seem that's not altogether easy at times. Half-hearted living sometimes seems more familiar and more comfortable. The goal of 'life to the full' sounds great from the armchair 'daydream' position! But when it comes to making real choices to trust and follow Jesus as he calls us towards that goal … well is it really worth it?

The answer to that question is one for you to discover this week as you let Jesus tell it his way. Please don't take life for granted. And don't limit your idea of life to a functioning body and mind. Great as those gifts are, there's much more to abundant life than that!

Sheila Pritchard is self-employed after twenty years lecturing in spiritual formation at the Bible College of New Zealand. She enjoys encouraging others in their spiritual journey through teaching, writing and personal mentoring. She also enjoys walking the beaches and bush tracks in beautiful New Zealand.

MAY 6–12

DAY 1

Life to the max!

Sit or stand in a posture of openness and invite God to fill you with all that he has for you today. Take a few deep breaths of receptivity to his Spirit and his Word.

John 10:1–10

How full would you say your life is at present? Beware, this is a trick question! I don't mean full as in busy. I mean full as in satisfying. How full of meaning and purpose and deep joy is your life? It may be hard to find a way to answer such a question in words. Jesus says he has come to give 'life to the full' or 'abundant life' or 'life to the max'. On a scale of 1–10 where would you place your level of abundant life? This is not a way of judging yourself. Rather, it is a way of knowing how much room you have for more!

If there is room for some more abundance in your life think about who you are listening to and who you are following. Advertisements, billboards and TV shout loud messages about what is supposed to satisfy – do you listen to them? Some people make convincing arguments about the latest way to be rich and happy. Do you follow them? Some things and some people actually steal and destroy fullness of life (v 10).

Jesus says that he is like a shepherd who really cares for your well-being. He's out ahead calling you on to fullness of life. The important thing is to learn to recognise his voice so you know who to follow (vs 4–5).

Listen in your heart for Jesus calling your name. Let him know you are grateful and willing to follow.

The Bible in a year: 2 Samuel 3–5; 1 Corinthians 3

MAY 6–12

DAY 2

Life laid down

Ask God to help you see more deeply than ever before what Jesus' death means for you.

John 10:11–21

I honestly don't know if there is anyone I would die for. I hope that I would be willing to die for someone in my family or for a vulnerable child I could save from a fire, but I honestly don't know for sure. I guess none of us knows until our life is really tested.

Jesus says quite confidently that he will voluntarily lay down his life for his sheep (vs 11, 15, 17–18). That's us! Long before he was actually confronted with death he had made the choice. He chose to be the kind of shepherd that put his life on the line so that those he cared for could be totally secure. The only thing that could motivate a sacrifice like that is love. The most central fact of the gospel is the one we find hardest to grasp. Jesus loves me *that* much.

As a way of bringing home the truth of what this means, let's journey to the foot of the cross. In your mind's eye stand there and take in what is happening. Let the truth of Jesus' words we've read today come to you from the cross. 'I know you by name. I love you. I'm choosing to lay down my life for you. I'm your shepherd. I care about your security. I will never abandon you. Yes, I will receive my life back again but my dying is to bring you safely home.'

Receive what Jesus the Good Shepherd is saying to you. Your response may be tears, words of gratitude or simply silent wonder.

The Bible in a year: 2 Samuel 6–7; Corinthians 4

MAY 6–12

DAY 3

Never-ending life

Take a moment to relax and become still. Notice how every breath brings you life. Breathe deeply and gratefully, thanking God for the wonder of life itself.

John 10:22–42

You may remember the story about a little Cuban boy who was a refugee in the USA. He had escaped there with his mother who tragically drowned on the journey. His father wanted him back in Cuba while his American relatives opposed that strongly. A heart-wrenching scene shown on TV news was this six-year-old boy physically being wrenched from the arms of his carers and carried, shocked and crying, into a police car.

I do not presume to judge where the little boy rightfully belonged. I remind you of the story only to contrast it with the words of Jesus who said, 'No one can snatch them out of my hand' (v 28). What utter security followers of Jesus enjoy! Picture yourself held firmly and securely in the hands of Jesus and the Father (v 29).

It is not only during this life on earth that we are securely held by God. No, what Jesus is getting at is that life connected to him is never-ending. Once we have decided to follow the Good Shepherd who lays down his life for us, our life is inextricably linked with his and we will never be separated again. 'Eternal life' does not begin *after* we die. Eternal life begins when the Spirit of Jesus enters our life so we are one with him (Romans 8:9–11). He lives his unending life in us (Galatians 2:20)!

Celebrate your never-ending life in Jesus with song or prayer or simply seeing yourself secure in God's strong hands.

The Bible in a year: 2 Samuel 8–10; 1 Corinthians 5

MAY 6–12

DAY 4

Even though he dies …

Recall a time when your trust in Jesus was really tested. Can you give thanks that in the end you saw his faithfulness? Pray today for the strengthening of your faith to meet any challenges that lie ahead.

John 11:1–27

I find this story agonising to read. I can't help putting myself in the place of Mary and Martha. How could a really good friend who loves you – and has so much power – just stay away when you need him most? Maybe you've felt like that sometimes too. One of the hardest things in our Christian life is to believe that when Jesus seems to 'stay away' it is for a good and loving reason.

Martha's conversation with Jesus is a masterpiece of faith growing before our eyes. She is honest in telling Jesus she believes he could have saved Lazarus from dying (v 21). In spite of the fact that he didn't do that she affirms her trust that he can do something now (v 22). Jesus stretches that faith by talking about resurrection (v 23). Martha rises to the challenge! She not only believes in resurrection (v 24) she proclaims that she believes Jesus is the Christ, the Messiah (v 27). That is an astounding statement. When Peter came to the same realisation (Matthew 16:15–20) Jesus affirmed him as a foundational person in the church. It's a pity we don't give Martha the same credit for her insight and faith!

Martha's grief and disappointment does not cause her to draw back but rather to be even more bold in her faith. How Jesus must have loved her!

What part of Martha's story challenges you most? Pray that you may be given grace to trust as she did.

The Bible in a year: 2 Samuel 11–12; Psalm 51

DAY 5

Off with the grave clothes!

Pause to remember that you are in the presence of the life-giving God. Come to his Word with expectancy.

John 11:28–44

I suspect that the raising of Lazarus was more of a shock to Mary and Martha than his death. However sad it is to see a loved one die, there is a normality about it. Everyone's life comes to an end at some point. The sisters, the onlookers and Jesus himself are all grieving. This too is normal.

Suddenly Jesus turns normality on its head. Opening a grave isn't normal (v 39). Calling a dead man to come out isn't normal (v 43). And it most definitely isn't normal to have to unwrap grave clothes (v 44)! I expect the mourning turned to dancing and the tears turned to laughter once the reality of what had happened sank in. Put yourself in the scene and try to imagine what a major turnaround was required. When you are adjusting to death and processing grief how easy would it be to reverse the process and welcome new life? Psychologically, emotionally and intellectually a lot would be required.

Jesus is continually offering new life to parts of our lives that seem to have died. Death and resurrection are powerful themes in all spiritual journeys. Sometimes we may find it hard to make the shift from grief at what we've lost to discovering new life as we unwrap the grave clothes.

Is there any part of your life that is wrapped in grave clothes? Maybe that death had to happen in order for new life to be revealed. Ask the Spirit to help you turn your attention to the new life which is possible.

Choose life!: Deuteronomy 30:11–20
A resurrection body: 1 Corinthians 15:35–44

The Bible in a year: 2 Samuel 13–14; Psalm 52–54; 1 Corinthians 6

MAY 6-12

Going deeper ...

Read 1 Thessalonians 5:23–24 and ask the Holy Spirit to reveal life-giving truth to you as you enter this meditation. Paul prays for peace, wholeness and holiness to saturate our spirit and soul and body. Most of the time it's only our body that is visible! Even then it can be possible to cover up our real state of health or strength with clothes, make-up or a firmly-fixed facial expression. To enter into life-giving prayer I invite you to imagine your 'whole spirit, soul and body' revealed in a picture or symbol. You might see yourself as the person you are now but with all the usually invisible aspects of yourself shown in some way. You may have some healthy vibrant parts and some withered or handicapped parts. Or you might see yourself like a person from a gospel story whose need somehow mirrors your own. You might even find you are given a more abstract symbol which captures the essence of your life now. Take time to allow the Spirit to bring the picture to mind ...

Now, if you are willing, ask Jesus to bring a new level of wholeness to the person or symbol. Don't try to make anything happen. Just watch. What does Jesus do? Does he say anything? Do you need to co-operate in some way? Are you willing to do that if required? Take time to let the picture unfold without hurrying.

When you are ready, find a way of noting what has happened. You might write about it, draw a picture or share it with a friend. Read the Scripture passage again.

Calling forth life

Abundant life is worth sharing! The more we experience and enjoy the life Jesus offers, the more we will want others to do so too. How can we call forth life in our families, neighbourhoods and communities? First of all let it overflow from you. Have you ever been in the presence of a person whose very quality of being is vibrant and radiates life? They don't need to say much to raise the level of energy and attract others to their liveliness. As you open yourself to abundant life, trust that this is how your life will influence others too.

Be a channel for God's life in unexpected places. A life-giving outlook sees and shares God in even the bleakest landscape. Much of our news media, television and movies keep the focus on the mud. Be counter-cultural. Celebrate beauty. Comment on what is good. Express thanks for kindness. Offer a warm smile as you pass a stranger. Such seemingly small acts can be rays of light in the life of another.

Calling forth life may also involve sacrifice and committed action. It did for Jesus. Ask the Spirit to show you if there is someone whose 'grave clothes' you can help to unwrap. Pray about joining a social action group or supporting those in the front line of giving life to the poor. The opportunities are endless. Be a life-giver! Take on the exhilarating challenge of asking every day: 'Lord, how can I give life, share life, call forth life today?'

The Bible in a year: 2 Samuel 15–18; Psalm 52–54; 1 Corinthians 7

MAY 13–19

God, where are you?

'Praying used to be so enjoyable,' someone told me recently, 'but suddenly it feels like talking on the phone to someone who's hung up!' I've certainly felt like that, how about you? I believe most of us go through dry, dull or even painful patches in our relationship with God, although few of us are honest enough to admit it! When I've been on a Christian holiday or conference, and feel 'on fire' spiritually, I long to stay like that permanently, but our spiritual journeys include boring stretches of colourless desert as well as 'green pastures' and exhilarating mountain tops! Yet, while the deserts may be inevitable they are dangerous places. Many Christians stay in them permanently, and their spiritual lives wither and become drab and unfruitful.

So what causes and prolongs these deserts? Are they our own fault; some kind of test God sets us; or the result of stress, depression, or physical illness? Can we get ourselves out by some formula or do we wait passively for God to rescue us? If we suspect a friend's Christian life has become hollow, how can we help them? These are some of the questions we will be asking this week.

If we live in countries where rain can ruin outdoor events we find it hard to identify with Bible references to dry deserts, scorching sun or refreshing showers! Yet the Bible often describes the lives of those who are spiritually blessed as 'a well-watered garden' full of beautiful flowers and delicious fruit. But someone who has stepped away from God's protection is described as a dry wilderness; a barren, fruitless wasteland (see Psalm 107:33–34 and Isaiah 51:3).

What kind of a garden is *your* life at the moment?

Jennifer Rees Larcombe runs a Christian charity called Beauty from Ashes which aims to help people who face bereavement trauma, rejection and loss of any kind. She is an agony aunt and has published twenty-three books. She has six children and loves gardening.

MAY 13–19

DAY 1

Help! I'm lost!

Imagine you are in a vast desert – lost, alone, a dust storm obliterating all landmarks – and your water bottle is empty. Grimly you trudge on, only to realise you are moving in futile circles. That nightmare is unlikely to become a reality but David obviously felt like that, inwardly, when he said to God, 'my soul thirsts for you … in a dry and weary land' (Psalm 63:1). Can you identify with him?

Psalm 107:1–9

Malcolm, travelling on the London underground, became thoroughly irritated by the 'bright' Christian student who enthusiastically shared his faith with a fellow strap-hanger. 'Then suddenly I realised my own Christianity had once been that important to me,' Malcolm said later. 'I began wondering why I had lost my enthusiasm.' He had drifted into his desert so gradually that he'd accepted it as normal, yet he was in danger of remaining a bored, duty-bound pew-filler for life. Look at verse 5. People dying of thirst in a desert are unaware that their 'lives are ebbing away' – they just want to lie down and sleep. 'Dying' Christians are also tempted to give up the effort involved in following Christ. The stranger's shining face alerted Malcolm to the danger and he followed the example of verse 6. He also asked the question 'why?' 'Gradually God showed me various things which had subtly pushed him out of the centre of my life and when he'd helped me deal with them, I experienced a remarkable personal revival.'

If you suspect your spiritual life is dry, don't just plod on; stop and send up an urgent, inward shout for help. Think back to when your relationship with God was last 'green and fresh', and ask him to pinpoint what went wrong.

The Bible in a year: 2 Samuel 19–20; 1 Corinthians 8

MAY 13–19

DAY 2

A physical cause?

Sue expected her vicar to hunt for secret sins when she told him how dry she felt spiritually; but he said, 'You need a holiday! With three kids and a new baby you're exhausted.' Would you describe yourself as stressed-out, burnt-out, worn-out? Feeling spiritually low can also follow an illness, or be a symptom of an undetected medical condition, such as mild depression, anaemia, problems with hormones, thyroid or the immune system. When was your last medical check-up? Before looking for spiritual causes for a desert, take time to look for a physical explanation.

1 Kings 19:1–18

Elijah had just successfully confronted the nation with the reality of God by staging a dramatic showdown with pagan idol-worshippers. No wonder he was exhausted! Verse 4 finds him alone in a geographical and spiritual desert. What did he need most (vs 5–6)? Our outward, physical health influences our inner, spiritual life enormously, but look at verse 8. Once Elijah was well enough he set off to seek God afresh, on the holy mountain. How did he feel (v 10)? Perhaps he wanted to go to the spot where, centuries before, God had given Moses the Ten Commandments which his people were now breaking. There at Mount Sinai, God restored Elijah's lost sense of proportion (v 18, compare v 14) and showed him what to do next (vs 15–17).

Deserts can be convenient places to hide from responsibilities, like turning up at church or running the youth group. You have to want to get out. Elijah was willing to risk anything to be close to God again (v 8). How much do you want to recover the excitement of your first love (see Revelation 2:4)?

The Bible in a year: 2 Samuel 21–22; 1 Corinthians 9

MAY 13–19

DAY 3

Deserts we cause ourselves

We all sin – we're human! Jesus died to take the punishment for those sins but his sacrifice is only effective when we repent and confess. Wrong attitudes, thoughts, behaviour patterns or relationships develop so gradually we can fail to recognise them as sin until our spiritual lives become barren. Could you dare to pray this? 'Search me, O God … point out anything you find in me that makes you sad' (Psalm 139:23–24, The Living Bible).

2 Samuel 11

David had always tried to please God but look at verse 1 and then compare it with Uriah's attitude (v 11). Why do you think David stayed in his palace (v 2a)? When life is tough we often cling to God, but success, ease and laziness can cause deserts.

Perhaps David convinced himself that he'd got away with his one-night-stand with Bathsheba – then came bad news (v 5). How do you think David felt about himself during his efforts to hide his sin (vs 8–9, 13, 15)? Perhaps he told himself that a God of love would understand? But how did God feel (v 27b)? For months David was so out of touch spiritually that God had to 'shout' to gain his attention (12:1–9). How do you feel when friends point to a 'dodgy' area in your life? Do you react like David (2 Samuel 12:13) or become angry and defensive?

How remarkable that God continued to use and honour a man who had sinned so horrendously! It was David's complete repentance that made this possible. He probably wrote Psalm 51 at this time; you could use it as your prayer if God shows you that hidden sins have been responsible for your desert.

The Bible in a year: 2 Samuel 23–24; 1 Corinthians 10

MAY 13–19

DAY 4

It's not fair!

Have you ever felt disappointed by God when he failed to answer a heart-felt prayer, or allowed too many disasters to hit you at once? Are you arguing with God over anything? Sometimes we try to ignore these kinds of feelings. Why not ask the Lord to help you face them honestly today?

Psalm 73

The psalmist had obviously been through a horrible experience (v 14). He wanted to know why, but when God remained silent his faith wobbled (v 2). His suffering didn't seem fair when he had tried so hard to please God (v 13). Meanwhile others, who could not care less, seemed to prosper (vs 3–5, 12). He wanted answers but only grew more confused (v 16). What was his turning point (v 17a)?

When doubts attack our minds we want to avoid church but it was going into God's house, perhaps through obedience and habit, which saved the psalmist. While it is wise to ask 'why' when things go wrong, God does not always explain. Trying to understand him with our human intellects only causes frustration, but peace comes when we 'grab' him, by faith, and nestle down in his written promise to love us unconditionally, and to make all life's experiences work for our ultimate good.

Looking back with hindsight, the psalmist almost laughs at himself (vs 21–22) as he realises God was there, holding him, all through his worst times. The verses he writes *after* he comes out of his desert are some of the most beautiful in the Bible (vs 23–26). Could *you* look back at some of your past faith-deserts and difficult life experiences and ask yourself what you gained from them spiritually?

The Bible in a year: 1 Kings 1–2; Psalm 55

MAY 13–19

DAY 5

How much do you love me?

Lou was on cloud nine after the Christian camp where she gave everything she was and had to God, and was filled by his Spirit. A year later she said, 'Everything keeps going wrong and God feels billions of miles away!' Dry patches often occur after we've made a deeper commitment to Christ; received a new spiritual gift, revelation or vision for the future. Could your desert be a test of faith? Would you say that you loved God for himself or simply for answering your prayers, or because you enjoy Christian music or the excitement of seeing his supernatural power?

Deuteronomy 8:2–14

What were the reasons God gave for taking his people through the desert (vs 2–3, 5)? Being humbled by God is not the same as being humiliated; he is simply making us rely on him instead of on our old self-reliant coping strategies. A spoilt, undisciplined child is determined to go his own way, regardless of others. God is too good a father to bring his children up like that (v 5). While some Christians are content to keep God merely as one compartment in their lives, a smaller group tell him they want to love him in *everything*. He may then want to discover if that love is pure and untainted by self-interest.

What was God's ultimate intention (vs 7–9)? Remember, he never wants our deserts to be permanent, so if you are sick of feeling dry, remind yourself that 'times of refreshing' (Acts 3:19) are just ahead. Remember, too, that desert experiences often happen before God gives us some new, exciting mission: think of Joseph, Moses, David and Jesus himself.

Loss, change and rejection: Genesis 21:9–20
Who are you trusting?: Jeremiah 17:5–14

The Bible in a year: 1 Kings 3–5; 1 Corinthians 11

Going deeper ...

One Sabbath morning Jesus was in the synagogue when he noticed a man whose hand and arm were withered (Mark 3:1–6). He was no longer able to earn his living or support his family. Jesus realised at once how hard this made life for him so, right in front of the outraged gaze of the religious bigots, he healed him flouting all their restrictive Sabbath rules. 'Withered' is the same word used in the Bible for dryness and deserts. A part of that man's life had become dry, dead and useless but, after one touch from Jesus, life, joy, energy and independence flooded back again.

Is there an area of *your* life that has withered and dried up, perhaps because of the 'disease' of sin, or one of life's accidents: the loss of someone or something you valued and loved or some other life-shattering event? Is it your creativity, your passion for the Bible, your first love for the Lord? Perhaps it is your love for someone else close to you, your personal happiness, the vision for service you were once given, your sense of fulfilment, confidence, faith, self-respect or respect for someone else. I am convinced Jesus still has the same power to touch, revive and restore these 'withered' areas. Why not face your inner desert and ask him to transform it into a garden full of flowers and fruit? All too often we just sigh and resign ourselves to these secret deserts. Jesus told us to ask (Matthew 7:7), and nothing is impossible for him!

Rescuing the victims

Suppose you suspect that a spouse, family member or close friend is in a spiritual desert – how can you help? Shut your mouth and put your hands together! In other words, don't bombard them with advice, intrusive questions, helpful books or tapes or endless streams of texts. Instead, pray for them and perhaps even fast. Someone in a desert is in danger! Never assume they will automatically be fine if given space. Take prayer seriously but don't let them know about it. Get up five minutes earlier each morning; perhaps set an alarm to remind you, several times a day, to stop and hold them before God. Don't gossip all round church but find one or two people you can trust, and ask them to pray as well.

And how can we avoid deserts ourselves? Perhaps we can't – dry patches seem an inevitable part of spiritual life. However, it is possible to travel safely through a geographical desert if you remember that people only die of thirst when they stop drinking regularly. So keep reading the Bible and drinking in the Holy Spirit in prayer. People get lost in deserts when they go off by themselves. So keep close to other Christians by going to church. The most dangerous thing to do in the desert is to lie down and give up. Conquering a desert builds self-confidence but spiritual deserts can build God-confidence because, in them, we often discover just how much he loves us (Deuteronomy 32:10).

Once we realise that, we become invincible!

The Bible in a year: 1 Kings 6–9; Psalm 56–57; 1 Corinthians 12

MAY 20–26

Old life versus new

Roman 6–10

Some friends of mine spent months planning their holiday. They meticulously studied the travel arrangements, poring over maps and timetables, to be sure their journey would be a success. They were anticipating a dream holiday. When they returned I asked them how it had gone. To my surprise they didn't look too cheerful. 'The journey was great,' they said, 'everything just fell into place. But when we got there we didn't know what to do with ourselves and in fact wondered why we'd gone there at all.'

In the first part of Romans, Paul has explained in detail how we make the journey from being God's enemies to being his friends – how we move from being sinners under God's wrath to being declared righteous by God. He has shown us that this journey can only be made by faith in Jesus, through whose death and resurrection we are justified and reconciled to God.

The next question is this: having made that journey into the 'grace in which we now stand' (Romans 5:2), what do we do now we're here? What are we saved *for*? This week's readings give us some answers. They tell us that we have been rescued from our old life of sin in order to live a new life which is 'alive to God in Christ Jesus' (6:11). We have not only been rescued from the *penalty* of sin but also from the *power* of sin so that we can now serve God 'in the new way of the Spirit' (7:6). So as we read this next section of Romans, let's remember the journey we have already made, from being condemned sinners to forgiven children, and let's now ask the age-old question: How should we then live?

Martin Hodson is the minister of the Red Hill Baptist Church, Worcester, England. He and his wife, Becky, have three boys and live in a house full of toys, music and visitors.

MAY 20–26

DAY 1

Dead to sin

Think about the significance of baptism. Most of us have been baptised; if you have, what does it mean to you?

Romans 6:1–14

We most often describe being a Christian in terms of life – for example, being born again or living a new life. But it's also about being dead – that is, dead to sin (v 2). Experience tells us that being dead to sin doesn't mean we never sin, nor that we're unconscious of the temptation to sin. So what does it mean?

We were baptised *into* the death of Jesus (v 3). This signifies that we are united with him by faith to such an extent that his death has now become our death (v 5). Sin has the power to make us live in fear of its penalty (death) but by being united with Jesus we have already died that death in him, so sin's power over our destiny is defeated. We are no longer slaves to sin (v 6) but share in the resurrection life of Jesus (v 8).

Since our spiritual status is 'dead to sin' we are now free to work that out in practice (vs 11–12). Sin remains an attraction to be battled with on a daily basis but it is not our master. We are free to decide to offer ourselves to God rather than to wickedness (v 13). Just as a master could not demand work from his slave once that slave had died, so sin cannot now demand that we do its work (v 14).

What leads you into sin? Perhaps it's pressure from other people, ingrained habits, or simple selfishness. Ask the Spirit to give you a new conviction that these things no longer have mastery over you and a new power to resist them.

The Bible in a year: 1 Kings 10–11; 1 Corinthians 13

MAY 20–26

DAY 2

A new slavery

'You are not your own; you were bought at a price' (1 Corinthians 6:19–20). Use the words 'I am yours' a few times as a simple prayer. Wait a while for the Spirit to deepen their meaning to you. Then use the same prayer, adding phrases he brings to mind, such as 'I am yours for ever/today/at work …'

Romans 6:15–23

For millions of people slavery is the way they are compelled to live; they may have been forced into bonded labour or become enslaved to debt or addictions. Slavery steals human freedom and dignity and is now almost universally reviled. Paul has already explained that without Jesus people are 'slaves to sin' (v 6) and its cruel control over their destiny. Now, perhaps surprisingly, he says that Christians are also slaves, slaves to righteousness (v 18) and to God (v 22). Jesus has set us free from sin not so that we can adopt an autonomous way of life with no obligations and no master but so that we can live wholeheartedly for God (v 17).

True freedom is not freedom to do as we like but freedom to be what our Creator intended. Slavery to God is infinitely better than all other forms of slavery. It is not based on coercion but on a choice to offer ourselves to him (v 16). It replaces ever-increasing wickedness with holiness (v 19) and results in eternal life (v 22).

If we're 'slaves' to God and righteousness, what obligations do you think we have to our Master – in terms of availability, obedience and loyalty? Don't let the language of slavery blind you to the fact that God is also a Father, a Saviour and a Helper.

The Bible in a year: 1 Kings 12–13; 1 Corinthians 14

DAY 3   Dead to the law

Grace has been cleverly summed up by someone as God's Riches At Christ's Expense. Think what riches you have received as a gift from God. Then think of the cost Jesus paid on your behalf. Try to recall a verse of Scripture or part of a song or hymn that mentions grace and hold that in your mind.

Romans 7:1–6

Legalism comes in many shapes and sizes. There's that feeling that we have to prove ourselves to God or to other people by the quantity of our good works. There can be a striving to live up to the (impossible) standards we perceive other people have set for us, or which we set for ourselves. There may be a critical spirit towards others which arises from our sense of failure to achieve our own legalistic goals. These are just some of 'the sinful passions aroused by the law' (v 5). God's law is, of course, good in every way; the problem is that our sinful nature causes us to break and abuse it.

Here Paul tells us that just as we have died to sin through being united with Christ, we have also 'died to the law' through his body (v 4). The illustration in verses 1–3 emphasises that the law no longer has power over us – to control our destiny or determine our standing before God. The reason we serve God is not to achieve our salvation or prove our worth, but to participate in 'the new way of the Spirit' (v 6).

Ask the Spirit to show you if you are letting the law usurp the place of grace in your life. Be especially attentive to a challenge about boastfulness or self-condemnation.

The Bible in a year: 1 Kings 14–15; 1 Corinthians 15

MAY 20–26

DAY 4

Struggling with sin

'If we claim to be without sin, we deceive ourselves' (1 John 1:8). Take a long hard look at yourself as you really are. Then look to Jesus and see the friend of sinners.

Romans 7:7–25

Popular wisdom says no one should be held back by the restrictions of earlier times. If you want it, go out and get it! There's plenty that's good about this attitude, but there are some boundaries that are permanent. God's law (as summed up in, say, the Ten Commandments) marks the boundary between good and evil; it was given so that we could recognise where righteousness ends and sin begins (vs 7, 13). However strong the pressure is from within us (v 8) or from around us to push beyond these God-given boundaries, they remain holy, righteous and good, and not subject to negotiation (v 12).

An honest glance at our own lives shows that keeping within those boundaries doesn't always come easily. Although we are dead to sin, we still experience the struggle between our old 'sinful nature' (v 18) and our new 'inner being' (v 22). Most of us can easily think of a specific example of the struggle Paul describes in verses 14–23, and like him we have probably felt 'wretched' at times because obedience to God has proved so difficult (v 24). But notice how Paul deals with this feeling: he doesn't wallow in it but immediately gives thanks to God for what he has already done through Jesus (v 25).

God knows we don't always triumph in the struggle against sin but he invites us to enjoy living in his forgiveness. Don't let the enemy get a foothold in your failure but remember God 'is faithful and just and will forgive us our sins …' (1 John 1:9).

The Bible in a year: 1 Kings 16–17; Psalm 58–59

MAY 20–26

DAY 5

The Spirit of life

Ask yourself, 'Who am I?' Think of the answers you could give based on the things you do and the roles you play in life. Now ask God, 'Who do you say I am?' and give time to hear his answer.

Romans 8:1–17

We admire the independent achievement of people who have climbed Everest without extra supplies of oxygen or walked across the Antarctic dragging their equipment behind them all the way. Here Paul explains that putting to death the sinful nature is not an independent achievement once we are justified by faith; that would be too awesome a challenge for anyone. Rather, God gives his Spirit to all who belong to Christ (v 9).

Notice how the Spirit works in us. He controls our minds when we offer ourselves to God (v 6), giving us a new way of thinking and a new set of priorities. His presence in us is the promise that we will share in the resurrection of Jesus (v 11), giving us a continual reminder that our destiny is glory and not destruction. He gives us the power to put to death our persistent sins (v 13) and he leads us into a more holy way of living (v 14). Perhaps most wonderfully, he gives us the confidence to call God our own Father in the most intimate of terms, '*Abba*', just as Jesus himself did (vs 15–16, see Mark 14:36), providing a continual reminder of our true identity in Christ.

An independent streak that's in us all can quickly tempt us to try living for God using our own resources. Instead, invite God's Spirit to fill you in a newly pervasive way and be ready to respond to his leading and to hear his inner testimony today.

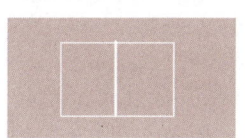

Free indeed: John 8:31–38
Now and not yet: 1 John 3:1–3

The Bible in a year: 1 Kings 18–19; 1 Corinthians 16

Going deeper ...

Lord God, what sort of Father are you? There are so many different kinds of human fathers – some are good, some are bad, and most are a bit of both. I know some people who practically idolise their fathers, and I'm not sure if that's very healthy. I'm worried that they are confusing what is true about their good old dad with what is true about you. I know some other people whose fathers treated them so horrendously and left them with such hurts that calling you 'Father' seems like an insult. When your Spirit stirs me to call you 'Father' (Romans 8:15–16), what am I saying?

Jesus, you've said that the Spirit will take from what is yours and make it known to me (John 16:14). I think this even includes your Sonship. The Spirit shows me something about your relationship with the Father and that's how I learn what kind of Father in heaven I have. I can't find the answer from human fatherhood; it only comes when I start to understand what you meant when you said '*Abba*, Father'.

I'm thinking about when you were baptised (Mark 1:11). The Father's voice spoke from heaven. 'You are my Son' – because fatherhood means belonging to God. 'Whom I love' – because fatherhood means committed, unreserved love. 'With you I am well-pleased' – because there was no hint of condemnation but an exhilarating sense of the Father taking pleasure in you. And this is what your Spirit testifies to in my heart when I say, '*Abba*, Father'.

Saved from sin

The word 'sin' has been a recurrent theme in this week's readings. Through faith in Christ we are saved from sin and in Romans 6–8 we have seen the past, present and future dimensions of this.

We *have been* saved from the penalty of sin. 'The wages of sin is death' (6:23). Everyone who sins deserves God's just penalty for sin, which is death. But Jesus has become a sin offering for us (8:3). He has died in our place and through faith in him we have received God's free gift of eternal life. We are no longer under God's condemnation (8:1).

We *are being* saved from the power of sin. Living as a Christian does not mean that we never sin. It would be a naive boast to suggest such a thing. Paul is honest about his ongoing struggle to subdue his old sinful self (7:14–25) but he is confident that things have changed. In Christ we are now dead to sin (6:2). It no longer has the right or power to control us. Though it may tempt us and trip us, it is not our master for we are now slaves to righteousness (6:18) and are ultimately controlled 'not by the sinful nature but by the Spirit' (8:9). There is no sin we may find in ourselves which we do not have the right to challenge and the resources to subdue.

We *will be* saved from the presence of sin. One day we will no longer fall short of God's glory but share in it (8:17). God will complete the saving work he has begun in us and we will live in his perfect, sinless presence for ever.

The Bible in a year: 1 Kings 20–22; Psalm 60–61; 2 Corinthians 1

MAY 27– JUNE 2

God's mercy

As a child I was taught that when you give thanks to God before a meal you should also pray to be made 'mindful of those less fortunate than ourselves'. This introduced me to the healthy principle that celebrating the good things we have can quickly turn into self-indulgence unless it is accompanied by a true concern for people who desperately need what we are now enjoying.

The readings this week move in precisely that direction. We begin with one of the most enthusiastic New Testament celebrations of the hope of glory and the security that comes from knowing that nothing in all creation can separate us from the love of God. Then, just as this exhilarating exposition of salvation reaches its climax, we turn immediately to think of those who have not received God's mercy. Paul discloses his agony of spirit over the fact that most of his own people, the Jews, have not been saved through faith in Christ. Most of us will share the same sort of agony over those of our own people – our family or close friends, or perhaps our nation as a whole – who have not become Christians and don't share in the blessings we enjoy.

This raises some difficult questions. Why have some been saved and not others? Why us and not them? The readings in chapter 9 begin to address these issues and will give us some deep ideas to grapple with. But above all, we will see in chapter 10 that the good news is not too difficult for anyone to receive, and that our greatest priority must be ensuring that it is made known. We who enjoy a spiritual feast cannot be complacent about those who remain spiritually hungry.

Martin Hodson is the minister of the Red Hill Baptist Church, Worcester, England. He and his wife, Becky, have three boys and live in a house full of toys, music and visitors.

MAY 27–JUNE 2

DAY 1

The big picture

How far back can you remember? How far into the future do you make plans? God is eternal. Worship him who is not confined by time.

Romans 8:18–27

As a teenager I went on a school trip to the National Gallery in London. Standing about two feet away from the canvas, I was trying to appreciate *The Hay Wain* by John Constable (which is 185 cm wide) when a curator came over to give me some useful advice: 'You need to stand a little further back to enjoy this one.' He was right. In these verses Paul invites us to step back and see the big picture of God's redeeming work, including what has gone before us and what is still to come, as well as what is right in front of us now.

When Adam and Eve first rebelled against God, sin spoiled the glory of God in human beings. God's curse on sin subjected the created earth to frustration (v 20, see Genesis 3:17–18). In the future, when God's redeeming work is completed, the glory of God will again be fully revealed in his children (v 18) and the creation will be liberated (v 21). In the present time, we have been saved in the confident hope that God's work will be completed (v 24). Think about what it means to wait both eagerly (v 23) and patiently (v 25) for the day when the glory of God will be fully restored in us.

We sometimes wonder if our praying is really 'in the will of God'. Read verses 26 and 27 again. As you pray for other people now, be conscious that though you may be unsure what to pray, the Spirit is interceding in accordance with God's will.

The Bible in a year: 2 Kings 1–3; 2 Corinthians 2

MAY 27–JUNE 2

DAY 2

God's work

Think carefully about one way God has blessed you. Do you realise that he did that *for you*?

Romans 8:28–39

TV programmes showing how to transform your home or garden are hugely popular at the moment. They leave some of us saying perhaps naively, 'I could do that myself'. Here Paul is resisting that do-it-yourself impulse when it comes to our relationship with God. What matters is that 'God works', and that he does so 'in all things' (v 28). Look in verses 29 and 30 at the list of things God has done which we couldn't do: he has given us a destiny to be like his Son, called us to himself, justified us and given us the certain hope of being glorified. No amount of hard work on our part could accomplish these things!

If that unrelenting desire in us to work for our own salvation makes us ask *why* God should work for our good, then the answer is clear: God is for us (v 31). We have positive proof of this because he gave up his own Son for us (v 32). We have absolute confidence in this because no one has the power to undo what God has done (vs 33, 34). We have perfect security in this because there is nothing we or anyone else can do that would make God stop loving us (vs 35–39).

The other day my young son got out of his depth in the swimming pool; he reached out to me and I took hold of him. I think he felt that he was holding onto me, but I knew that beneath the surface I was holding onto him with a far greater strength. Delight in God's hold on you.

The Bible in a year: 2 Kings 4–5; 2 Corinthians 3

MAY 27–JUNE 2

DAY 3

Passion for the lost

There are some difficult theological questions around that I can't fully answer. Sometimes I have to say, 'Lord, I don't have an answer to that, but I know you do.' Think of any tough questions you keep wrestling with. Can you tell God you believe that he has the answers?

Romans 9:1–21

One of the marks of an evangelist is a passion for the lost. This was certainly true of Paul. He was the 'apostle to the Gentiles' but he also had an 'unceasing anguish' for the salvation of his own people, the Jews (vs 1–3). Here we see three vital features of the evangelist's outlook. Firstly, he identifies the things which have already made people think about God. In this case it is the tremendous privileges the Jews have received from God (vs 4–5). Secondly, he confronts the claim that people don't need Jesus because they have become God's children by some other means. He shows that simply being descendants of Abraham does not guarantee this privilege to the Jews (vs 6–13). We are more likely to find ourselves explaining why just living a good life, or believing sincerely in any religion, doesn't make you a child of God.

Thirdly, he anticipates the objections people will raise: if God chooses to have mercy on some and not others, isn't he being unfair (v 14)? He recognises it as a great mystery and concludes humbly that God being God has a right to have mercy on whom he pleases (v 18) and that human beings are in no position to judge God (vs 20–21).

Whose salvation do you long for with anguish in your heart? Pray for them and ask the Spirit to lead you to play your full part in making Jesus known to them.

The Bible in a year: 2 Kings 6–7; 2 Corinthians 4

DAY 4

The new people of God

MAY 27–JUNE 2

'Lord Jesus Christ, Son of God, have mercy on me, a sinner.' Pray this prayer a few times, thinking especially of what impact God's mercy has on you.

Romans 9:22–33

Who do you think of as 'the people of God'? Paul had grown up in a setting where the phrase was used exclusively to mean the Jewish race. At the heart of this passage is the truth that the 'people of God' has a far wider meaning. It refers to both Jews and Gentiles whom God has called to know him by faith in Jesus (v 24). God has patiently withheld his wrath from both unbelieving Jews and sinful Gentiles so that they can become equally 'objects of his mercy' in the new inclusive people of God (vs 22–23). Two prophecies which God had given Hosea, originally about the Jewish people, now also apply to Gentiles (vs 25–26).

The question of why most of Paul's fellow-Jews are still unbelievers and therefore not among the new people of God remains in the background. Tackling this issue, he shows that though this is disturbing, it is not surprising since the Scriptures predicted that only a remnant would be saved (vs 27–29). Also, as long as anyone pursues righteousness by works and not by faith, the good news of salvation as God's gift through faith in Jesus will be a stumbling-stone rather than a foundation stone (vs 32–33).

Praise God for the diversity of people in the congregation where you worship. Pray for a big vision of the people of God, and ask him to give you a special sensitivity to anyone who doesn't feel included in the fellowship.

The Bible in a year: 2 Kings 8–9; Psalm 62–63

MAY 27–JUNE 2

DAY 5

The word of faith

As you recognise God's presence here now, hold out empty hands before you as a sign that you have nothing to bring to win his approval. Focus your thoughts on what Jesus has done to make you righteous before God.

Romans 10

God does not expect the impossible from us. He has made us and he knows what is within our reach and what is beyond it. Paul's heart's desire for the Israelites to be saved (v 1) is coupled with the frustration that in their zeal for God they have set themselves an impossible task – to establish their own righteousness by obeying the law (vs 3–4). By contrast, the righteousness that comes through faith in Christ is received by things we *can* do – confessing openly that Jesus is Lord and believing in our hearts that he died and rose for us (vs 9–10). This is not too difficult for anyone to do … if they have heard the 'word of faith' (v 8).

The necessity of telling others this message is eloquently expressed in verses 14 and 15. There is no one blueprint for fulfilling this need. For one person it means telling a work colleague what they believe about Jesus; for another it means going on an evangelistic mission or camp; for some it means faithfully living out the gospel in their home or teaching it to their children; whilst for others it means travelling thousands of miles to live in a totally different culture. The message of Jesus must be heard (v 17). That needs missionaries – and that means *all* of us.

Pray for the wisdom to discern between the seemingly impossible things which you can accomplish by faith and the truly impossible which God doesn't want you to attempt in vain.

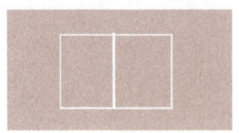

Everyone's invited!: Luke 14:15–24
No barriers: Galatians 3:26–29

The Bible in a year: 2 Kings 10–12; 2 Corinthians 5

MAY 27–JUNE 2

Going deeper …

Look again at Romans 8:38–39. Invite the Holy Spirit to deepen the conviction that absolutely nothing can separate you from God's love. What he has given you through faith in Christ Jesus is his gift to you for ever. Nothing has the right or authority to throw you into spiritual isolation or to return you to the status of a condemned sinner. Nothing will persuade God to love you less or weaken his hold on you. Spend some time thinking through this list of things which God has declared are incapable of separating us from his love:

Death – when you leave behind everything else you have known in this world.

Life – anything that happens to you while you're still in this world.

Angels – next to God they have the greatest power, but not enough to separate you from his love.

Demons – Satan's agents may attack you, but they cannot suppress God's love.

Present – whatever is putting pressure on you this week.

Future – the things that might happen which cause you anxiety.

Any powers – the people who wield authority at work, in your family, or in the nation.

Height – in the heights of success or joy, when you feel you could do anything.

Depth – in despair, loneliness or grief; deep confusion or profound loss.

Anything else – whatever might attempt to impede God's love for you.

Why did he do it?

Why did Paul give up so much to be an evangelist? Why did he sacrifice his reputation as a learned and respectable Jewish teacher to proclaim Jesus Christ as Saviour for both Jews and Gentiles? Why did he endanger his life by travelling over dangerous seas and along bandit-infested roads? Why did he continue making arduous missionary journeys despite his own persistent ill-health? Why did he repeatedly endure opposition and persecution? Read 2 Corinthians 6:3–10 and 11:23–33.)

The answer is plain from this week's readings. He had a passion for Jesus and a passion for the lost. He was passionate about Jesus because through faith in him he had been justified and now had the Spirit of God and the hope of glory in his heart. Through Jesus he had become certain that God was at work in all things and that no circumstances could ever separate him from God's love. This gave him a passion for the lost. How could he keep such a great gift to himself! That would be selfish, callous and contrary to the express command of Jesus. He longed for his own people to receive God's mercy, but if God had promised that everyone who called on him would be saved, then everyone, regardless of race or background, must be given a chance to hear the good news.

I'm committed to zealous and active Christianity because this is the right response to an awesome gift and a desperate need.

The Bible in a year: 2 Kings 13–16; Psalm 64–65; 2 Corinthians 6

JUNE 3–9

Love's young dream

Exodus 5–18

The life of faith often starts with great excitement and expectation. We have met with the living God! Everything looks different. Surely others too will come to know this wonderful reality into which we have entered and our family, church, school, neighbourhood, town and country will be changed for the better.

Yet just as the experience of falling in love does not last, so the initial excitement of faith does not last. The process of change, however, need not be negative, a cooling of love, a fading of vision – the frisky, gambolling lambs becoming just dozy sheep (though sadly this often does happen). Rather, there needs to be a process of deepening, of understanding more fully what it is that love, and the life of faith, really entails. Then we can more truly and lastingly enter into its many dimensions.

Our readings this week (and next) feature the people of Israel in their infancy as a nation. On one level their situation is bad. The land of Egypt, which they entered as a place of refuge from famine years ago, has become a place of oppression and captivity. On another level, however, they would be full of hope. Moses has just met with God at the burning bush, been given a new understanding of the name and nature of God, and has been commissioned by God to bring Israel out of Egypt. On his return to the people of Israel, they have greeted him with joyful belief (Exodus 4:29–31). Surely now they will see wonders, surely now everything will be changed.

What they (and we) need to learn is to take seriously both the obstacles in the life of faith and the resources of God. This week the obstacles primarily take the form of opposition from others: Pharaoh and the Egyptians.

Walter Moberly is a lecturer in theology at the University of Durham and is married to Jenny. He is a doting and sleep-deprived father of John-Paul and Rachel, and author of a number of books including *The Bible, Theology and Faith: A Study of Abraham and Jesus*.

JUNE 3–9

DAY 1

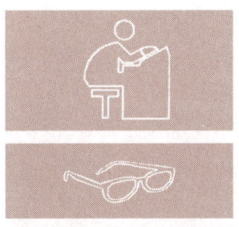

Why, oh why?

Fresh from his encounter with God, Moses – like any believer – must have had the highest expectations of what would happen when he confronted Pharaoh …

Exodus 5

Moses wastes no time and confronts Pharaoh with a confident proclamation of God's demand. Pharaoh simply dismisses Moses' words out of hand (vs 1–2). Moses climbs down, and uses words that might be more acceptable to Pharaoh. No longer does he use God's new name (Lord), he requests permission to go, and he gives the kind of reason which might make sense in terms of common assumptions about the gods (v 3). But Pharaoh is no more impressed by the second speech than the first (vs 4–5).

Pharaoh responds further. All this stuff about the Israelite God is simply a lie (v 9), a pretext to escape from their work because the real issue is their laziness (vs 8, 17). So he ensures that their work is harder. This increase in Israel's workload has the further – no doubt desired – effect of turning Israel's other leaders, the foremen, against Moses and Aaron (vs 20–21).

The remarkable feature of this narrative is the – apparent – absence of God. Just when his presence and power would have been expected, there is nothing but the heedless cynicism of Pharaoh and a situation that gets worse rather than better. Moses comes to the Lord with a complaint (of a sort common among the psalms, though this is the first instance in the canonical story). Why, oh why, has God done the opposite of what was expected (vs 22–23)?

Can I learn to face unexpected disappointment and bring it to God?

The Bible in a year: 2 Kings 17–18; 2 Corinthians 7

JUNE 3–9

DAY 2

The nature of God

If once we have been badly disappointed, dare we hope again?

Exodus 6:1–12

God responds to Moses' complaint, but, as ever, neither justifies himself nor explains why things have turned out as they have. Rather he renews his commitment to deliver Israel from Egypt (v 1). God also reminds Moses of what he had learned at the burning bush. Moses has been allowed to know the very name of God – in Hebrew 'YHWH', meaning 'I AM' (Exodus 3:14–15), reverently spoken of as 'the Lord'. This knowledge was not given to the patriarchs, who knew God as El Shaddai ('God Almighty') (vs 2–3).

In Hebrew, a name regularly says something about the character of its bearer, and a change of name depicts a change of character (Jacob becomes Israel, see Genesis 32:28). Thus a new name for God signifies a new and deeper access to the nature of God (as supremely shown in Jesus). What is involved? Firstly, the faithfulness of God, who stands by his covenant commitment, even when made long ago (vs 4–5, 8). Secondly, God's deliverance of Israel from slavery to live as the free people of God (vs 6–7). Thirdly, the need to trust now what will only be realised in the future (v 7).

Yet such was the disappointment of Moses' initial encounter with Pharaoh that Israel cannot respond to this renewed promise. And even Moses has lost his assurance and reverts to the kind of excuse he made when God first spoke to him (vs 9–12, compare 4:1–10).

Which is bigger: our vision of God, or our sense of hurt and self-pity?

The Bible in a year: 2 Kings 19–20; 2 Corinthians 8

DAY 3

The long haul

Once it has been understood that God's will may not be done instantly, it is time to settle down to the long haul, realising that this may include facing and overcoming prolonged conflict with hostile opposition. 'Lord, help me to stand firm.'

Exodus 6:28–7:13

Moses' renewed anxieties about his ability to confront Pharaoh, after his initial failure, are met by God's provision of his brother Aaron, who will do for Moses what a prophet does for God, i.e. speak on his behalf (6:28–7:2). But this help is accompanied by a warning that their task will still be long and hard, for Pharaoh will be as unresponsive as he can be (7:3–5).

The confrontation with Pharaoh will not just be a matter of words. It will also be a contest of powers. Part of God's initial assurance to Moses, when commissioning him, was to work signs through him, especially the turning of his staff into a snake (Exodus 4:1–5); the size and shape do not change, but that which was an inert support is changed into a dangerous living thing. Moses and Aaron are now to do this in Pharaoh's presence (7:8–10). This would surely seem a persuasive sign of the power of God!

Yet Pharaoh's Egyptian experts can do the same (v 11). Miraculous power is not necessarily the preserve of those who follow the Lord. However, although others may indeed have mysterious power, Israel's power is greater – Aaron's staff swallows up the others (v 12). Yet Pharaoh is unimpressed (v 13). Signs of power may achieve little; the struggle will be prolonged.

Am I willing to serve God in the long haul?

The Bible in a year: 2 Kings 21–22; 2 Corinthians 9

JUNE 3–9

DAY 4

Showdown

'Lord, you often do things that I don't even begin to understand. Please give me understanding.'

Exodus 11

After a lengthy contest between Moses and Pharaoh, the final plague comes upon Egypt. It will be the most terrible – the death of every Egyptian first-born son. Why so terrible an affliction? Within the text, the idea of killing male children (not just the first-born son, but all of them) came from a Pharaoh himself (Exodus 1:15–22). Thus the Egyptians are to experience something of what they have inflicted upon others. Further, in the ancient world the first-born son was all important as a symbol of hope for the future, and the loss of a first-born led to the most bitter and anguished of all griefs (Jeremiah 6:26; Amos 8:10); this, therefore, will touch the inner being of Pharaoh and the Egyptians in a way that no other plague or adversity could.

Most significantly, however, this plague will underline a concern that runs throughout the plagues narrative – that the Lord makes a distinction between Israel and Egypt (11:7); that which afflicts Egypt does not afflict Israel (8:22–23; 9:4–7, 26). The key to the narrative has already been provided earlier (4:22–23). Israel is the Lord's first-born son, the people in whom the Lord specially delights and for whom he has special purposes. If Pharaoh continues to keep them in a slavery which is a kind of living death, he will lose his first-born while God's first-born is spared and goes free.

We often use the language of life and death lightly in relation to God's call and our response to him. Can we respond faithfully in those times when life and death in their totality really are at stake?

The Bible in a year: 2 Kings 23–25; Psalm 66–67

JUNE 3–9

DAY 5

Sacrificial worship

Old Testament accounts of ritual detail tend to bore and baffle the modern Christian reader. This is in part because we are no longer concerned to do what the text says and celebrate Israel's festivals (as Jews still do today). If it is also symptomatic of a failure of understanding, let's ask the Lord to help us overcome it.

Exodus 12:1–28

We expect to come directly to the affliction of Egypt's first-born and Israel's deliverance. We are in for a surprise. Before the rather brief narrative of affliction and deliverance (vs 29–42), we have a lengthy account of how Israel is to commemorate it. Israel's worship of God in every generation (vs 14, 24) is the primary focus of the text.

Such is the significance of God's deliverance that the whole calendar is to be reshaped around it (vs 1–2). The offering of a lamb is similar to that of regular sacrificial worship (Exodus 29:38–46), but with distinctive features. It is a communal occasion for families together (vs 3, 4), dress is to be symbolic (v 11). Blood of the slaughtered lamb, as a sign to avert the entrance of death (vs 13, 23), is to be put at the place of access to their gathering (v 7), the place otherwise marked by the prime words of Israel's faith and identity (see Deuteronomy 6:4–9). It will symbolise God's judgement of Egypt's oppression and idolatry (v 12), and the consecrating of Israel as God's special people.

Because of Jesus, Easter has become our Passover celebration (see 1 Corinthians 5:7–8). Is our worship as full and faithful as Israel's was commanded to be?

Unconditional trust: Exodus 13:17; 14:14
Unreserved trust: Exodus 14:15–31

The Bible in a year: 1 Chronicles 1–3; 2 Corinthians 10

Going deeper …

The confrontation between Moses and Pharaoh revolves around signs of power. One of the most remarkable features of the text is how unpersuasive Pharaoh finds these. To some extent Pharaoh personifies a widespread human tendency to be blind and stubborn when one should be open and amenable.

The significance of signs of power is a live issue in the New Testament, as it is in many churches today. Jesus in the Gospels and Paul in Acts regularly perform astonishing acts of power, yet the positive response that they receive is limited. In John's Gospel, Jesus' supreme act of power, the restoration of Lazarus to life, moves the religious leaders to make a firm resolution that this man who so troublesomely gives life to the dead should himself be put to death (John 11:43–53). Jesus is painfully aware that signs of power can fail to touch the heart and mind and bring the one thing needful, turning to God. He is scathing about people's failure to heed what is before their eyes (Matthew 11:20–24). Elsewhere he says that the only sign his contemporaries will be given is the mysterious sign of Jonah, whose story anticipates the death of Jesus (Matthew 12:38–42; 16:1–4).

That the death and resurrection of Jesus is God's supreme sign and act of power is central to Paul, who sees its outworking in his own life, where divine power is fully realised in human weakness (2 Corinthians 12:7–10). How truly do I understand what it means that God's power is supremely realised in human weakness which replicates that of Jesus on the cross? And am I prepared to live it out?

The heart of faith

Learning to grow in the life of faith in the light of the book of Exodus is not always straightforward. Although there are many important ways in which Israel is a pattern or model of the church, there are major differences. But aspects such as opposition to Israel, and Pharaoh's unresponsiveness to Moses' speaking and acting for the Lord, ring many bells in contemporary Christian life. It is striking how long it takes before Israel is able to leave Egypt. It is equally striking that God would clearly have it so. God never promises that the deliverance will be speedy, and the warning that he will harden Pharaoh's heart is also a warning about how long and hard the process of deliverance will be.

When our life is like this, we usually wish it were otherwise. We project our impatience onto God and forget that his ways are not our ways (Isaiah 55:8–9). The lesson is a hard one. Paul clearly longed that the thorn in his flesh (quite likely the opposition from the 'false apostles') should be removed precisely so that he could serve the Lord without being hindered. The Lord taught him something about the very heart of Christian faith (2 Corinthians 12:7–10). God can transform and use even the most difficult and unwelcome situations and, in so doing, will teach us truths deeper and more enduring than we would otherwise learn.

The Bible in a year: 1 Chronicles 4–10; Psalm 68; 2 Corinthians 11

JUNE 10–16

Living as God's people

The church is an interesting community to belong to. Quite apart from the fact that we Christians dare to base our lives on a reality which many of our contemporaries regard as mistaken and misguided, life has a way of becoming more complex and demanding once we are Christians. As we learn to take God into account in all we do, everything becomes (at least subtly) different. However, this learning takes time and, like babies learning to walk, tends to need lots of help from those more experienced and involves lots of falling over and learning the hard way. This is one reason why the life of the church is often a less impressive witness to God than we long for it to be. We are still learning to live a life of faith in which, even with the best will, we often get things wrong, and often we are struggling with our inner desires and priorities which still simply resist trusting transformation at the hands of Christ.

In all these regards Israel in the Old Testament is remarkably similar. Israel is graciously called by God to be his people, utterly distinct from Egypt. Israel is called to be holy, as the Lord is holy (Leviticus 19:2). Yet the task of learning to live in a holy way, of becoming in practice what they already are by virtue of God's call, is far from straightforward. Last week we saw the persistent opposition which Israel faced, and their tendency quickly to lose heart. This week they are free from Egypt, but their problems are not over. Rather, their own deep-seated reluctance, indeed opposition, to living as God's people must now be faced. There is much learning to do.

Walter Moberly is a lecturer in theology at the University of Durham and is married to Jenny. He is a doting and sleep-deprived father of John-Paul and Rachel, and author of a number of books including *The Bible, Theology and Faith: A Study of Abraham and Jesus*.

JUNE 10–16

DAY 1

New every morning

We regularly pray, 'Give us this day our daily bread.' 'Lord, help me understand what this really means.'

Exodus 16:1–21

Freedom is sweet. Or is it? Although the Israelites are now free from Egypt, they are in the unmapped territory of the desert, where things are not regular and straightforward as they were in Egypt (which they remember only selectively). Food, basic provision for their human needs, is now problematic and, apparently, scarce. Do they respond in expectant trust? No, they respond with the habits of the old life, not the new – they grumble (vs 1–3).

God undertakes to meet their needs, but in a surprising way. Bread will come from heaven, i.e. from God, so that they can learn what it means that they have a heavenly Father. But although God will provide all they need, his means of providing will test them. That is, it will challenge their hearts and minds, so that they may truly learn what it means to live as God's people (vs 4–5). Moses and Aaron announce this, making clear that what will happen is to teach them what it means that their God is the Lord (vs 6–12). God's provision is initially puzzling – they cannot recognise it for what it is, and so Moses has to tell them (vs 13–15). Moses then teaches the first two lessons about their daily bread. Firstly, what God gives meets the needs of all, neither more nor less, regardless of the varying labours of those who work to gather it (vs 16–18). Secondly, manna does not keep, but must be gathered and consumed within the day, despite the natural desire to store and hoard (vs 19–21).

Do I try to live off God's grace in the past rather than receiving it afresh each new day?

The Bible in a year: 1 Chronicles 11–14; 2 Corinthians 12

JUNE 10–16

DAY 2

The principle of rest

Christians often downplay the importance of the Sabbath rest within the Old Testament. Ask the Lord to show you the true meaning of rest.

Exodus 16:22–36

Just when the Israelites might perhaps have thought they were getting the hang of living with manna – each person receiving the amount they need, and the discipline of 'dailyness' – they have to learn that it works differently when the Sabbath comes. For, when the sixth day comes, they are to gather a double amount (v 5) and it will keep fresh. This is so that on the Sabbath itself Israel can rest without needing to gather.

But just as the discipline of living by daily bread conflicts with the natural desire to store and hoard, so the trusting that nothing needs to be done on the Sabbath conflicts with other natural expectations – the need to keep on 'doing', lest (as we may fear) God does not actually provide. The Sabbath symbolises God's grace, his provision is the key thing. But some within Israel disregard Moses and assume that the regular pattern still applies on the seventh day (v 27). They fail the test (v 4). This leads to a stinging rebuke for Israel's failure yet again to follow the divine instructions (vs 28–30).

Finally, some manna is to be preserved as a lasting reminder of the lessons it teaches (vs 31–36).

The manna teaches one of the most basic of all spiritual lessons (Deuteronomy 8:2–3, used by Jesus, Matthew 4:1–4). Have I yet truly learned this lesson?

The Bible in a year: 1 Chronicles 15–16; 2 Corinthians 13

JUNE 10–16

DAY 3

Trust and obey

It would be so nice if we learned straightaway the lessons which we are taught. Ask the Holy Spirit to be your guide today.

Exodus 17:1–7

Israel appears to have learned little (or, more accurately, nothing?) from the manna. For this story raises the other obvious difficulty in the desert, once that of food is dealt with. What should they drink? Again, the issue revolves around something that symbolises what is fundamental to life in the new and strange situation in which the Israelites find themselves as the people of God. That they should look to God in expectant trust is still alien to their deep selves, and so they respond as before, the only difference being that they 'quarrel' as well as 'grumble'. The fact of their new life as God's people features much less significantly in their thinking than the problems they face (vs 1–3).

Moses is dismayed and bewildered. He senses that the people's resentment of their situation could easily turn into deadly violence against himself (being a leader in Israel or the church is not a recipe for an easy life!). But Moses knows the lesson of the manna, that true human life is nourished by attentive obedience to God (Deuteronomy 8:3), and so brings the problem to God, who offers a solution (vs 4–6). The solution is as striking as it could be. Rock is by its nature hard and dry, the very opposite of water. For God thus to provide water symbolises God's power to transform even the most difficult and unpromising situations. The episode is given a lasting memorial in the naming of the place (v 7), to which Scripture elsewhere often refers.

Read Psalm 95:7b–11. If today God speaks to you, will you have learned to trust and obey, come what may?

The Bible in a year: 1 Chronicles 17–18; Galatians 1

JUNE 10–16

DAY 4

A piece of the action

In a week of readings where Israel's problems are primarily 'internal', we are reminded that opposition from others continues. Does opposition make you seek God?

Exodus 17:8–16

The conflict arising from the Amalekite attack is faced in two ways: what Joshua does, and what Moses does (vs 8–9). The relationship between these is crucial. What happens on the battlefield is seen to depend on what happens on the hilltop where Moses is (v 11). The place where most obviously 'the action is' may not be the place which is most important.

What is Moses doing? The sequence of verses 10b–12 does not mention prayer (nor does it even mention God!). A wooden reading of the text could see it just as a magical manipulation of power (some similar difficulties attach to the story of the woman with unstoppable bleeding who touched Jesus, Mark 5:24b–34). Yet Jews and Christians down the ages have, surely rightly, understood the depiction of Moses as implying the dynamics of prayer. The most obvious linkage is the outstretched arms of Moses, for such is a regular posture of prayer (1 Kings 8:54; Psalm 134:2). The arms reach up to God, and the staff (v 9) is the sign (almost like a sacrament) of God's transforming power. The crucial thing is that Moses' posture, with all it implies, is maintained, for this engagement (like most spiritual battles) is not over in a moment but takes time. And Moses is only able to remain steady because of the support of Aaron and Hur (no individualism here).

Have I learned the importance of the hilltop?

The Bible in a year: 1 Chronicles 19–21; Psalm 69

JUNE 10–16

DAY 5

Listening to wisdom

Learning to live as God's people requires willingness to learn a lesson wherever it is found.

Exodus 18:1, 13–27

Moses has a problem. The life of Israel contains disputes of one kind or another, and these need proper adjudication and resolution – the work of a 'judge', one of the most important and godlike responsibilities within Israel (and elsewhere). This work needs the kind of wisdom that God gives (if you have time, compare Solomon's prayer, God's response, and the striking outworking in 1 Kings 3:4–28). So far Moses has tried to carry this responsibility alone.

Jethro gives sound advice: Moses is to retain his primary role as divine mediator and lawgiver (vs 19–20), while delegating the practical judicial applications to others (vs 21–23). Moses recognises the wisdom of this (vs 24–27). Those who are to assist Moses must be qualified for it (v 21). They must 'fear God', the prime term in the Old Testament for appropriate human response to God (the Old Testament equivalent to 'faith' in the New Testament). This will show itself in their trustworthiness and perhaps, above all, in their abhorrence of 'unjust gain', i.e. any form of using their position of responsibility to get money out of people. Usually Moses is guided directly by God. Here he has the humility and wisdom to recognise truth 'from below' (even from an in-law!).

Learning from God should not be set against, or become a substitute for, learning from wise people. Does my faith make me more open to recognise and accept wisdom when it comes my way, or am I proud, fearful, or insecure?

The journey of faith: Exodus 15:22–27
Responding to God: Exodus 18:1–12, 27

The Bible in a year: 1 Chronicles 22–23; Galatians 2

Going deeper …

The story of the manna is the first extended narrative of Israel's life as the people of God, once rescued from Egypt. One may reasonably therefore see its lessons about the life of faith as foundation. Deuteronomy 8:3 sees the significance of the manna as teaching the basic truth that 'man does not live by bread alone, but by every word that proceeds from the mouth of God'.

Deuteronomy 8 draws out the significance of the manna. It contrasts the desert, where the lesson of the manna is learned, with the Promised Land. God is giving Israel a land characterised by all the good things that the desert lacks (vs 7–9). This good gift of God raises a new problem, however. When Israel enjoy plenty in the land, will they neglect and unlearn the spiritual lessons they learned in the desert (vs 10–16)? Will they cease to understand that all they do is given and enabled by God (vs 17–18)? That would be the high road to disaster (vs 19–0).

Often it is only in hard times that we learn to take God seriously. A searing encounter with darkness can cut through our hardness and complacency and open our hearts and minds to God. Yet if the darkness passes, do we remember its lessons? How do we retain vital, and disturbing, spiritual truths in a culture of affluence and entertainment? There are no easy answers. Yet the challenge to be faithful, is as urgent for us as it was for Israel.

Lifelong learning

There are many different ways of thinking about the church. One time-honoured image, well-rooted in Scripture, is that of the army, marching to fight for God and good against evil. Another image is that of the hospital, a place where the sick and wounded can find healing. Perhaps the image which most appropriately arises out of this week's readings is that of a school, a place where people can learn what it means to know God, and themselves, and be enabled to grow into the kind of people that God intends us to be. The fact that the process of learning is long and hard, and frequently unwelcome!

Lifelong learning is an increasingly common slogan in our culture, and there is obvious value to it (though the accompanying lifelong debt might be less attractive!). Most churches have courses of basic instruction for those new to the faith. But how many churches have serious programmes of continuing education, which remind us that growing in faith is a lifelong process, and that the issues involved in responsibly relating our faith to the world in which we live need constant working at? Do we see our churches as schools where we can learn true patterns of human existence, distinct from distorted patterns of life focused on money, sex, and power? What is our vision of a Christian counter-culture?

The Bible in a year: 1 Chronicles 24–29; Psalm 70–71; Galatians 23

JUNE 17–23

Jesus in his people

Acts 3–4

The ascension of the resurrected Jesus Christ, and Christ's subsequent gift of the Spirit of God to his church, radically changed the spiritual framework for all his disciples. They were no longer observers and supporters of the life and ministry of Jesus: they themselves were that life and ministry.

Christ lives in his people today, not in symbolic sentimental fashion, but directly by his Spirit. In these two chapters the evidence of this spills into public view, beyond the disciples' upper room experience of the Spirit that had previously drawn comment (Acts 2:7–13). Now two unsophisticated disciples, carrying the new responsibility of Jesus' ministry, pass by a beggar on their way to worship. And their whole city is impacted by the ensuing events (Acts 3).

A middle-aged cripple who expected no more than a handout to survive the day is surprised beyond measure by the unpremeditated act of those who had been with Jesus. The ripple effect of the encounter changed more than a beggar's life. Both joy and hostility were triggered in their city, and God's people became more aware than ever of their awesome authority to serve sinners through the unspeakable grace of God in Jesus Christ.

The dynamics of those days can be distilled into five principles: believing action, spiritual unity, confrontation, regular prayer, and encouragement. Christianity's founding documents give us more than divine truth and promises. As is the case in these two chapters, they demonstrate by concrete examples the true character of the faith in which we share.

Paul Hartwig is a Baptist Minister who is presently taking a break from pastoring to complete his PhD through the Baptist Seminary in Cape Town.

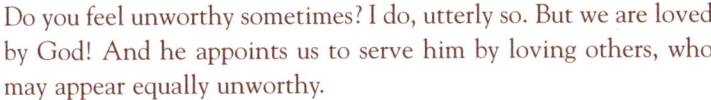

DAY 1

Love has method

Do you feel unworthy sometimes? I do, utterly so. But we are loved by God! And he appoints us to serve him by loving others, who may appear equally unworthy.

Acts 3:1–10

Born crippled and now more than 40 years old (4:22), his disability went beyond his body. It was his way of life; deliberately contrasted to Gate Beautiful at which he begged. Peter and John responded to his appeal (v 4). Spokesman Peter spoke the action, ordering the helpless cripple to walk, and immediately acted himself. He took the man's right hand and lifted him up.

No one experiments with God. He is not tested by us. This was no hopeful prayer and then a watching to see whether healing happened. Peter invested himself in this action. Having gained the man's attention, he issued an instruction of faith (v 6) and acted to involve himself in it (v 7). Faith is not simply the absence of doubt or a supply of positive feelings. Faith, as the channel of God's power, is always expressed in action. Jesus 'spoke' to the fig tree, 'touched' the leper, 'rebuked' the fever. Love, living love, always has a verb of faith; a 'doing word'.

Their faith, confidence, and bold trust in their Lord, expressed in sharing his compassion, was just a channel, a vehicle, for the resurrected and ascended Christ to continue his work in and through them. He did, and he does. He continues faithful!

Thank the Lord that he is interested in your circumstances. Ask him to make you continually aware of this. As you begin this day, pray for strength to do his good pleasure.

The Bible in a year: 2 Chronicles 1–2; Galatians 4

JUNE 17–23

DAY 2

Togetherness builds faith

Peter's public disloyalty and failure under pressure must have been painfully recent in his mind. He was restored to faith, but this did not happen in isolation.

Acts 3:11–26

This awesome miracle happened on the way to somewhere. God's miracles are never a destination to be aimed at. Peter and John were on the way to pray and praise. 'Solomon's Colonnade' (v 11) was the Christians' gathering place for public worship (5:12).

God is in charge of the miraculous. We are responsible for our faithfulness in devoting ourselves to the Bible's teaching 'and to fellowship, to the breaking of bread and to prayer' (Acts 2:42); and so stimulating 'one another on to love and good deeds', not neglecting our 'meeting together' (Hebrews 10:24–25). Christ lives in his church, and he is not divided. In Christ, there are no divisions of class, race or religion: we are all new people. We've been accepted by Christ and should readily accept one another.

What a sermon Peter preached – and in the Temple, at that! No wonder there were negative repercussions. Peter's passion pours out for 'lost sheep' milling around this miracle. He confronts them with: 'You disowned the Holy and Righteous One' (v 14); 'You killed the author of life' (v 15); and later refers to their 'wicked ways' (v 26). But this is not an attack. He reassures them that they acted in ignorance, as did their leaders (v 17); and calls for their immediate repentance.

How concerned are you for the welfare of your brothers and sisters in Christ?

The Bible in a year: 2 Chronicles 3–5; Galatians 5

JUNE 17–23

DAY 3

Confronting responsibility

Friction is not fun. Most of us do everything we possibly can to escape from it. Pretending it doesn't exist is one way of running away. We go in circles and do not grow unless we speak the truth, the real truth, with love.

Acts 4:1–22

After a night in prison, these two fishermen-preachers confront the religious authorities with their responsibility: 'Judge for yourselves whether it is right in God's sight to obey you rather than God. For we cannot help speaking about what we have seen and heard' (4:19–20). Not to have confronted the people and their leaders would have been to lie.

It's never easy to confront. But all those that we love need it from us at times. Being prepared to confront someone can be a sign of really loving them. It's part of the 'tough love' that is talked about nowadays. Love that confronts is never without respect for the value of the person concerned. And respect means limiting the confrontation to a minimum. The aim of confrontation should always be to build up, never to break down. Careful preparation and much prayer will pave the way for a positive outcome.

Neglecting the things that divide us does not bring unity, only a papering over of the cracks. What deep unity we will enjoy if we deal honestly with the things that divide us!

Pray for discernment to know when you should confront someone, and ask the lord to give you the courage to act. Pray for gentleness and tact in broaching the matter.

The Bible in a year: 2 Chronicles 6–7; Galatians 6

JUNE 17–23

DAY 4

Praise in practice

The beggar at Gate Beautiful did not need lessons in praise. He was 'walking and jumping and praising God'. Spiritual eyes that are opened to see God and his works cannot help but praise him.

Acts 4:23–31

To praise God is not to list reasons for thanksgiving. Praise goes beyond that. Praise actually sees God in all his wonder! Praise does not affect God: it affects us! Praise is the practice in which conscious awareness of his character and attributes is cultivated.

A crisis is often a call to prayer. Peter's and John's report to the believers of the hostility and threats of further harassment by the authorities, provoked a response of intense, united payer in this first Christian community. 'They raised their voices together in prayer to God' (v 24). This impassioned prayer caused the early church to experience a new level of God's powerful presence: 'After they prayed, the place where they were meeting was shaken. And they were all filled with the Holy Spirit and spoke the word of God boldly' (v 31).

The God of these early believers was not relegated to the realm of the spiritual. The Creator himself had met them in Jesus Christ, and, fittingly, the physical building where they had gathered quaked at the power of his presence through the Holy Spirit. There was no false distinction between the physical and the spiritual. It is the Sovereign Lord, Creator of all that exists, to whom they pray, and therefore there can be no limit, none whatsoever, to his gracious response.

Be still before the Lord. Let his glory flow over you. Praise him!

The Bible in a year: 2 Chronicles 8–9; Psalm 72

JUNE 17–23

DAY 5

Giving encouragement

Christ's naming of Peter to indicate his potential, rather than by family or history, is such an example to us. At his very first meeting with Simon, Jesus called him 'Peter', meaning 'rock' (John 1:42). But, just like Jacob – whose name was changed to Israel (Genesis 32:28) – it really took time and much failure before Peter was able to live out his new image before God.

Acts 4:32–37

His name was Joseph of Cyprus (v 36), but the apostles called him Encourager ('Bar-Nabas'), because they saw that potential in him. And Joseph of Cyprus becomes one of the most significant catalysts of God's work. His giving set the selfless tone of communal life in Christianity's first church.

Later, when the believers in Jerusalem distrusted the conversion of Saul of Tarsus, this Joseph of Cyprus (Barnabas) saw the potential of the young man, went against the stream of opinion, and introduced him to the apostles (Acts 9:26–27). Later again, when there was a need for leaders in the new church in Antioch, Barnabas remembered Saul and opened the door for him to be a teacher of the church (Acts 11:25–26). This served as a springboard for Paul's first missionary journey, which had awesome results.

What could your spiritual name be? Maybe you can think of appropriate spiritual names for close Christian friends. You could encourage them by passing these on to them. It might help them realise and develop their potential.

The power of love: 1 Corinthians 12:31–14:1
Completing his work: Acts 1:1–11

The Bible in a year: 2 Chronicles 10–12; Ephesians 1

JUNE 17–23

Going deeper …

Feeling flat, unmotivated? We've all been there – Peter too. Before Christ's resurrection, Peter's experience with Jesus was one huge anticlimax of personal failure. Peter found God's power in his life because it had a place to grow.

John, the loyal disciple, and Peter, the passionate hothead, were on their way to the place of prayer when God healed the crippled man through these simple servants of Jesus. To Jesus, the temple was a place of prayer. That's why he twice took radical action in its courts, saying (Mark 11:17).

Daily prayer was Christ's own path to power, 'To know the word that sustains the weary, (God) wakens me morning by morning, wakens my ear to listen like one being taught' (Isaiah 50:4). Christ's early mornings with God set the precedent for all who follow him.

When the opposition looked into Peter's and John's lives, it saw 'unschooled and ordinary men', but recognised them as having 'been with Jesus' (Acts 4:13). Time with the Lord made them different. 'Through Jesus, therefore, let us continually offer to God a sacrifice of praise – the fruit of lips that confess his name' (Hebrews 13:15). Worship the Lord! Ask him to fill your mind with himself, and enable you to hear him speaking. Hand him each moment of your day that it may be empowered by his presence.

Prayer our priority

Conclusion

If Jesus was right in what he said about Satan, then anything that has potential to draw us closer to God and empower us for effective living is also subject to distraction and opposition. The five factors listed in the introduction: that we have looked at this week give us balance and strength to handle whatever is necessary for effective living. But the key is prayer that is a feature of our lifestyle, much more than a polite list of requests bracketed with praise and appreciation. Prayer, as the devotion of Christ shows us, enables our spiritual hearing. In prayer, we meet with the great Chairman. The agenda of our meeting ultimately belongs to him. Praise and adoration should be our language, and our requests should at best be our response to the concerns of his heart. He cares! Therefore, not to be directly aware of our Lord's attitude toward an issue is to miss the cues in this prayer conversation.

Our awareness is directly affected by the amount of time given to our focus on him. For this reason Jesus spent the whole night in prayer before he chose his twelve disciples (Luke 6:12–13). The sinless One, full of the Holy Spirit, needed time before God to hear fully the detail of God's way for him. How much more do we!

No time? Priorities are really the problem, not our responsibilities. The greater our responsibilities, the greater the need for time in prayer with him.

The Bible in a year: 2 Chronicles 13–17; Psalm 73; Ephesians 2

JUNE 24–30

Dreaming dreams

Many organisations and churches exist today because somebody was a dreamer. Hebrews 11:1–3 speaks of the heroes of faith who changed the course of history through their ability to dream. In verse 1 we read of 'bulldog' faith. Then in verse 2 the Old Testament saints are commended for it. At first glance, verse 3 seems to be about God creating the universe. But this would contradict verse 2 which tells us that this chapter is about the exploits of the Old Testament saints! Verse 3 is the continuation of verse 2 and is not about creation. The writer is still talking about the saints who, in 'bulldog' faith, sought God's purpose for their lives. Notice the words 'universe' and 'formed'. The word 'universe' in verse 3 is the Greek word 'aionos', which refers to generations or decades. The word 'formed' in Greek means the reshaping of something that already exists. So verse 3 is not about the act of creation, but about the act of transformation!

Now read the following version of verse 3: 'Through faith we understand that different time periods (decades, generations, centuries) within the history of mankind have been completely remoulded by the word of God.' So, this whole chapter is about people who received a word from God, obeyed it, and against all odds, changed the course of history.

I'm going to share some ideas with you and challenge you. What I've written is not intended to make you relax and accept mediocrity. It's meant to propel you like an arrow towards your destiny. One word from God can change your destiny – believe in your dream. Become the best you can be.

Alf Friend is the National Bible Ministry Co-ordinator of Scripture Union. He retired from headmastering in 1998.

JUNE 24–30

DAY 1

Fulfilling God's purpose

How do I fulfil God's purpose for my life? Ask yourself, 'What would I like to do in my life?' Then ask the Holy Spirit to guide you and prepare your heart.

Hebrews 11:1–28

You need to get a word from God on fulfilling his purpose for your life (v 3 – see introduction). God told Noah to build an ark because a flood was coming. In spite of accusations, allegations and opposition, he stood by that word from God (v 7). Moses was told by God: 'I want you to go to Pharaoh and tell him to let my people go' (vs 23–28). Because this one man, in his generation, stood by a word from God, the course of history was changed!

Abraham, Isaac and all the heroes of faith each received a word from God and were instrumental in changing history. If God speaks a word to your heart, and tells you to start a business, to study or to do something constructive, don't wait for a fifty page prophecy. Remember, standing by one word from God can change an entire generation!

Pray and wait on God until you receive a definite word from him. When thoughts or impressions come to your mind, or maybe a strong awareness of something, write it down, then continue to pray it through.

The Bible in a year: 2 Chronicles 18–20; Galasians 3

DAY 2

Planning God's purpose

In planning God's purpose for our lives, we need to know what God has called us to do. In Joshua 1:3–4 God said: 'I will give you territory as long as you stay within these boundaries.' In other words, if you stay where God has called you to be, you can be absolutely confident of supernatural help!

Joshua 1:1–18

In planning God's purpose for your life, four principles are of utmost importance. Firstly, you need to take one step at a time (v 2–3). You see, God was going to give them their inheritance, one step at a time. Secondly, you need to be 'specific and realistic about your vision' (v 4). God knows you need clear direction in order to keep on track! God did not say, 'take any piece of land'. Today most people are looking for bold leaders who will set goals, make decisions and then breathe vision into the people around them. You need to put your dreams into words: talk about them! Thirdly, ask God for strategy (v 1). Monitor carefully the ideas entering your mind. Keep a journal in which you write down your goals and your dreams.

Lastly, set goals and plan for every area of your life. Set goals in your service of God, in your personal life and in your vocation. Commit your goals to God. Remember to stay focused on your ultimate Goal!

The Bible in a year: 2 Chronicles 21–23; Ephesians 4

JUNE 24–30

DAY 3

Pursuing God's purpose

'We do not want you to become lazy' (Hebrews 6:12a). It's a command!

Hebrews 10:23–25; 11:32–40

In order for you to fulfil your dream, your 'word' from the Lord, you need to understand chapter 10:23. You need to hold your dream 'unswervingly'. Don't let go! Don't let time or your friends rob you. The whole tenor of verses 23–25 is action: 'spur one another on … towards good deeds … Let us not give up …' The heroes listed in chapter 11:32–38 'were all commended for their faith' (v 39), but they were men and women of action: they 'conquered … administered justice … routed foreign armies.'

One person who pursued God's purpose for her life was Mother Teresa. She cared for the poor and underprivileged, mainly in India. One day she visited the prisons in New York. Immediately afterwards she went to see the mayor and asked him to phone the governor. 'Governor,' she said, 'I'm just back from Sing Sing and would like to open an Aids centre for prisoners.' The governor immediately consented. 'I have a building in mind. Would you like to pay for it?' 'OK,' he replied. Mother Teresa turned to mayor Koch, 'Today is Monday, I'd like to open it on Wednesday. We will need some permits cleared. Could you please arrange this?' The mayor's reply was, 'Yes, as long as you don't make me wash the floors!' A lady of action who pursued God's purpose for her life!

How diligently are you pursuing God's purpose for your life? Is there a sense of urgency, or are you merely going through the motions?

The Bible in a year: 2 Chronicles 24–25; Galasians 5

JUNE 24–30

DAY 4

Obstacles to God's purpose

Can you do more than you are doing right now? Our spiritual success isn't measured by what we do, but by whether we are doing what God has asked us to do.

Proverbs 6:6–11

Let me share some obstacles as you pursue God's purpose. The first obstacle is *laziness*. How do you know if you are being lazy? According to Proverbs 6:9–11 the symptoms are: sleeping long hours, idleness, sluggishness, and lethargy. Lazy people often complain that they never have any energy. Remember: 'dreamers never sleep'. When you do nothing, you lose your energy. Laziness is a choice! Why look to the ant (v 6)? Because he is constantly working.

    The second obstacle is *unrealistic fantasies*. Laziness leads to unrealistic fantasies: instead of working hard, we sit and fantasise about accomplishments (Proverbs 28:19). *Success is obtained through hard work.* By working your land, not by living in a world of fantasy, you will reap a harvest.

    The third obstacle is *slothfulness*. Laziness is a *discipline* problem, whereas slothfulness is an *attitude* problem. The lazy person rebels against God by choosing to do nothing. The slothful person chooses to do God's will *outwardly* but *inwardly* retains a lukewarm attitude to the things of God.

The world is full of doom and gloom. In Numbers 13, Moses sent twelve men to spy out the land. Ten spies saw giants (vs 31–33), while Caleb saw fruit (vs 28, 30). What would you have seen? Be positive and achieve your goals in life.

The Bible in a year: 2 Chronicles 26–28; Psalm 74

JUNE 24-30

DAY 5

Pursuing the next level of your dream

Where are you right now? Are you handling positively the winds of adversity and change? Are you being stretched further than before, or content to stay where you are? Ask God right now to give you the inner strength to move to the next level of your dream.

Numbers 13:1-3, 17-33

May I share some steps that will stretch you?

Analyse: Analyse your feelings and future desires. Be thorough: an incorrect analysis will put you on the wrong path. In verse 21, they analysed the land promised to them.

Aim: Set your aims high, but be realistic! The Israelites' goal was possession of the promised land (v 2).

Adjust: If you're not heading in the right direction, adjust your course. You might be shooting a lot of little arrows aimlessly. You can use the same energy to take aim with one big arrow and achieve your dream.

Align: Align yourself with people who will stretch and teach you. The ten spies came back with a negative report (vs. 31–33), but Caleb came back with a positive report (v 30). When you align yourself with people who are positive, they will challenge your thinking, your small-mindedness and wrong perceptions.

Affirm: It is important to affirm your destiny to others; to describe your dreams enthusiastically. Talk about your goals and what action you will take. This will stretch you, and commit you to your words.

Apply: 'Faith without works is dead.' Get your hands dirty. Some people find life an empty dream because they put nothing into it. The Israelites took possession of the promised land.

Prayerfully go through the six steps again. Which of them do you need to take?

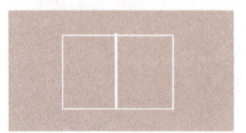

Have a positive outlook: Nehemiah 1:11; 2:8, 20; 4:20
Be decisive and determined: Nehemiah 4:1–15

The Bible in a year: 2 Chronicles 29–30; Ephesians 6

JUNE 24–30

Going deeper ...

'Circumstances do not make you what you are, they reveal what you are' (John Maxwell). As you pursue your dream, there will be obstacles; there will be storms and pressures; but when it feels as though you're going through 'hell on earth', what should you do? Look for the exit and run? Keep on moving as fast as you can?

My destiny was far too important to surrender. My desire to shepherd God's flock meant everything to me. I had no Plan B to fall back on. It was this or nothing. So I decided to weather the storms. I persevered, rose above the circumstances and concentrated on building an effective church for the glory of God.

Challenges and crises are part of life. They are common to all of us. We can't live with them and we can't live without them! Crises come in different shapes and sizes. There are small, medium and large challenges in life. They have different intensities and different timings. Crises often inflict stress and strain, but how we react to them determines what we will be once they are gone.

The key is my attitude. 'Consider it pure joy whenever you face trials of many kinds, because you know that the testing of your faith develops perseverance' (James 1:2–3). Listen, when trials come; it's development time; character time; perseverance time. So, maintain your joy.

Dreamers never sleep

Some people dream of worthy accomplishments, while others stay awake and do them. It's the person who crosses the line who wins the medal. Follow your dream, don't get stuck in your nightmares.

'If you can dream it, you can do it. Always remember this whole thing was started by a mouse' (Walt Disney). 'Don't let anybody steal your dream' (Dexter Yager).

Remember the best time to start pursuing your destiny is *now*! The best time to shake off your miseries and take the first step is *today*! The twenty-first century can, for you, be a time of yielding to the dreams and destiny of your life. Don't procrastinate! When people say: 'I could *never* do that,' they are cutting off their future. They are trapped in today. What do you think is the greatest obstacle to having this 'Dare to Dream' attitude? *Fear*. Fear of the unknown, of failing. Fear is cruel, it stifles, cripples and oppresses. Listen, courage conquers fear. Courage means stepping out despite the way you feel. Let me encourage you today to follow your dream. Don't give up. Not for *anything*! And you don't have to step out alone!

'Do not be anxious about anything, but in everything, by prayer and petition, with thanksgiving, present your requests to God. And the peace of God, which transcends all understanding, will guard your hearts and your minds in Christ Jesus' (Philippians 4:6–7).

Conclusion

The Bible in a year: 2 Chronicles 31–34; Psalm 75–76; Luke 1:1–38

JULY 1–7

The hour approaches

John 11–14

Our readings this week begin just after the great turning point in Jesus' public ministry – the raising of Lazarus. We might have thought that from this moment on, Jesus' ministry would have taken off. After such a mighty demonstration of supernatural power, we might have expected the Jewish leaders in Jerusalem to recognise who he was and to proclaim him as the Messiah. Not so. Here a resurrection miracle leads to martyrdom.

In 1998, a Buddhist monk died in Myanmar. A few days later, his funeral was held, at which he was to be cremated. From the smell, it was obvious that his body had already started to decompose. Hundreds of monks and relatives of the dead man attended the funeral. Just as the body was about to be burned, the dead monk suddenly sat up, shouting, 'It's all a lie! I saw our ancestors burning and being tortured in some sort of fire. I also saw Buddha and many other Buddhist holy men. They were all in a sea of fire! We must listen to the Christians; they're the only ones who know the truth!'

The events shocked the whole region. Over 300 monks became Christians and started to study the Bible. The resurrected man continued to warn everyone to believe in Jesus, because *he* is the only true God. Tapes of the monk's report were distributed throughout Myanmar. The Buddhist hierarchy and the government were soon alarmed, and they arrested the monk. He has not been seen since (story distributed and confirmed by mission agency, *Asian Minorities Outreach*).

If we pray for miracles we need to understand that they may not be the end of our problems, but the beginning! We need to understand this truth, 'As the Master shall the servant be' (Amy Carmichael).

Mark Stibbe is vicar of St Andrew's, Chorleywood, and a popular speaker in the UK and abroad. He is the author of many articles and books, including 'Thinking Clearly about Revival'.

JULY 1–7

DAY 1

A believing heart

If you had heard about Jesus raising Lazarus from death, how would you have reacted? Would you have believed in Jesus? Or would you have hardened your heart against him? Spend a few moments praying for a believing, open and receptive heart.

John 11:45–57

Jesus has just raised Lazarus from death. It's his seventh miracle in John's Gospel and seven was the perfect number in those days. So this was a perfect miracle! Yet in spite of this, some of the eyewitnesses betray Jesus to the Pharisees (v 46). This leads to a meeting of the Sanhedrin in which the chief priests express alarm about what they themselves admit is a miraculous sign (v 47). They are worried that this very public sign will enlarge Jesus' following and lead to severe Roman reprisals (v 48). At this point, enter Caiaphas, the high priest (v 49). He tells them that it is better for Jesus to be put to death than for the whole nation to be destroyed (v 50), which John then tells us was a prophetic utterance (vs 51–52). From this point on, the council decide to have Jesus executed, forcing Jesus and his disciples to hide in the desert (vs 53–54). The crowds look for him in the city, but he is nowhere to be found (vs 55–57).

It's a mystery how people could see Jesus personally, hear his teaching, witness his miracles, observe his compassion, and still not believe. It's a mystery how Jesus' act of giving life to Lazarus could result in people wanting to put Jesus to death.

Coming to faith in Jesus is a miracle. Stubbornly refusing to believe in him – in spite of good evidence – is a mystery.

Spend time praying for those you know who don't yet believe in Jesus.

The Bible in a year: 2 Chronicles 35–36; Luke 1:39–80

JULY 1–7

DAY 2

Extravagant worship

To worship something is to attribute worth or value to it. In this story we see a woman using perfume worth a year's wages as an act of worship. That's how much she thought Jesus was worth. How much do you think Jesus is worth? How extravagant is your worship of him? Spend some time simply telling Jesus how much you adore him.

John 12:1–11

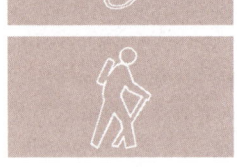

It's time to meet Mary and Martha again. We saw them last when Jesus raised Lazarus. They were Lazarus's sisters and both came to meet Jesus outside the tomb. Both reacted to him differently there. Here we see the sisters again as a dinner party is held in Jesus' honour after the great miracle of Lazarus's resurrection (v 2). Martha serves Jesus; Lazarus reclines at the table; Mary pours expensive perfume on Jesus' feet, wiping them with her hair. The whole house is filled with the fragrance (v 3). Judas objects, saying that the money should have been spent on the poor (vs 4–5), a comment motivated by greed, not compassion (v 6). Jesus reprimands him, and applauds Mary for her extravagant act of worship (v 7). John ends the story by saying that so many people were putting their faith in Jesus that the chief priests now decide not only to kill Jesus but Lazarus also (vs 9–11).

Every time we meet Mary (Lazarus's sister) she is at Jesus' feet. She sits at his feet to listen to his teaching (Luke 10:39), she weeps at his feet in desperate intercession (11:32), and she worships at his feet with extravagant love (12:3). Unlike Martha, Mary has learned that passion is more valuable than performance. Have you?

The Bible in a year: Ezra 1–2; Luke 2

JULY 1–7

DAY 3

Can I borrow your life?

Have you noticed how many times Jesus borrowed something in order to achieve the Father's purposes? He borrowed a stable for his birth. He borrowed a donkey for his triumphal entry. He borrowed a tomb for his burial. Now he wants to borrow us. Like the donkey in the story we're about to read, we are called to be carriers of the presence of Jesus wherever we go. Today, Jesus is asking, 'Can I borrow your life?'

John 12:12–19

The hour of Jesus' return to the Father is drawing very near. The events of the last story happened six days before the Passover (when Jesus would die). Now we come to the triumphal entry of Jesus into Jerusalem, which happens 'the next day' (v 12). Those who have come up to Jerusalem for the feast join Jesus on his journey from Bethany towards the city, performing actions and shouting words that show they think Jesus is the Messiah (v 13). Then Jesus does something totally unexpected. Instead of entering Jerusalem like a victorious military king, he enters riding on a donkey in great humility. Zechariah had prophesied that this would happen, but even so the disciples were mystified at the time (vs 14–16). Only after the resurrection would they understand what was happening. In the meantime, Jesus enters the city and so many believe in him and follow him that the Pharisees declare that the 'whole world' is following him (vs 17–19).

Sometimes we pray fervently for something, but when the answer comes it reminds us that God's ways are not our ways. Spend some time telling the Lord that your life belongs to him, and that he can 'borrow' it to do anything he wants, even if it's unexpected.

The Bible in a year: Ezra 3–4; Luke 3

JULY 1–7

DAY 4

A time for dying

Dietrich Bonhoeffer (a twentieth-century Christian martyr) wrote, 'When Jesus calls a man he bids him come and die.' The Christian life is a constant process of dying to self. As you prepare to read, ask the Holy Spirit to reveal areas of your life where you still need to 'die'.

John 12:20–36

We begin with a story about some Greek pilgrims who come up to Jerusalem to celebrate Passover. Hearing that Jesus is in the city, they go looking for him and two of the disciples introduce them to Jesus (vs 20–22). Jesus now declares that the time of his death has come (v 23). He came to die for the whole world, not just Israel, and the arrival of the Greeks reveals that the 'hour' has come. In the next breath he talks about the impossibility of a grain of wheat bearing fruit without being buried in the ground (v 24). He encourages his followers to die to self (vs 25–26) before confessing to his Father that his heart is troubled at the prospect of the cross (v 27). After hearing from the Father, Jesus declares that the purpose of his death is to defeat Satan (v 31) and to draw all people to himself when he is 'lifted up' (vs 32–33). The crowds object because they thought the Messiah would be immortal (v 34). Jesus then warns that there is only a little time left for them to see the light (vs 35–36).

If we are praying for revival, we had better understand that there is a price attached. Spiritual harvests always come through death. Are we prepared to count the cost? The good news is this: when we come to the end of ourselves we arrive at the beginning of God.

The Bible in a year: Ezra 5–6; Psalm 77

JULY 1–7

DAY 5

Intimacy with the Father

The key to Jesus' ministry was intimacy with the Father. Everything he ever said or did flowed out of heart-to-heart communion with his Father in heaven. Spend some time just being in the Father's presence, soaking in his love, preparing to listen to his voice.

John 12:37–50

These verses mark a turning point in John's Gospel – the end of Jesus' public ministry. Here John reveals how Jesus' ministry has caused a polarisation between unbelief and belief. On the one hand there are those who chose of their own free will not to believe, with the result that they brought judgement upon themselves (vs 37–41). On the other hand, many did believe in Jesus, but because of their fear of people, decided to keep it a secret (vs 42–43). Jesus points to the Father, the one who sent him (vs 44–46). He tells the crowds how important it is to listen to his words because they come from the Father (v 48). Indeed, throughout Jesus' ministry it was the Father who told Jesus what to say and how to say it (v 49), and these words were life-giving (v 50). So Jesus ends his public ministry by reminding us that he taught exactly what the Father had told him to say.

The greatest priority we have in life is to cultivate daily our intimate communion with the Father. Jesus alone reveals God as Father and taught us to pray 'Our Father'. The word translated 'Father' is actually better translated 'Papa' or 'Daddy'. Each day we need to set aside time to worship the Father. Jesus said that we are to worship 'in spirit and in truth' (4:24). The word translated 'worship' here means 'to approach someone in order to kiss them'. Spend some more time now in intimate worship of the Father.

The Father's pleasure: Mark 1:9–11
Blessing and battle: Mark 1:12–15

The Bible in a year: Ezra 7–8; Luke 4

Going deeper ...

Our readings this week have centred on the theme of costly worship. It is costly witnessing to and praying for unbelievers. It is costly spending time worshipping Jesus. It is costly giving up our lives and serving the Lord Jesus. It is costly dying to self so that we can be fruitful for God. It is costly listening to the Father and obeying him.

King David said that he would not make an offering to God that cost him nothing (2 Samuel 24:24). The psalmists said that we are to bring a *sacrifice* of praise into the house of the Lord (Psalm 107:22, 11; 6:17–19). True worship is not about what I can gain but what I can give (Hebrews 13:15–16). It involves being a contributor not a consumer.

How much time, energy and passion do you give to the Lord in private and public worship? Are you, like Mary, prepared to spend your resources and yourself on intimate adoration of Jesus? This is a tough question. I have to discipline myself daily to spend time with God. When I get down to prayer, my head starts to spin with all the problems and challenges that confront me and it's all too easy to bypass thanksgiving and praise.

When I go to church, I can be so burdened that I switch into receiving rather than giving mode. But the breakthroughs come when we make a sacrifice of praise. God intervenes in our lives when we praise him in spite of our circumstances or feelings. Whatever you're going through right now, start worshipping the Father.

Ministering out of intimacy

The most fruitful ministry flows out of intimacy with the Father. This is the constant witness of revival history. John Wesley, before he began preaching to the nation, experienced his heart being strangely warmed by the fire of the Father's love. Howell Harris, a contemporary of Wesley, experienced exactly the same thing. In fact, John Wesley described Harris as the most powerful evangelist he had ever met. Harris traced his effectiveness to a moment described in his journal: 'June 18th, 1735. Being in secret prayer I felt suddenly my heart melting within me like wax before a fire, with love to God my Saviour. I felt not only love and peace, but also a longing to be dissolved and to be with Christ; and there was a cry in my inmost soul, with which I was totally unacquainted before, it was this – "Abba, Father; Abba, Father". I could not help calling God my Father: I knew that I was his child, and that he loved me; my soul being filled and satiated, crying, "It is enough – I am satisfied; give me strength and I will follow thee through fire and water". I could now say that I was happy indeed. There was in me "a well of water, springing up into everlasting life", yea, the love of God was shed abroad in my heart by the Holy Ghost.'

National revivals begin with personal revivals (see Romans 5:5). Jesus began his preaching *after* his baptism, where the Father revealed his love for him. True ministry flows out of intimacy. Abandon yourself afresh to the river of God's love for you.

The Bible in a year: Ezra 9–10; Nehemiah 1–2; Psalm 78:1–39; Luke 5

JULY 8–14

Which way?

Currently in the West, we live in a society which demands us to conform to the idea of 'political correctness'. It is deemed extremely intolerant if Christians make the claim that Jesus is the only way to God, yet that is exactly what Jesus taught us and what the apostles were martyred for proclaiming.

The chapters we are about to study stress the uniqueness of Jesus. He completely undermines three thought patterns that lie behind our political correctness. The first of these is pluralism. This says that there are many ways to God. But Jesus says, 'I am the way.' The second of these is relativism. This says that nothing is absolutely true, and that everything is relatively true. But Jesus says, 'I am the truth.' The third of these is hedonism. This says that there are many ways of enjoying life and experiencing pleasure. But Jesus says, 'I am the life.'

Many of us are praying for revival today. Those who have lived in such seasons will tell you that true revival is a sovereign work of the Holy Spirit in which Jesus is revealed as the glorious Son of God to both the church and the world (John 16:8–15). In a true revival, the church is given great boldness to declare that Jesus isn't just *a* way, he is *the* way. True revival puts the definite article back into our evangelism and brings an end to that political correctness that says all religions are equal.

If you look at road signs in a Highway Code book you'll see there is one that says 'One Way'. That is what we believe about Jesus. He is the one and only Son of the Father, and the one and only way to the Father. Pray as you read these chapters that the Holy Spirit will awaken you to this great truth.

Mark Stibbe is vicar of St Andrew's, Chorleywood, and a popular speaker in the UK and abroad. He is the author of many articles and books, including 'Thinking Clearly about Revival'.

JULY 8–14

DAY 1

The Son became a slave

We now begin the second half of John's Gospel, sometimes called 'The Book of Christ's Passion'. We are about to study two chapters that begin the last twenty-four hours of Jesus' life. We are going to be reading about some of the most sacred facts in human history. Ask the Holy Spirit to fill you with fresh gratitude for the Calvary love of God.

John 13:1–17

The hour has now come. It is 'just before the Passover Feast' (v 1) – the time when the Passover lambs were to be slaughtered in the temple. More importantly, it is the hour when Jesus, the Lamb of God, will die for the sins of the world (see 1:29). Jesus now performs an act of prophetic symbolism. He shows the full extent of his love through an enigmatic action at the evening meal. He gets down from the table, strips off his clothes, puts a towel around his waist and begins to wash his disciples' feet (vs 3–5). Peter objects because Jesus is performing a duty that was considered menial even for a slave (vs 6–8a). Jesus explains that he must be cleansed, so Peter accepts (vs 8b–9). Then Jesus puts on his clothes, and sits down again (v 12), saying that all this is an example for them (v 15). What kind of example is this? It is a picture of Jesus' whole ministry – descending from the realms of glory in heaven, humbling himself like a servant, dying on the cross that we might be made clean, before returning to heaven to be seated at the right hand of the Majesty on High.

Jesus has fully demonstrated the extent of his passion for you. What is the full extent of your passion for him? Ask the Holy Spirit to increase your intimate adoration of the Son of God.

The Bible in a year: Nehemiah 3–4; Luke 6

DAY 2

Rest and revelation

Make sure you're in a quiet place and pray: 'I don't just want to know the Book of the Lord. I want to know the Lord of the Book.'

John 13:18–30

Jesus has already warned that there is one at the meal table who is unclean and who is going to betray him (vs 10–11). Now he tells his followers that there is a traitor in the camp (v 18). Jesus delivers this prophetic word so that his listeners will later know that he is the Son of God (v 19). He challenges them to go on accepting him, and not to reject him (v 20). The author writes that Jesus was 'troubled in spirit' as he thought and spoke about the betrayer. At this point, the disciples come into focus (v 22). Two are described. The second of these is Judas, the betrayer (vs 26–30). As Jonathan Edwards once wrote, 'his associates never seemed to have entertained a thought of his being anything other than a true disciple'. But the true disciple in this story is not Judas but John, the beloved disciple (vs 23–25). He is seen reclining with his head resting on Jesus' chest. This suggests intimacy and friendship in Middle Eastern culture. As he leans back against Jesus, John hears his hushed words concerning Judas (v 26).

The clear lesson that John's example teaches us is this: resting in the presence of Jesus is the key to receiving revelation. Intimacy is the key to insight. Among the disciples at the table, only John senses the heartbeat of the Son of God and hears the whispers of the Saviour. How much time do we spend in such a posture? Resolve to find a secret place where you can spend time listening to Jesus, receiving his revelation for you and your church.

The Bible in a year: Nehemiah 5–6; Luke 7

JULY 8–14

DAY 3

The course of true love

Simon Peter suffered terribly from 'foot and mouth' disease. Every time he opened his mouth he seemed to put his foot in it! We too can be like this. Meditate on Ecclesiastes 5:1–3 and resolve to listen to God before you speak to him.

John 13:31–38

Our previous passage ended with Judas leaving the meal table and the terse statement, 'And it was night' (v 30). Darkness has truly arrived with the departure of the betrayer. Now Jesus announces that the time has come for his glorification (vs 31, 32). Keep in mind that John's Gospel describes the crucifixion as 'the lifting up of the Son of Man'. Jesus is lifted up physically on the cross. But he is also lifted up figuratively, in the sense that the cross begins his ascent back to glory. The hour of the cross is therefore the hour of his glorification. It is not a literal period of sixty minutes but a period of time involving Jesus' suffering, death, resurrection and ascension. If the advent of this hour means glorification for Jesus, it means the opposite for Peter. Jesus tells the disciples that they cannot go where he is going (v 33) and that they are to love one another as he has loved them. Love will mark them out as true disciples (vs 34–35). Peter, mystified, asks if he can follow Jesus now, adding that he will lay down his life for Jesus (v 37). Jesus warns him that he will do no such thing. Before the cock crows, Peter will deny Jesus three times (v 38).

The word translated 'love' in verses 34 and 35 denotes sacrificial, self-forgetful love. True love involves costly acts of kindness. The more his followers show this kind of love to one another, the more the world will see Jesus. So how loving is your church? What difference can you make?

The Bible in a year: Nehemiah 7–8; Luke 8

DAY 4

The Father's house

John's Gospel makes it clear. Jesus came to give us life, and life that lasts for ever. Ask for a glimpse of eternity in your heart as you prepare to read.

John 14:1–14

Jesus has told his disciples that he is about to depart (13:33). They are troubled by this, so Jesus reassures them (vs 1–2). He will prepare a place for them and then return to fetch them (v 3). The discussion then turns to the route to this house (v 4). In response to Thomas's complaint (v 5), Jesus says that he is the way to the Father's house (v 6). In fact, there is complete unity between the Father and the Son (vs 7–10). The greatest evidence for this is Jesus' miracles (v 11). The disciples will now be responsible for manifesting the Father's love, because Jesus is leaving them. Indeed, Jesus promises they will do even greater miracles than he has – greater in number if not greater in kind. The key will be to ask in his name (vs 13–14); in other words, to ask for those things that are consistent with the person of Jesus (because the name and the person were one and the same).

Not long ago a lovely elderly man in my congregation died of cancer. He had literally shone with the love and the joy of the Lord. When I visited him in hospital shortly before his death, he told me that his sons were decorating a room on the ground floor of his home in which to spend the last days of his life. George looked at me with a twinkle in his eyes and said, 'I've got another room prepared, in my Father's house. That's where I'm going.' Ask Jesus to give you the same level of assurance.

The Bible in a year: Nehemiah 9–10; Psalm 78:38–72

JULY 8–14

DAY 5

The Father loves you!

Do you need a word of comfort today? Some of the most reassuring words in the Bible are contained in the passage we are about to read. Invite the Comforter to draw near to you.

John 14:15–31

As his enemies close in (vs 30–31), Jesus begins his teaching on the Holy Spirit. Every other great leader in history has left his followers comfortless at the leader's death. Not so Jesus. He promises that his disciples will not be left fatherless (v 18). To those who obey him, Jesus promises another Counsellor to be with them, whom the world cannot know (v 17). The key to receiving this gift will be to love and obey the risen Jesus (vs 15, 19–21). The Father will come and manifest himself to those who love the Son (vs 22–24). The Holy Spirit will cause all true disciples to share in the unending love of the Son for the Father. So Jesus comforts his friends by saying that there is no need to fear. The Holy Spirit is coming and he will adopt all true believers into the flow of intimate love that Jesus has for the Father (vs 25–31).

The Holy Spirit is the Spirit of adoption (see Romans 8:15). If you were orphaned at birth – as I was – you will know how precious this truth is. Just as my adopting father entered an orphanage and adopted me, so our Father in heaven has entered the orphanage of this world and adopted us. He has done this in the person and work of his Son, through the power of the Spirit.

Ask the Father to fill your heart with more of the fire of his love so that you can know the revelation that 'the Father himself loves you' (16:27).

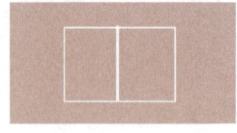

Giving God's love away: 1 John 3:11–20
A Father to the fatherless: Psalm 68:1–6

The Bible in a year: Nehemiah 11–12; Luke 9

JULY 8–14

Going deeper …

Recently I decided I had had enough of being on the defensive about being a Christian. I suddenly realised that most of the non-Christians I meet are very blunt about my beliefs. So I decided to be very blunt about what they believe. I can challenge them about theirs (which, I've found, are rarely thought through). So I've started being more confrontational. At a party recently I asked an unbeliever if Jesus was lying when he said that he was the way to the Father. She said, 'I suppose not.' Then I asked why she was looking in astrology and Eastern religions for what she could only find in Christianity. If nothing else, it made her stop and think.

One of the recurring themes of this week's readings has been the call to witness. When Jesus washes his disciples' feet, he is witnessing to them through an act of practical and humble service. Judas failed terminally as far as being a faithful witness was concerned. Peter failed but was later to be restored.

Witnessing about Jesus is a calling that we all have. Some are set apart to be evangelists, but *all* are called to be witnesses. We can witness through washing people's feet (practical evangelism), through laying hands on lost people and praying for them to be healed (power evangelism), through words (proclamation evangelism) and by living out our faith with integrity (presence evangelism). The Holy Spirit is beginning to awaken the church to obey the call to witness to the lost. How will you respond?

In love with the Father

Conclusion

A small boy, not yet three years old, ran down the corridors of the large building. Armed guards ignored the child as he ran by. The boy went past several members of staff, who took little notice, except that some smiled at him. Going past a secretary's desk, the child did not even see her wave, so focused was he on his objective. The guard at the door made no attempt to impede the advance of the eager child, who opened the door and stepped inside. With a great smile, the boy ran across the floor of the Oval Office and jumped into the arms of the most powerful man on the planet. Key statesmen had to wait a few moments while President John F Kennedy and his son, John-John, hugged and kissed each other at the beginning of the day.

That's quite a picture … a small child in the arms of the most powerful man in the world. The beauty of it is this: the child knew who he was. He knew that he was John F Kennedy's son and that John F Kennedy was his daddy. So he approached his dad with confidence and embraced him with affection.

You and I are the adopted sons and daughters of a glorious Father. When we are born again, we become children of the God Almighty. He has chosen to reveal himself, through Jesus, as *Abba* – Daddy. He wants you to rest in the knowledge that you are *Abba*'s child. There are two ways to do this. Believe what the Bible says, that you are chosen, adopted and loved (Ephesians 1:4–6). And, open your heart to the fire of God's love.

The Bible in a year: Nehemiah 13; Esther 1–3; Psalm 79; Luke 6

JULY 15–21

Amazing grace

As a young person all I knew about grace was the last line of a piece of doggerel: 'Grace is a little girl who never washed her face,' and that it was something some people said before meals. Then came the day, in my eighteenth year, when I experienced the grace of God and was born again of the Spirit.

Some years later I encountered a book entitled *Grace Is Not a Blue Eyed Blonde!* Flippant and insensitive the title may be, but the book emphasises an important truth: God's grace is no flimsy thing – it has the power to transform the sinner and grant victory to the struggling Christian.

John Newton was a sailor who lived a particularly debauched life. Returning from a slave-trading expedition, the ship Newton was aboard was struck by a furious typhoon. One side of the vessel was battered to pieces and water poured in so fast that it couldn't be pumped out. He later wrote, 'I began to think of that Lord Jesus whom I had so often ridiculed.' Miraculously the ship remained afloat. Seizing a Bible, Newton went to his cabin where he read the story of Paul's conversion. The thought that God might also extend mercy to him, began to grip Newton. His life changed dramatically. Years later, then an Anglican minister, he wrote the famous hymn, 'Amazing Grace … that saved a wretch like me'.

God's grace is indeed amazing. As we ponder some of the most wonderful passages in the New Testament this week, I pray that we will not only gain a good theological understanding of the grace of God, but also powerfully experience it in a new way.

Roger Witter is the Manager of Church Resources for Scripture Union. This involves responsibility for all Alpha material in South Africa. The year 2001 was a good year for him, as he is an avid Liverpool fan.

JULY 15–21

DAY 1

God's nature

What do you really think God is like? Take some time to get in touch with your feelings about him. Is he a severe or angry God whose demands you are constantly trying to keep? Or do you find him loving and encouraging, even when you fail?

John 1:14–18

After they met Jesus, something amazing happened to Jesus' followers. Their understanding of God changed radically. It was as though someone had switched the lights on (John 1:9). In Jesus they encountered God as he really is: 'full of grace and truth' (v 14). In the Bible, the word 'name' often means a person's character or nature. John speaks of those who believed in Jesus' name (v 12), referring to the fact that God revealed his true nature in Jesus. Is the Old Testament picture of an unapproachably holy God whose standards are absolute, wrong? 'No,' John would tell us, 'but that's only half the story.' 'The law was given through Moses: *grace and truth* came through Jesus Christ' (v 17).

Behind all the commandments in both the Old and New Testaments, stands an utterly loving God. Until Jesus came no one really understood that. Jesus – he who 'was with God in the beginning' (John 1:2) – made him fully known (v 18). In the Old Testament we see the absolute standards which God's righteous nature demands. In the New Testament, however, we discover that the same God has himself provided a way for those demands to be fully met. *That's Grace!*

Ask the Holy Spirit to give you a fresh, new revelation of what God is really like.

The Bible in a year: Esther 4–5; Luke 11

JULY 15–21

DAY 2

God's initiative

Did you find God, or did he find you? Who took the initiative?

Ephesians 2:1–10

The Christian's position has changed. We have been transported from the lowest (v 3) to the highest (v 6). What we are now is very different to what we were. What happened? Who did it? 'You were dead' (v 1). Dead people are incapable of doing anything! 'But God … made us alive … it is by grace you have been saved' (vs 4–8).

What is grace? Grace is God doing for us what we cannot do for ourselves. More than that, it is what God does for us *freely*. Grace is a gift. You don't deserve it and cannot earn it. But *why* does God do it? 'Because of his great love for us' (v 4)! Yesterday we saw that grace is a manifestation of God's nature revealed to a sinful human race. He 'who is rich in mercy' (v 4) takes the initiative to save us.

So emphatic is Paul that our salvation has nothing to do with ourselves but everything to do with God, that he twice repeats his statement: 'By grace you have been saved' (vs 5, 8). Even our believing is not of our doing – God gives us the faith (v 8). But what of the present and the future? God even provides the good deeds we do after we have been saved (v 10). It is God, and God alone, who takes the initiative in our salvation – from beginning to end. *That's Grace!*

What should we do? 'Remember,' says Paul twice (Ephesians 2:11, 12). And give thanks!

The Bible in a year: Esther 6–7; Luke 12

JULY 15–21

DAY 3

God's enablement

How do you live the Christian life? Does it take great effort, or do you find it easy?

Galatians 2:20; 3:3

Years ago I entered a particularly bleak time in my Christian life. I felt I was a hopeless Christian. Living for Christ seemed unbelievably difficult. I was confused and depressed. Then one day I heard the Lord quietly speak: 'You say serving me is hard; I say it is easy (Matthew 11:28–30). I suggest you decide which of us is right!' That incident marked the beginning of a process which completely changed my life.

After our new birth, living as a Christian *remains* a matter of faith (v 20). Our salvation begins with the gift of faith (Ephesians 2:8) and continues in the same way. Paul says, 'I do not set aside the grace of God' (v 21). 'I *live* by the faith of the Son of God' (v 20, KJV). By his faith, not mine!

We do not start with grace, but then have to continue by our own efforts (3:3). God's plan of salvation covers everything. It is by grace from beginning to end. The God who gave us the faith to believe in the first place, will give us the faith to continue. Salvation is not a matter of trying, but of trusting. We are not urged to keep a grip on God – he keeps a bulldog grip on us. No one (Satan included) can snatch us out of his hand (John 10:28). *That's Grace!*

Whatever your response to the questions above, spend quality time with God asking him to make the truths of today's passage real to you.

The Bible in a year: Esther 8–12; Luke 13

JULY 15–21

DAY 4

God's empowerment

Having looked at how we get saved and stay saved, we look now at how we do God's work? What has been your experience? Has it mainly been something you do for him, or something he does through you?

1 Corinthians 12:4–11

Writing to the Corinthians in Greek, Paul uses a derivative of the word for grace, 'charis'. It is most commonly translated 'gifts of the Spirit', but literally means 'grace gifts'. Spiritual gifts are just that, gifts which God freely gives us to do his work. They are given to all God's people to use for all God's people (v 7). There are different gifts, used in different ways, for different purposes (vs 4–6).

Even what we *do* for God is all of grace, worked in and through us by the Holy Spirit. He is the one who empowers believers for the particular service God has lined up for them (v 11; Ephesians 2:10). Paul encourages the Philippians to 'continue to work … for it is God who works in you' (2:12–13). So once again, God has graciously taken care of everything. He and he alone saves, keeps and empowers us. *That's Grace!*

What is God's plan for your life? What special service is the Lord calling you to (v 5)? Which are the spiritual gifts you need in order to fulfil God's plan (v 4)? If you have not already begun to do so, ask the Lord to show you what he has in mind for you. If you have, keep looking to the Holy Spirit to lead you day by day.

The Bible in a year: Job 1–2; Psalm 80

JULY 15–21

DAY 5

God's intervention

Can you remember times when God came to your aid in special ways? Perhaps the Lord intervened in a spectacular way. Or perhaps it became apparent over a period of time that his strength was carrying you through difficult days.

2 Corinthians 12:7–10; Hebrews 4:14–16

There is another aspect of grace which we all enjoy. I refer to the ways in which God is gracious to us. Sometimes the Lord's intervention comes in miraculous ways. At other times it is imparted quietly and steadily.

Throughout the Old Testament we find references to people who, like Noah, 'found grace in the eyes of the Lord' (Genesis 6:8, KJV). Paul refers to his preaching of the gospel to the Gentiles as being a privilege granted to him through special grace from God (Ephesians 3:8). The greetings and farewells given in most of the New Testament letters contain the thought of believers receiving grace from God (e.g. Colossians 1:2; 2 Corinthians 13:14).

Paul faced an obstacle in his life which was so troublesome that he pleaded with God repeatedly to take it away (2 Corinthians 12:8). God didn't, but in a wonderful way he enabled Paul to handle it (v 9a). This experience of the grace of God deeply affected Paul's view of life (vs 9b–10).

Although without sin, our Lord was tempted just like us. He not only sympathises with our human weaknesses, but is eager to help us in our times of need (Hebrews 4:15–16). *That's Grace!*

Need mercy and help? God himself invites you to approach the throne of grace, and to do so with confidence.

The right response: Romans 6:1–4
The real reason: 1 Corinthians 15:9–10

The Bible in a year: Job 3–4; Luke 14

JULY 15–21

Going deeper ...

Do you sometimes feel like giving up trying to live the Christian life? That is precisely what God wants you to do. It is when we finally turn from ourselves to God that we discover a Christianity that works. 'You who are trying ... have fallen away from grace' (Galatians 5:4). The Christian life is not a matter of *trying*, but rather of constantly *receiving* the grace of God. It starts when we receive God's gift of *saving* grace, and it is meant to continue day by day as we receive the Lord's *enabling* grace. If we try to continue by our own struggling efforts, God's question to us is, 'Are you so foolish?' (Galatians 3:3). If we needed God's gift of grace to begin, how much more will we need it to continue?

Is your Christian life one of love, joy and peace (Galatians 5:22), or do you find the going heavy? 'Come to me, all you who are weary and burdened, and I will give you rest,' Jesus says (Matthew 11:28). Why not spend some time before the Lord now? Ask him to make his all-encompassing grace real to you, as you think back over the Scriptures we have covered this week. Jesus is 'full of grace and truth' (John 1:14) and longs to make your life and service victorious, meaningful, and joyous. As you wait on him, allow the Holy Spirit to reveal to you God's amazing grace.

It's always grace!

Grace versus law is one of the central themes of the New Testament. Several passages pursue the same subject using contrasting words, e.g. 'Spirit' and 'flesh'. The principle nevertheless remains the same: God's gracious provision is contrasted with attempted human accomplishment. What does God require of us? Are we meant to try or to trust? Or is it perhaps a mixture of both? God's answer is clear: 'The righteous will live by faith' (Galatians 3:11; see verses 2–3, 14, 25). 'The only thing that counts is faith expressing itself through love' (Galatians 5:6). Christianity is a matter of response rather than responsibility. When we truly believe that God himself has provided everything for our salvation: past, present, and future, our hearts automatically respond with love and obedience. Indeed, the New Testament message runs even stronger: we are 'dead', i.e. completely out of the picture! It is Christ who now lives in our bodies (Galatians 2:20).

The truth is that we cannot live the Christian life, nor are we expected to. God's message to us is that *we* cannot, but his Son can! The real secret to godly living is 'God-living' – God himself through his Son living *his* life in us. The principle remains the same for Christian service: God himself does the work (1 Corinthians 12:4–6). Choosing our own agenda, or relying on our own efforts and abilities, invariably brings weariness and disillusionment. Allowing Jesus to work out God's plan for our lives in and through us (Ephesians 2:10) is the intended way. From beginning to end (and all the way between) it is always grace: *Amazing grace!*

The Bible in a year: Job 5–8; Psalm 81–82; Luke 15

JULY 22–28

Faith in action

James

Have you ever met a person who has both their 'head in the clouds' and their 'feet planted firmly on the ground'? If not, then you are about to meet one! For James was just such a person: deeply practical and realistic about this life, but also very much in touch with the Lord. It is a powerful combination, which makes the letter of James both down-to-earth and also spiritually challenging.

Who was James? He writes as if everyone should know him: 'James, a servant of God and of the Lord Jesus Christ …' (1:1). This suggests that he was either James the brother of John or James the brother of Jesus, who became the leader of the Jerusalem church (see Galatians 1:19). Since James the brother of John was martyred in AD 44, James the brother of Jesus is the most likely candidate. The Jewish tone of the letter fits this leader of the 'Jewish party' in the early church, and he may well have been writing to believers who had literally been 'scattered' (v 1b) by the persecution which arose after the martyrdom of Stephen (Acts 11:19).

In many ways the book of James is a 'picture book', full of vivid illustrations, which bring to life the practical advice that James gives to struggling believers. Themes do emerge, but they are not always connected in a logical way. This led Martin Luther to call James 'an epistle of straw' in comparison with Paul's letters, with their reasoned arguments and detailed theology. Yet few New Testament writers have written as powerfully as James about Christian lifestyle. If this is God's straw, then I will happily use it to build my 'house' any day!

Andrew Marsden is the vicar of St Sebastian's Church in Wokingham. He is married with two children. He finds keeping the balance between family life and parish ministry a delicate one!

JULY 22–28

DAY 1

Faith under trial

Have you ever asked, 'Why me?' or 'What have I done to deserve this?' Did your Christian faith help or hinder you at such times?

James 1:1–18

Before you are tempted to dismiss verse 2 as unrealistic, remember that James is a man who was at the heart of the persecution of the early church in Jerusalem. He has been 'under fire' in a way that many of us can only imagine, and his advice is that we should welcome our troubles as an opportunity for God. God does not bring afflictions on his people, for he does not will anything that is evil (v 13). On the contrary, his work is always good (vs 16, 17). Yet God is able to use our suffering to deepen our trust in him (v 4).

What is our part in all of this? We are to persevere (v 4), throwing ourselves on God's wisdom rather than relying on our wealth (vs 9–11) or any other form of human security. Our trust in God is to be unwavering. The 'double-minded' Christians whom James condemns (vs 5–8) are those who have a foot in God's camp, and a foot in the world. They are often irregular in their commitment, compromised in their lifestyle and critical of fellow believers. They are like an unstable nuclear reactor core: ready to blow at any time.

Have you ever prayed for God to give you perseverance? In James it is not a 'meek and mild' quality, but a steadfast trust in God and in his promises as they are worked out in our lives. Why not try asking for it?

The Bible in a year: Job 9–10; Luke 16

JULY 22–28

DAY 2

Practical faith

Think back to the time before you became a Christian. What difference has your Christian faith made to the way you live?

James 1:19; 2:26

This passage is held together by the theme of faith being worked out in action. It is all too easy for Christians to 'hear' the word on a Sunday in church, and fail to put it into practice from Monday to Saturday (1:22–25). By 'the law' (1:25; 2:8–13) James probably means not just the Old Testament law, but that law as it is fulfilled and completed in Jesus. It is by doing the will of God, as supremely revealed in the life and teaching of his Son, that we will know freedom and blessing (1:25).

In practice, this means being ready to listen to others rather than rush in with our own opinions (1:19–21). In church, at work and in the local community it means treating others fairly and without discrimination (2:1–7). If we break the 'law' at any point, we are denying the will of the Lawgiver. We are to be like him, showing mercy to others, just as he has shown us mercy in Jesus (2:8–13).

The difference between James's teaching here (2:14–26) and Paul's on 'justification by faith' (Romans chapter 4) is more apparent than real. For both writers, faith and works are indivisible, and faith that does not show itself in a changed life is no faith at all (2:26; see also Romans 13:8–10).

For some people faith is a matter for home and church, but never impinges upon their work environment. Are there any 'no go' areas for God in your life?

The Bible in a year: Job 11–12; Luke 17

JULY 22–28

DAY 3

Faith and speech

When was the last time that you deliberately said something to encourage someone?

James 3:1–12

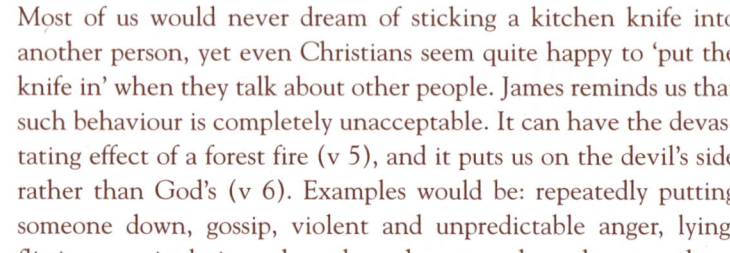

Most of us would never dream of sticking a kitchen knife into another person, yet even Christians seem quite happy to 'put the knife in' when they talk about other people. James reminds us that such behaviour is completely unacceptable. It can have the devastating effect of a forest fire (v 5), and it puts us on the devil's side rather than God's (v 6). Examples would be: repeatedly putting someone down, gossip, violent and unpredictable anger, lying, flirting, manipulating others through our words, and many others.

Yet the tongue can be used for so much that is good. James compares it to the bit that turns the whole horse, or the rudder that directs a ship (vs 3–5a). It can be used for Christian teaching (but remember the word of caution in verse 1), for evangelism, for encouragement, to bring reconciliation and above all to give praise to God (v 9a).

Ultimately our words reveal what we are like inside. Jesus said 'Out of the overflow of the heart the mouth speaks' (Matthew 12:34), and this is James's point when he says that fresh and salt water cannot both flow from the same spring (v 11). If the water is brackish, then the spring needs to change from within.

'No man can tame the tongue ...' (v 8), but God can. Ask the Holy Spirit to pinpoint those areas of your speech that are like salt water, so that you can repent and invite him to change you from within.

The Bible in a year: Job 13–14; Luke 18

JULY 22–28

DAY 4

Divided in faith

Think about some decisions that you have made recently. In each case, what led you to make the decision as you did?

James 3:13–4:12

One of James's themes is the 'double-minded man' (1:8), the kind of person who has one foot in God's camp, and one foot in the world. In the same way he now asks us to consider our motives. If we are motivated by 'envy and selfish ambition' (3:16), this will lead to disorder in the church and in our families. The 'wisdom of heaven', however, is not self-seeking and pushy, but – like Jesus – humble and self-effacing (3:17–18).

For James, the root of all human division lies in our 'selfish desires', which, if unchecked, can lead to physical violence (4:1–2a). He would have agreed with the UNESCO (United Nations Educational, Scientific and Cultural Organisation) Charter that 'wars begin in the minds of men'. Often we pay lip-service to the lordship of Christ, but our prayers are selfish and not truly submitted to his will (4:2b–3). Such people are spiritually 'adulterous', and James makes clear that 'friendship with the world' is incompatible with friendship with God (4:4–5). The only solution for a church or an individual Christian who has compromised their faith in this way is humble repentance (4:7–10).

There are many 'worldly' values that can become alternatives to 'the wisdom of heaven'. Here are some examples: money can motivate and direct us rather than Christ; we can seek excellence as opposed to righteousness of life; we can be individualistic rather than building community; or we can fill our time with activities but miss God's calling. Ask God whether any of these apply to you.

The Bible in a year: Job 15–17; Psalm 83–84

JULY 22–28

DAY 5

Faith and lifestyle

'Target setting' is all the rage today. What are your personal targets in life?

James 4:13–5:20

Often we make short-term targets based on personal need rather than on God's will. James encourages us to live our lives in the light of our eternal destiny. We do not know when we will die (4:13–17), and God's judgement is a reality (5:1), but there will be a harvest for Christians who wait patiently for their Saviour's return (5:7). In this passage James gives us some 'qualities for the last days', targets to aim at in our Christian lives.

So often we ask God to bless our human efforts when all the time he is calling us to develop obedience to him (4:13–17).

Today's passage contains verses which are almost certainly an attack on the rich oppressors of the church, but it is also a stark reminder to today's wealthy church of the importance of generosity. In the 'now' society in which we live patience is rarely esteemed, yet it is one of the prime qualities required of Christians (5:7–11). Prayer is to be our response in times of trouble, and it should be as natural for us to seek healing prayer as to call the doctor (5:13–14). The faith required is not a faith in miracles themselves, but a faith in the God who brings miracles, the same deep trust in God that was shown by both Job (5:11) and Elijah (5:17–18).

'The prayer of a righteous (person) is powerful and effective' (5:16). Righteousness in James has to do with character. Which of the qualities listed above do you need to ask the Holy Spirit to give you?

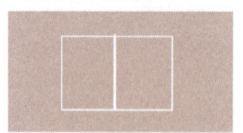

The beginning of wisdom: Proverbs 1:1–7
The source of wisdom: Proverbs 2:1–6

The Bible in a year: Job 18–19; Luke 19

Going deeper …

'Sticks and stones may break my bones, but words will never hurt me.' Most physical wounds heal, but no amount of time will heal many of the emotional wounds that we inflict with our tongues. The tongue, says James, is 'full of deadly poison' (3:8). Words can kill emotionally.

James tells us that it is inappropriate for Christians to speak words of praise to God one minute and to curse other human beings the next (3:9–10). But do we curse people in the twenty-first century? Surely that belongs in the past, to pagan religion and the occult? What are we doing when we speak ill of someone behind their back? Or when we lash out at people with our words? This 'wisdom', says James, is 'earthly, unspiritual, of the devil' (3:15). The power of such words may be greater than we realise.

Invite the Holy Spirit to come and take control of your speech; invite him into your heart, the source of our speech (Matthew 12:34). Repent if the Holy Spirit brings to mind any specific times when you have hurt others through your words.

As the Holy Spirit takes control of your will and your emotions, invite him to go deeper, to bring to the surface the wounds that you have suffered from the words of others. Ask God to help you to forgive the people concerned, to break the power of any words spoken over you, and to heal your damaged emotions.

Faith for living

James is a letter 'for all seasons'. It has something to say to us when we are undergoing trials and temptations, challenging us to rejoice in our suffering and to hold fast to the goodness of God. It speaks of the relationships that are appropriate between members of the body of Christ, where there is to be no partiality or favouritism. It tells of the importance of a faith that is shown to be genuine by the good works that accompany it. It challenges us deeply about the way we speak, and the motives of our hearts. It calls us to a lifestyle that is in tune with our eternal destiny as believers in Christ.

However, the words of James are in vain if they have not changed your life. This is, after all, 'the perfect law that gives freedom.' As you turn away from James, look once again at 1:22–25. What do they mean to you in the light of all that you have studied in the last week? Write down the things that God has been saying to you this week. You may not feel changed, but I hope that you have been challenged. Commit yourself to pray regularly for God to bring about the changes you know need to take place in your heart and in your life. James reminds us that God is looking for humble people (4:6) who recognise their own failings, and weaknesses. The Lord is swift to help those who know their need of *him*. What kind of person are you?

The Bible in a year: Job 22–23; Psalm 85; Luke 20

JULY 29– AUGUST 4

Singleness/marriedness

Marital status. It's a way of classifying people into convenient groups, but not a system of classification that God uses. Within churches there can be a great divide between the two groups – sometimes the marrieds are considered to be more spiritual and singles are somewhat of an embarrassment who don't fit into the normal social system. I have ghastly memories of a church picnic where families clustered in tight-knit groups on the vicarage lawn and I wandered like a lost lamb searching in vain for an opening in the defences. I vowed never to go again.

In his time, Jesus broke the mould of Jewish culture. Tradition demanded that he marry and have children whilst still a young man. Yet he didn't. He also claimed that marriage is not an eternal state, but only temporary (see Matthew 22:30). We'll all be single in heaven, so marital status won't matter there one little bit. But it does matter here in the world and in the church. It matters when people are isolated and lonely, when their private griefs are not acknowledged or their gifts are not allowed full expression. The church should be the place where all find acceptance, love and value for who we are, and not on the condition that we are happily married with 2.4 obedient children. In God's sight all are equally precious and loved whether single, married, divorced, childless, separated or widowed.

Over this next week we'll look at some of God's wise and encouraging words about how we relate to him and how singles and marrieds have a significant contribution to make to God's kingdom and to each other. If you're hurting in any way over this issue, don't switch off, but allow God to reach in and soothe the wounds.

Christine Platt has worked for the discipleship movement, The Navigators, for twenty years. Ten of those years were spent in Abidjan. Currently, she works as a health visitor in South Wales. She enjoys helping people to go deeper in their relationship with Jesus.

JULY 29–AUGUST 4

DAY 1

Am I of value?

When do you feel of most value to God? Serving him in some church activity, at work, watching the television or preparing a meal? What does this reveal about your understanding of how God sees you?

Psalm 139:1–18

King David's words erupt from his tumultuous experiences with God. David really blew it in some of his relationships. He knew betrayal, blame, disappointment as well as elation and victory. Yet, despite all that, he reminded himself that God knew him completely (vs 1–4), and loved him unconditionally. This enabled him to forgive himself and revel in his value as a human being (v 14).

Life events can give our self-esteem a battering from which we feel we may never recover. The quick fixes the world offers – comfort eating, tobacco, alcohol, drugs, self-harm – offer only momentary relief and leave us feeling worse than ever before.

Some single people feel inferior because they haven't attracted a life partner, whereas some married couples gain all their self-esteem from each other's love and approval. Neither situation is healthy. God wants us to be confident in our immeasurable value just as we are, without any appendages of human relationships or status symbols.

Where do you stand on this? Try relating this psalm to yourself. Choose one phrase that speaks to your heart's need. You could memorise it and remind yourself of it throughout the day. Ask God to embed this truth into your mind so that when your self-esteem is battered you will have a solid foundation to fall back on. Thank Jesus that you are a unique individual, tenderly shaped by his loving hands and held close to his heart.

The Bible in a year: Job 24–26; Luke 21

JULY 29–AUGUST 4

DAY 2

Can God really be trusted?

Are there areas in your life at the moment where you are struggling to trust God – his love, his plan, his purposes? Be honest with him. Tell him exactly how you feel.

Psalm 73:1–3,13–28

Trust is a small word with huge implications. A tightrope walker pushed a wheelbarrow on a thin cord over Niagara Falls. 'Do you think I can do it again?' he yelled to the onlookers. 'Yes!' they screamed. 'Then one of you come and sit in the wheelbarrow!' Needless to say, nobody volunteered. They thought he could do it but weren't willing to risk their lives. They trusted, but not completely.

The psalmist was having a crisis of trust (v 2). His life circumstances seemed all wrong to him (v 13). He just couldn't put it together (v 16). He was tempted to retreat from God in anger and disappointment (vs 21–22), but recognised that God was the only one who had any answers (v 25), so he 'entered the sanctuary of God' (v 17). For him that would have been the temple. He made time to be quiet and focus on God which gave him new insight and perspective. Seeing his circumstances from God's point of view invigorated his faith – he almost bursts in verse 26: 'My flesh and my heart may fail, but God is the strength of my heart and my portion for ever.' Yes!

Do you think God can be trusted to meet you at your point of need right now? He is the God who says, 'I love you deeply and want the best for you – trust me!' He may not change the circumstances, but he surely can give you his perspective and help. Talk to him.

The Bible in a year: Job 27–28; Luke 22

JULY 29–AUGUST 4

DAY 3

Life is now!

In days gone by, even if there was no eligible suitor on the horizon, young women would spend months and years preparing for marriage by collecting household items in their bottom drawer – often towels and linens lovingly embroidered by their own hands. Are you missing out on today's energy and opportunities by concentrating on a hoped-for future state?

Ephesians 5:1–21

Jane, a deeply committed Christian, confided in me: 'I think God is calling me to be a missionary, but I want to get married before I go.' She was being tempted to put life on hold until the magic moment of marriage. Others might think, 'Everything will be all right when I get married.' These are 'empty words' that 'deceive' (v 6). God is God of the now and he asks us, whether married or single, to live and relish today.

Coming from darkness to light heralds a massive transformation in a person's life. Values, attitudes and motives all undergo change, and we have much to learn about how to live as children of light (v 8). We need to be careful how we live *today* (vs 15–16). God's grace is available for us today, not for five years hence. As a single person I find it helpful to accept the reality that it is God's will for me to be single *today*, so I take the day and try to make the most of it, rather than dwelling on long years of singleness ahead.

Jesus came that we might 'have life, and have it to the full' (John 10:10). Consider any attitudes or actions that reveal you have put life on hold. Ask for God's help in living wholeheartedly each day.

The Bible in a year: Job 29–30; Luke 23

JULY 29–AUGUST 4

DAY 4

Sex and children

Our sex-obsessed society and one's own sex drive can make life exceedingly trying for single people. Ask God today for fresh insights about your body and your relationship with him that will enable you to walk with him through the sexual minefield that we live in.

1 Corinthians 6:12–20

When I was studying anatomy and physiology as a nursing student I was amazed at the intricacy of the digestive system, for example all the various enzymes kicking into play at the right time. It illustrated for me that our physical bodies are 'fearfully and wonderfully made' (Psalm 139:14). Your body is a gift from God. He has chosen it for his home (vs 15, 19). That means it becomes a sacred place. Think how carefully you choose and look after the home in which you live. You bolt the door against anyone who is out to destroy it or break in. You protect it from damage because you want to continue to enjoy it. Almighty God wants to enjoy you, his home, which he has bought at an unimaginable price (v 20).

God provides the sexual relationship as a way of expressing love and commitment within marriage and so that children are born into a stable and loving environment. Life doesn't always work out that way, and God is able to help those of us who are bruised, battered and hurting in this area.

Any attempt to enjoy sex outside the God-ordained parameters is destined to bring grief to God and to us. His command is 'Flee from sexual immorality' (v 18).

Take a few moments to thank God for the gift of your body, and ask for his help in consecrating it to him (v 20).

The Bible in a year: Job 31–32; Psalm 86–87

JULY 29–AUGUST 4

DAY 5

Friendship and fun

In lives packed with commitments, time for fun and friendships can sometimes seem a bit of a luxury. Think about your close friends and the efforts you are making to deepen those friendships. Are friends a priority for you or something you fit in when you have time?

Ecclesiastes 4:7–12

This man described in Ecclesiastes was a loner. His life, although successful materially, became meaningless (v 8). All of us, married and single, need friends. Some married couples say that their partner is their best friend. That's great, but other friends are vital to prevent that relationship becoming too exclusive and possibly stifling. It seems to me that single people have to make more effort to build and deepen friendships and that takes time and courage. Singles often move around more with their jobs. They move alone and need to build new networks of friendships. This can all get a bit tiring, especially for people who are not extroverts. When married people move at least they take their family unit with them, although I know that some married people are intensely lonely within their marriage and being uprooted from friends would be painful.

The contrast in these verses between the loner and the friend is a salutary warning to make time for positive, mutually enriching friendships (vs 9–12). Perhaps you've been hurt by a friend – it takes courage to forgive, rebuild and initiate other relationships, but to have friends, one needs to *be* a friend (vs 10–11).

Ask God to show you ways of being a really good friend to those around you. You might find 1 Corinthians 13:4–7 stimulating verses to pray over.

Jesus came to dinner: Luke 10:38–42
Teamwork: Acts 18:1–3, 19, 24–26

The Bible in a year: Job 33–34; Luke 24

JULY 29–AUGUST 4

Going deeper …

'Each one should use whatever gift he has received to serve others, faithfully administering God's grace in its various forms' (1 Peter 4:10). 'Each one'? All of us, married, single, young and older have received one or more gifts. Have you identified yours? Ask friends and people you respect in your church community what gifts they discern in you. God's instruction is clear. Gifts are to be used to serve others and bring honour to God (1 Peter 4:11).

For those with a 'shrinking violet' tendency it can seem boastful to even imagine we are gifted. Others might be pushed or feel drawn into a role for which they are not gifted. I'm sure we've all endured sermons given by preachers who undoubtedly have gifts in other areas but not preaching! Some church communities might not be open to recognise gifting in young people, singles or women. Those with demanding family responsibilities may be frustrated by not having time or energy to exercise their gifts outside the family context.

The exhortation to use our gifts is clear but as with all scriptural instructions, it does not stand alone. The timid among us must remember we have the promise of the Holy Spirit's power (2 Timothy 1:7). Those who are thwarted in the expression of their gifts by church tradition or politics may need to wait patiently or change churches, but 1 Corinthians 13:4–7 is still the standard for relationships. Those with busy family commitments need to see the family as an arena for using their gifts, and to trust God for other opportunities in the future (Ecclesiastes 3:1). Let's revel in the confidence that God has given the gift and he will not let it go to waste.

Get hooked up!

Conclusion

'What can I do to make you love me?' is a common refrain in many of our hearts. In our society of broken relationships, confused children and isolated adults, God's people can be channels of healing love to those around them. We have ready access to the *only* inexhaustible source of love.

Have you ever had an intravenous drip? These are given when patients can't take fluid or drugs for themselves. Christians can be like the tubing – connecting the source to the needy recipient. Not many people are going to walk into a church and ask questions about God. We have to take God to them where they are. To be an effective 'tube' we need to be connected to God's love ourselves and ask him to fill the emptiness and soothe the sore places. He wants to help us to become complete and secure in him. 'Let us then approach the throne of grace with confidence, so that we may receive mercy and find grace to help us in our time of need' (Hebrews 4:16).

As we receive this mercy and grace we can infuse it into family, friends, neighbours and workmates so they too might know and experience God's unconditional love for them. By the grace of God, we can make a difference to people's lives.

The Bible in a year: Job 35–38; Psalm 85; Philippians 1

AUGUST 5–11

A gospel for all people

Acts 5–8

Is there anyone you find difficult to get on with? If so, maybe it's because they're different from you in some way. When someone is different from me, it is easy to make all kinds of assumptions about them which can often lead me to reject them as wrong or inadequate or even as an enemy. This can be true about people of different nationality, upbringing, sex or even character-type. We don't understand how they think or how they live, and it's very easy to slip into believing their ways are less valid than our own. The early church was a dynamic place where key issues touched on exactly this kind of reality. This week we will perhaps see what our radical God has to say about it all.

Up until the coming of Christ the Jews were, quite simply, God's chosen people. They were set apart as special and unique, with strict rules controlling every detail of daily life, and their whole sense of self-identity was built upon this separateness. Although God had made it clear that they were meant to be a 'light for the Gentiles' (Isaiah 49:6b), they had actually become very exclusive and saw themselves as superior. It was therefore inconceivable to them that God might be doing a new thing which actually challenged their special status. The church's concept of Jesus Christ threatened their very existence and struck at the heart of their Jewishness. It could not be tolerated.

God is seeking to challenge and reassure us this week as he yearns to use us to build his kingdom. Are you ready for a journey back to Jerusalem just after Christ's death and resurrection? It's potentially life-changing!

Sue Sainsbury is married to John and spends most of her life 'swapping hats', juggling the various roles of research student at London Bible College, assistant minister's wife, auxiliary nurse and writer.

AUGUST 5–11

DAY 1

God at work

Are you a follower of Jesus? What do you expect the lifestyle of a bunch of Christians to look like? Take a few moments to reflect on last week: what effect did Jesus have on your thoughts, expectations and actions? Bring your thoughts to him in prayer.

Acts 5:12–42

Let's resist the temptation to go down the guilt route of 'my life doesn't look at all like theirs' or the dismissive route of 'those things just don't happen today', and ponder what was going on here.

God was at work doing incredible things through his obedient servants: miracles (vs 12, 19), healings (vs 15–16), teaching (v 21a). The ordinary people loved it (vs 13–15 – what faith!), the religious leaders hated it (vs 17–18, 33), and the apostles carried on regardless (vs 29, 42).

The heart is in verses 30–32. This is the gospel – what God has done in Christ and what Christians do in response. They are forgiven and have been given the Holy Spirit. The passage is a kind of living film clip showing us what this dynamic actually looks like. What an amazing picture of the power of God at work in people's lives. For the apostles, there must have been much joy in knowing themselves to be used by God. But they were also pursued (v 26), imprisoned (v 18) and flogged (v 40) because of it.

What a challenge to watch these disciples rejoice because they were given the honour of being dishonoured for Christ (vs 41–42). Think about what all this means in our lives. One thing is clear – God wants to use us. Ask him to give you courage to speak about 'the Name' and live 'this new life' (v 20) to the full, today.

The Bible in a year: Job 39–42; Philippians 2

AUGUST 5–11

DAY 2

Tensions rising

Do you ever shut God out of the differences of opinion or the moments of tension in family life, work or church? Take a few moments to thank him that he's completely interested and available to help.

Acts 6:1–14

Yesterday we saw some 'big stuff' happening: God works through miracles. Today we are reminded of inevitable tensions when human beings do anything together. God also works through wise organisations. A big issue at the time was how the Jews had responded to being taken over by the Greek empire 300 years earlier. Some had totally rejected Greek culture (Hebraic Jews) while others had embraced it (Grecian Jews). The result being that one lot felt superior and unpolluted by outside influence while the others felt looked down upon (v 1). Both parties were now Christians and all knew that caring for the vulnerable was a cherished priority of God (see Deuteronomy 10:17–18). Typical of one of Satan's ruses, not only does this dispute threaten to distract the apostles from teaching about Jesus (v 2), it could also do much damage to the early church in the eyes of the watching world.

Thankfully, the apostles modelled wise leadership, depending on humble delegation (vs 3–4) and acknowledgement of others' gifts (vs 5–6) rather than the injured insistence that they do it all themselves. And the 'So' in verse 7 shows a direct consequence of this godly handling of a difficult situation as outsiders witness how the Christians care for each other and handle internal disputes.

Are there situations of conflict in your life? Ask God for his wisdom and pray that whatever Satan intends for evil, God will use for his own glory.

The Bible in a year: Job 41–42; Philippians 3

AUGUST 5–11

DAY 3

Telling the story

Imagine that you're listening to an 'enemy': someone totally opposed to everything you hold dear. As they talk, they speak such words of truth that you have to agree with everything they say. How do you feel: confused, nervous, angry? Remember those feelings as you 'listen' to Stephen.

Acts 6:15–7:53

It's important here that we remember who Stephen's talking to – the very 'holiest' people of his day. These were the Jews most committed to serving God, and a follower of Christ was, in their opinion, an arch-enemy, someone who believed in a different God. But here was Stephen calling them 'brothers and fathers' (7:2) and claiming to hold the same heritage. They had seen his godly beauty (6:15) and must have been pretty confused and tense.

Try to count how many times Stephen refers to the ancients as '*our* fathers' as he draws them in, telling them their own story. Suddenly, though, the tone changes and he's saying '*your* fathers' (7:51). He's turned the story around and they've become the bad guys (7:51–53)! This is the worst thing anyone could ever say to them; utterly beyond comprehension and utterly 'blasphemous'. But it was true.

At times people (including ourselves!) act as if they are certain they know everything about God. However, sometimes God uses people we least expect and knocks us sideways with truth. In this story it's easy to associate ourselves with Stephen because he's the hero. Is God asking you to be a Stephen in some situation in life? Or is he asking you to hear truth from an unlikely source? Pray that he'll give you insight and humility.

The Bible in a year: Proverbs 1–2; Philippians 4

AUGUST 5–11

DAY 4 — Silver lining

Of course this doesn't always happen, but have you experienced something bad in life which, when you looked back, turned out to be really positive? Praise God for his intervention.

Acts 7:54–8:8

How could Stephen's death possibly be a good thing? He was clearly godly, gifted and acknowledged as a key player in the church community. When talking with the risen Jesus, the disciples were certainly excited about the power they would receive to be his witnesses (1:8), but perhaps persecution and death were not so high on their agenda (7:60; 8:1). Surely such suffering was a waste – yet it proved to be the channel for the glorious spreading of the richest truth. (This may prompt memories of someone else, see John 12:24.)

Looking back, we can see just how clever God is in helping the first Christians to do what he always intended. Persecution under Saul meant the early church had to run for their lives (8:1). Up until then the Christians' message had only been impacting the Jews in Jerusalem but now they had to go wherever they could and speak to whomever was there (8:4), with marvellous results (8:7–8). The message for the world goes out because the Christians simply *can't* stay at home. How frightening at the time, but how very clever of God!

Jesus clearly wasn't messing about when he asked his disciples if they were prepared for the consequences of following him (see Luke 14:27). Consider honestly before God how prepared you are to live for him and what you would be ready to die for. Ask him to give you purpose and courage to live in the light of that today.

The Bible in a year: Psalm 89; Proverbs 3–4

AUGUST 5–11

DAY 5

Whoosh …!

There's no stopping a ripple on a pond's surface once it's started. Thank God that there's also no stopping the coming of his kingdom now it's begun.

Acts 8:9–40

So far we've only been in Jerusalem but here we go … whoosh! … on to Samaria and the ends of the earth (see 1:8)!

Samaritans were of mixed blood and were a kind of half-way station between the Jews and the rest of the world, so were regarded as second-class people by the purist Jews. When Philip found the Samaritans accepting Christ (v 12), it must have been quite something for the apostles back home to hear about. Would the Jewish Christians accept the Samaritans as equal in Christ? True to all we've seen of them this week, the apostles didn't let prejudice get in the way of their obedience to God (vs 14–17).

This led to them really being on the move. Off went Philip, *clearly* guided by God (v 26), and God used him and the words of the prophet Isaiah to bring an Ethiopian eunuch into the kingdom (vs 34–36)! Despite his wealth and privilege the Ethiopian official was blind and imprisoned by his lack of understanding. Isn't this the most beautiful way of serving a fellow human being – opening their heart and mind to the wonders of God? How will they know unless someone explains (vs 30–31)? We are left in no doubt that the *Jewish* Christ is radically relevant for the *whole* world.

Thank God for opening your eyes and pray for the people he used to bring you to Christ. Then ask him if there's someone he wants to send you to. Remember, he may be especially interested in some people you might not even think of!

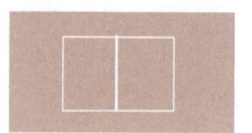

Consequences: Roman 10:5–15
Responsibility: Acts 28:23–28

The Bible in a year: Proverbs 5–6; Colossians 1

AUGUST 5–11

Going deeper …

Have you ever seen a huge, three-dimensional adult jigsaw puzzle? Imagine the most colourful, complex one possible. Imagine examining all the tiny pieces, holding each one carefully in your fingers, looking intently at its shape and the shape of those you've already placed. Where does this specific piece fit? Do you need others in place before you can find a home for this one? God has uniquely shaped each of us by giving us different gifts, perspectives and priorities. But not for our own benefit; rather to fit together like jigsaw pieces to build a beautiful and *complete* picture.

Read Acts 6:1–7 with this in mind. If you read this thinking you have nothing to offer, pray about who you could talk to. Perhaps your house group leader, a close friend or your minister could counsel you. God has given us *all* gifts and he yearns for you, to use yours. Imagine the frustration of missing a piece of the jigsaw. One tiny piece lost means the whole picture is spoiled.

I've had a strong sense of God wanting to speak into the West's individualistic culture. I believe he's saying that even we Christians can focus purely on ourselves ('me and my relationship with Jesus') rather than concentrating on being the interdependent *body* he designed us to be. Satan is holding us back from being the radical, effective, corporate witness of God we can only be together. 1 Corinthians 12 is a picture of an incredible, completed 'jigsaw'. Read it with your ears open to the Holy Spirit, then weigh what you hear and pray about what you think God might be saying.

Obedience not prejudice

Conclusion

It was wonderful to begin this week with the central truth: 'We must obey God rather than men' (5:29). Whatever the consequences and despite any preconceived ideas we might have, God has to come first. We cannot make up our minds about who God will touch or heal or who does or doesn't deserve to learn about God. It's totally up to him and yet he wants to do these things through us.

We must protect ourselves from assuming that we are the only ones who are blessed and called by God. Real faith, real worship involves having the priorities Christ had, doing the things he would have us do. His purpose in calling us to be his people was to preach good news to the poor, to proclaim freedom for prisoners, to recover sight for the blind, to release the oppressed … We're to seek an intimate relationship with God with our whole being and to pass on to others the beauty we find.

This week's snapshot of the early church in action should inspire us to reach out to *all* people as they did. To do this effectively we need to be radically Christlike, challenging the subtle tendency in all our lives to reject those who are different. We're designed to work as a body; lots of different-shaped pieces with different functions, all pulling together. This is what God *intends*.

Commit yourself to be obedient to God. Strive to embrace those different from yourself, engage with their world, and love them – for Jesus' sake.

The Bible in a year: Psalm 90; Proverbs 7–10; Philippians 4; Colossians 2

AUGUST 12–18

The perfect church

2 John; Titus

There's a well-known saying, 'If you ever find a perfect church, don't join it – you'll only spoil it!' As a Bible college student I had a pretty good idea of what my ideal church would be like. The trouble was, I couldn't find it anywhere. All the churches I tried seemed flawed in one way or another. At some churches the worship was wonderful but the teaching shallow. At others the welcome was warm but the worship less than enthusiastic. In the end I gave up 'floating' and plumped for the church I had started off at. I'd realised that churches are only as good as the people in them and if we want them to be better we have to get stuck in and make them better …

Letters like 2 and 3 John and Titus were written to people in imperfect churches. People like us. What we know as pastoral epistles were not written as comprehensive 'handbooks' on church life. Church life is worked out in face-to-face relationships, as the apostles Paul and John both knew (see Titus 3:12; 2 John 12). Church is something we *are*, not something we *do* (see 1 Corinthians 12:27). What Paul writes to Titus, and John to the 'chosen lady and her children' and to Gaius is advice tailored to the specific circumstances in which they find themselves. But the principles behind what they write are helpful for all of us who live with the joy – and pain – of church life.

This week, let's pray for discernment and for a new work of the Holy Spirit in our lives and churches. You can tell a healthy church because the life of Jesus shines through the lives of its members. May we all, with unveiled faces, reflect the Lord's glory and be transformed into his likeness with ever-increasing glory.

Mary Moody is the editor of *Closer to God* in the United Kingdom. She studied theology at London Bible College (where she met her youth worker husband, Andrew) and has worked for Scripture Union for four years.

AUGUST 12–18

DAY 1

An undiscerning church

'Grace, mercy and peace… will be with us in truth and love' (2 John 3). Meditate on these gifts from Jesus. What difference have they made to you?

2 John

By AD 90, when most of the original apostles had died off and John was a very old man, the church was in great danger of losing sight of the true gospel. There were lots of 'juicy', super-spiritual philosophies being peddled, some of which sounded like a development of the apostles' teaching, but for the more 'advanced' believer. One heresy that John was particularly concerned about said that Jesus was only temporarily the Christ or Son of God (v 7) – his divinity came on him at his baptism and left him again at the crucifixion. But if Jesus was not both God and man, how could his death have been effective for our salvation?

It is likely that 2 John was written to a local church, one that was inadvertently welcoming teachers of heresy. This church has members who are getting on well in their Christian lives (v 4), but their love for one another and their understanding of the gospel needs to be grounded in obedience to God (v 6). Our primary loyalty is always to him. If we jump on a super-spiritual bandwagon without first measuring any new teachings against what's revealed in Scripture, we may end up running ahead of Jesus' teaching (v 9), driving at breakneck speed in precisely the wrong direction. God's reward comes to those who persevere in the truth and do not give false teaching a foothold (vs 10–11).

Am I walking in the truth, in obedience and in love, or am I 'running ahead'?

The Bible in a year: Proverbs 11–12; Colossians 3

AUGUST 12–18

DAY 2

A warring church

'God is our refuge and strength … Be still, and know that I am God' (Psalm 46:1, 10). Calm your heart in God's presence.

3 John

Gaius was a 'dear friend' of John's who had benefited from his ministry (v 4). He was renowned for his hospitality towards visiting evangelists (vs 5–8). But walking in the truth (v 3) is an uphill struggle when you're caught in the middle of a warring church.

Diotrephes was an influential man – possibly a church leader – who had turned against John, and let everyone know it! He refused to allow any of John's co-workers a platform in the church (v 10). Diotrephes was a Christian and not a false teacher, but his powerful personality and desire for status had got out of hand (v 9). He was devouring fellow Christians to feed his own ego; destroying and scattering the sheep of God's pasture (see Jeremiah 23:1). Demetrius may well have been the messenger carrying this letter. While Diotrephes spreads his malicious lies about John, 'the truth itself' speaks well of Demetrius (v 12). The test of a person's heart is in their actions (v 11). Now Gaius must decide what action *he* will take. Will he stand up to the domineering Diotrephes by welcoming Demetrius and perhaps sharing the contents of John's letter with the 'friends' from within the congregation (v 14b), at risk of being thrown out of the church?

Christians too often find themselves in the middle of a warring church. If this rings bells with you, talk it over with God, asking him to search for and tend his scattered flock. Now pray: 'The Lord is my shepherd …' (Psalm 23:1).

The Bible in a year: Proverbs 13–14; Colossians 4

DAY 3

A compromised church

We should not let the world squeeze us into its mould. Today let's pray, 'Give me an undivided heart …' (Psalm 86:11).

Titus 1

Titus is another letter written by an apostle (Paul, v 1) to one of his spiritual children (Titus, v 4). It shares some common themes with 2 and 3 John: hospitality, faith and conduct, false teachers … All this in the context of a very young church (v 5), which was surrounded by a culture saturated in immorality (v 12). In Crete, Titus was to finish Paul's work of building a strong church from scratch. So, having thrown him in at the deep end, Paul writes to Titus with some guidelines.

In the shifting sands of a self-obsessed culture, Titus can rely on one thing: his relationship with God (v 2). In the context of the grace and peace he has received (v 4), he has been left alone to handle a volatile situation. Paul has charged him with appointing a leadership team strong enough to steer a church that was already compromised and had spent too much time listening to self-appointed leaders with destructive motives (vs 10–11). The elders, says Paul, will need to live transparently pure lives (vs 6–8) and preach the unadulterated gospel (v 9) in order to have the authority they need to rebuke the opposition within the church's own ranks (vs 13–16). However, if they cultivate the qualities listed in verse 8, allowing what is good to flourish in their lives, there will be little room for the weeds of domination, drunkenness, violence and manipulation (v 7).

Having an open home (v 8) encourages authentic, transparent relationships. Who could you ask round this week?

The Bible in a year: Proverbs 15–16; 1 Thessalonians 1

AUGUST 12–18

DAY 4

An immature church

Try meditating a while on the Jesus prayer: 'Lord Jesus Christ, Son of God, have mercy on me, a sinner.'

Titus 2

Christians should set an example by doing what is good (vs 7, 14; 3:8, 14). But first we need to recognise 'what is good' when we see it! The culture we grow up in moulds our perception of what is right and wrong. And where that culture is based on pagan values, or where all moral decisions are subjective (whatever feels right at the time), new Christians will have some relearning to do. This was exactly the situation of the young church in Crete. They were so used to lies, deception and Jewish myths (see 1:10, 12, 14) that they wouldn't recognise 'sound doctrine' (v 1) without the living visual aid provided by Titus.

With the new elders in place, Titus would be ready to lay some moral foundations for an immature church, with some straight-forward and hard-hitting teaching (v 15). This would have a knock-on effect throughout the church and society: the qualities to be exhibited by the various groups within the church are the complete opposite of those seen in the surrounding culture. Instead of lies, evil and gluttony (1:12) it was to be temperance, truth, integrity, love and self-control (vs 2–10). How would this transformation be possible? How would the church move from *recognising* what is good, to *doing* it? Only by the grace of God (vs 11–14).

We must never lose sight of God's mercy. If a pure life seems like an impossible dream to you, ask Jesus to be your teacher, day by day, hour by hour, minute by minute.

The Bible in a year: Psalm 91; Proverbs 17–18

AUGUST 12–18

DAY 5

A divided church

Jesus prayed for all believers: 'May they be brought to complete unity to let the world know that you sent me and have loved them even as you have loved me' (John 17:23). It is our task to make the love of Christ known. How is your church faring?

Titus 3

Like divorce, church splits can be an acrimonious business – and it's not just the central figures who get wounded in the fallout. Perhaps that is why Paul's language is so strong when he talks about divisive people in verses 9–11. We've all met them! And when we're tired or disillusioned, what they're saying about the church leadership or other members can sound awfully plausible ... But, hang on a minute, whatever happened to submitting to leaders, slandering no one and showing true humility (vs 1–2)?

Sometimes, realistically, the only way of achieving this is to shun troublemakers (v 10). They may also need warning that they are on a dangerous path: it is the peacemakers who 'will be called sons of God' (Matthew 5:9), and Jesus' prayer for all believers was, first and foremost, for unity (John 17:20–23). However, before we go wading in, we should remember our own weakness (v 3) and be sure to rebuke in a loving and non-judgemental way. Our motivation for doing what is good, and for speaking the truth, is not so that we can feel superior. It is our response of loving obedience to the kindness, the mercy and the rich generosity of God our Saviour.

Reread verses 4–8, pondering the significance of each phrase. The Holy Spirit's work in our life has made us heirs to a wonderful inheritance. Will we live like sons and daughters of the King of kings?

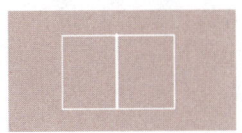

A healthy church: Ephesians 4:1–16
A radiant church: Ephesians 5:25–27; Revelation 19:6–9

The Bible in a year: Proverbs 19–20; 1 Thessalonians 2

Going deeper …

In the body of Christ, each of us has a leadership role. Whoever comes to Christ is called to lead others to Christ ('make disciples', Matthew 28:19). If this makes us feel inadequate, we shouldn't let it stop us! God is merciful (see Titus 3:3–7). Let's do some 'spring cleaning' now, allowing the Holy Spirit to explore the darkest corners of our lives. Set aside twenty minutes and make two lists from Titus 1:7–8 on two separate sheets of paper: one a list of habitual sins to conquer; the other a list of godly qualities to cultivate. If you can think of other things to add to either list, do that.

Pray through each item on the first list, asking God to highlight weaknesses in your life and confessing them to him one by one. As you receive his assurance that you are 'blameless' in his eyes through the saving work of Jesus, tear up your list of sins and ask for his strength to overcome future temptation. Read 1 Corinthians 10:13 and memorise it or write it on a piece of paper to keep with you.

Now pray through the second list, asking the Holy Spirit to 'grow' this fruit in your life. In some areas you will hear the Lord's encouragement. In others, you'll both know that there is plenty of room for improvement. But don't be discouraged. It is only the life of Christ within that enables us to live a Christ-like life. A Christ-filled life is an eternal, overflowing, flourishing, abundant life. And it is incredibly attractive to others. Invite the Holy Spirit to do his cleansing and empowering work and *be free!* The rest is in his hands.

Church life

Each of us who belongs to the body of Christ should reflect Christ's life. But it's God's intention that the greatest reflection of his glory should be seen when we come together. In Jesus, we are being 'built together to become a dwelling in which God lives by his Spirit' (Ephesians 2:22). However, false teachers and compromised lives, gossip, self-aggrandisement and divisiveness remain an ever-present threat to Christian unity. It shouldn't surprise us that the enemy's greatest ploy is to pit us one against the other. We know that 'the devil prowls around like a roaring lion looking for someone to devour' (1 Peter 5:8). What does a lion do when searching for prey? It tries to separate the weak and vulnerable from the rest of the herd and *then* pounces. We need to resist his tactics (see 1 Peter 5:9) and strive for unity.

Let's be vigilant, and learn to live a life of love and service within the church (Ephesians 5:25). Humility, honesty and hospitality go a long way towards building true fellowship. Whatever our current church situation, authentic face-to-face relationships are vital. We must not be afraid to 'tell it like it is', but always with an attitude of love. Truth and love go hand in hand.

As the children of God shine like stars in the darkness of a crooked and depraved generation, holding onto the word of life and living blameless, pure lives, others will be drawn to the light of Christ in us. Be the best you can be!

The Bible in a year: Psalm 92–93; Proverbs 21–24; 1 Thessalonians 3

AUGUST 19–25

Words of comfort

John 15–16

Rachel carried a floppy white rabbit everywhere, until she lost it. Daniel sucked a ragged corner of his blanket, until it was removed to the washing machine. Steven sucked a finger whilst twiddling his hair, until he outgrew the habit. Did you have a comforter to bring security from childhood fears? No doubt it's been put away in the cupboard with other childhood memorabilia. What comforter do you use now to bring security in the face of adult 'monsters': long hours at work, keeping fit, being well-insured, maintaining your home, evenings of drinking? Do these comforts work? Previous weeks' readings showed that Jesus has provided another Comforter (John 14:16, 26), who has life, personality and effective dynamism to help us in ways which no childhood (or adult) comforter could achieve. This Comforter is with us for ever; never to be lost, removed or outgrown.

This week, as you read, notice how Jesus names some monsters common to many of us: failure, barrenness, hatred, misunderstanding, confusion. He does so to encourage people just like us! Disciples, fearful of a future without Jesus. People in need of guidance about how to live for him in a world full of distractions and 'monsters'. Jesus speaks of his longing, and our need to stay close to him. See how persistent and focused love can be. Recognise that Jesus does not promise an easy life, but does equip us. Grasp his Comforter to pick you up when you stumble, aid your developing faith and enable you to walk with Jesus. Consider that the reasons he gives for this teaching are that you may avoid going astray, and learn how to deal with life circumstances which give you trouble and rob you of peace. Commit yourself to God's good purposes for your life as Jesus reassures you: 'Take heart! I have overcome the world' (John 16:33).

Ann Nias is married to Richard and they have two adult children. Her 'occupation' is the running of a mums' and toddlers' group, Alpha courses, woman's outreach and Bible study groups. Her hobbies include gardening, walking and embroidery.

AUGUST 19–25

DAY 1

Life that remains

Consider the ways in which you have grown since you became a Christian. Thank God for your progress.

John 15:1–8

I have inherited a huge, well-kept garden, which is a daunting responsibility. What needs pruning, and when? How do I look after fruit bushes? When should I replant onions? Is that plant dead or just resting? Who ate the hostas? Thankfully God the Gardener (v 1) is neither ignorant nor daunted by the task of producing good fruit (v 8) from the branches of the Vine. He is the expert in treating blight caused by sin, in pruning the straggly growth of waywardness, in nurturing those drooping flowers of good intentions and feeding the dry sticks of poor nourishment (vs 2–4). Sometimes the remedy seems drastic, like pruning (see Hebrews 12:11), but it is necessary to bring us into line, re-establishing healthy growth and fruit. During a dry spell we snap easily and feel in danger of being cut off from God but his injection of the Holy Spirit brings new life.

However, the real secret is that the Gardener talks to his plants (v 3)! We respond by depending totally on the life of Jesus, who calls it 'remaining in me', so that we resemble him and produce vine-like fruit. What does he promise to those who do so (vs 4–5, 7)? But look at the outcome for those who try to go it alone (vs 2, 5b–6)! What does it mean to you to remain in Jesus?

Prayerfully invite God to identify anything hindering your growth, blighting your attitudes, obstructing your fruitfulness, spoiling your relationship to the Vine. Ask him to remove them and renew the Spirit's flow. Consider any changes you could make to ensure closer contact with Jesus.

The Bible in a year: Proverbs 25–26; 1 Thessalonians 4

AUGUST 19–25

DAY 2

Love that remains

Rejoice in your status with Jesus. You are loved. You are his friend. You are forgiven. You are included in his plans.

John 15:9–17

In a world where love is a much maligned, mishandled and misunderstood commodity, can Jesus' perspective on love still be taken seriously? Unfashionably, he links love with obedience (vs 9–10) and joy (v 11), which are not the usual indicators. His route to joy is demanding territory, requiring that we copy Jesus' example. We obey God, like he did (v 10). We love others like he loved us (vs 12–13). Recall what this involved by reading Philippians 2:5–8 and Romans 5:8 thoughtfully. What humbling might be involved before you can love others in obedience to God, like Jesus did? There may be a cherished position, privilege or status you need to lay aside, or a habit or relationship which suggests disobedience and is blocking your joy.

Obedience and self-sacrifice may be unfashionable, but who would turn away from a way of life which guaranteed love and joy? We are privileged to be loved unconditionally, so loving others is not just an option, it is a command (vs 12–17). Jesus has *chosen* and *commanded* us to lead fruit-bearing lives (v 16). This fruit will look, and last, like the fruit of his own life, and will taste of forgiveness, unselfishness, patience and kindness, with a core of love.

Be honest with God about someone you currently have difficulty loving. Pray for them and for yourself, asking God to show you an appropriate opportunity to demonstrate love to them. This is initially an act of obedience, but Jesus says it is the path to joy.

The Bible in a year: Proverbs 27–28; 1 Thessalonians 5

AUGUST 19–25

DAY 3

Truth that remains

Do I doubt the existence of dolphins just because I have never seen one? Does electricity really pass from switch to light bulb, even when I can't see it doing so? Is a fact less true because someone refuses to believe it? Jesus said, '… blessed are those who have not seen and yet have believed' (20:29). Thank God that he has brought you from unbelief to faith.

John 15:18–16:4

I remember attending a wedding where some of the guests were emboldened by alcohol before the service began. Their sniggering, shuffling silence during the hymns, and open derision of the minister's words made it an uncomfortable occasion for me. I guess they were uncomfortable too; uncomfortable with the house of God, the man of God and the message of God – just like the people in today's reading (15:21). Don't be discouraged if you experience opposition as a believer, because you are being treated as Jesus expects you to be (16:2–3) and like he was treated (15:18–20). Jesus understands how tough it can be to be ostracised at work or criticised at home and is concerned that we keep on track in spite of it (16:1), with the help of the 'Spirit of truth' (15:26).

Jesus said, 'Blessed are you when people insult you, persecute you and falsely say all kinds of evil against you because of me. Rejoice and be glad, because great is your reward in heaven' (Matthew 5:11–12).

Take heart! The truth of Jesus remains the truth even though some people known to you do not believe it. Pray for them often, but just now encourage yourself by listing some of the truths about Jesus which you believe, and thank him for each one.

The Bible in a year: Proverbs 29–30; 2 Thessalonians 1

AUGUST 19–25

DAY 4

The Helper who remains

Different versions of today's passage call the Holy Spirit 'the Comforter', 'the Helper', 'the Counsellor' or 'the Friend'. What do these names suggest to you of the Holy Spirit's work? Meditate on them for a while.

John 16:5–16

What could possibly be better than having Jesus alongside you in person? What could be worse than him leaving you? This dilemma brought grief to the disciples when Jesus announced he was leaving (vs 5–6). Yet Jesus makes the amazing claim that 'It is for your good that I am going away' (v 7). God's plan is much bigger than people's cleverest contrivance. No longer would Jesus' impact be confined to those who lived within easy reach of Galilee at a certain period in history; now he would inhabit believers worldwide, living inside them by the dispersal of the Holy Spirit to each one.

In verses 8–11 Jesus speaks of sending the Spirit to convict us of sin, righteousness and judgement. Look at the verbs he uses to convey the activities of the Holy Spirit ('guide', 'speak', 'hear', 'tell', 'bring', vs 13–15). Consider examples in your own life of the Spirit's activities as described here: guiding your mind to understand the truth; listening to God then speaking his words to you; telling you of future events in God's plan; bringing glory to Jesus in an amazing way!

Peter writes of Jesus, 'His divine power has given us everything we need for life and godliness …' (2 Peter 1:3). Jesus emphasises, 'the Spirit will take from what is mine and make it known to you' (v 15). Ask the Holy Spirit to dispatch everything you need today from the storehouse of Jesus.

The Bible in a year: Psalm 94; Proverbs 31

AUGUST 19–25

DAY 5

Joy that remains

Spend a few minutes meditating on these verses about joy: 1 Thessalonians 5:16; Galatians 4:15 and Psalm 51:11–12.

John 16:17–33

The disciples are confused by Jesus' words and grieved by his imminent departure (vs 17–18), but Jesus predicts an outbreak of joy (vs 20, 22, 24).

The disciples thought joy was based on Jesus' presence with them, so the prospect of his departure robbed them of their joy. Jesus confirms that our joy is indeed based upon his presence in our lives, rather than how our lives are progressing, therefore it is undisturbed by circumstances or people: 'no one will take away your joy' (v 22). But he also confirms that periods of joylessness are part of the Christian experience (vs 21–22) and are meant to achieve a purpose (see also James 1:2–4), after which joy will be restored.

Perhaps you are in a joyless phase now. If so, what has robbed you of your joy? You may have been too busy or preoccupied to keep in touch with God. Maybe sin has crept in and you have not yet asked his forgiveness. Jesus is always seeking to develop new depth in us. Having a personal relationship with him where we daily read his Word to be inspired, depend on the Spirit to be enabled, and talk to God, hearing his answers, will fuel our joy because we will know that Jesus is with us.

Lack of joy can lead to a formidable guilt trip for Christians, but remember how Jesus was aware of the same problem in his disciples. Turn to him now, concentrating on his presence instead of your failings, and ask him to restore or increase your joy.

Chosen to bear fruit: Galatians 5:22–23
A chosen people: 1 Peter 2:9–12

The Bible in a year: Ecclesiastes 1–3; 2 Thessalonians 2

AUGUST 19–25

Going deeper …

'You did not choose me, but I chose you' (John 15:16). How often does your junk mail announce that you have been 'chosen' to receive a prize? By the time you've read the small print, you don't expect to receive anything. But to be chosen to play in a team, offered promotion, or asked your opinion does make a difference, often changing your perception of yourself and your environment. How much more significant, then, to discover you have been chosen by God (Ephesians 1:3–6).

- You are precious … wanted … included … valued.
- You can feel involved … secure … purposeful … content.
- You need never feel rejected … excluded … worthless.
- We are not chosen on the basis of merit (1 Corinthians 1:26–30).
- We are not influential (v 26), but Jesus' death is.
- We are not clever (v 26), but Jesus is our wisdom.
- We are not strong, but weak (v 27).
- We have nothing to offer, but God has everything (vs 28–30).
- Jesus has become 'our righteousness, holiness and redemption' (v 30).

Pause and 'think of what you were when you were called'. Make a 'before and after' list. This is your testimony what it means to be chosen by God.

The challenge

In the Bayeux tapestry, Bishop Odo is famously depicted as 'comforting' his men, stirring them into action with the end of his stick because as a man of God he was not allowed to use a sword! The Bible is the sword of the Spirit (Ephesians 6:17). Have the readings this week challenged you into action? There has been the challenge to stay close to Jesus; to love one another sacrificially; to continue to believe in spite of opposition; to rely on the Holy Spirit to develop the life of Jesus in you, and to base your joy on Jesus' presence with you.

We have not focused on Jesus' promises about prayer, but note the generosity of his offers that God will give us whatever we ask for as long as we live in close obedience and friendship with him (John 15:7, 16; 16:23–24). Allow this privilege to energise and encourage you. Spend time dwelling on these final words of Jesus: 'I have told you these things, so that in me you may have peace. In this world you will have trouble. But take heart! I have overcome the world' (John 16:33).

Think about how the things you've learnt can help you 'in this world' today. How can Jesus' words be of practical significance in your daily life? Highlight one of those 'things' which has especially caught your attention this week: perhaps to try a new way of staying close and 'remaining' in the Vine; or setting aside time to pray for those you know who do not share your faith. Resolve to work on it with Jesus, so that in him 'you may have peace'.

The Bible in a year: Ecclesiastes 4–7; 2 Thessalonians 3

AUGUST 26–SEPTEMBER 1

State of the heart

As a child, visiting Scotland's Sweetheart Abbey, I was fascinated by the ancient story of the crusader who died fighting for Jerusalem. Friends placed his heart in a golden casket and brought it home to his wife who built the Abbey around it. 'Why didn't they bring all of his body?' I asked ghoulishly. 'His heart represented all that he was on the inside,' was my grandmother's reply. She was using the word 'heart' as the NIV does; not to describe the pump behind our ribs but the part of us that thinks, feels, makes decisions and reaches for God.

We spend so much time caring for our outward, physical bodies, but it's our hearts God notices. Remember how the old priest, Samuel, was sent to Farmer Jesse to pick one of his sons as the next king? Their muscles dazzled Samuel as they lined up – seven gorgeous hunks – but God said, 'Man looks at the outward appearance, but the Lord looks at the heart' (1 Samuel 16:7). God could see the selfishness and pride behind the sun-tanned smiles. He wanted 'a man after his own heart' (1 Samuel 13:14), someone who would think, feel and act as he would. So Jesse finally sent for his youngest, and least favoured son, David. This shepherd may not have been as handsome as his big brothers, but one of his songs explains why he was chosen. 'The Lord is my strength and my shield; my heart trusts in him … My heart leaps for joy and I will give thanks to him in song' (Psalm 28:7).

So, this week, let's explore what the Bible says about this inside part of us it calls our heart and discover how we, too, can be people 'after God's own heart'.

Jennifer Rees Larcombe runs a Christian charity called Beauty from Ashes which aims to help people who face bereavement trauma, rejection and loss of any kind. She is an agony aunt and has published twenty-three books. She has six children and loves gardening.

DAY 1 — Pure heart

'Above all else, guard your heart, for it is the wellspring of life' (Proverbs 4:23). That was the text of a sermon that made a huge impact on me. We were all asked to close our eyes and ask God to show us a picture of our hearts. I 'saw' my heart, inside my chest, totally drained of blood because a knife had ripped it open. Startled, I went for prayer ministry and faced the pain I had been suppressing after a friend's betrayal. I also realised my lack of forgiveness was draining my spiritual life dry. The 'picture', although disturbing, ultimately brought healing. Could you dare to stop and ask the Holy Spirit to show you how your heart looks at the moment?

Psalm 24

Imagine David, sitting on a hillside, revelling in all God had made (vs 1, 2); longing to be close to the Creator but feeling unworthy (v 3). What do you think it means to be pure in heart (v 4)?

The Bible uses the word 'pure' most often in connection with gold, which has to be heated in a crucible until all the rubbish surfaces and can be skimmed off. Perhaps a pure heart is one that has no selfish motives, no sin it refuses to relinquish, and which loves unconditionally and unreservedly – as God loves.

David longed for a pure heart but, like the rest of us, he messed up badly on occasions. We cannot make our own hearts pure. We constantly need to ask for God's help as David did. Why not 'borrow' some of his prayers? 'Search me, O God, and know my heart … Create in me a pure heart, O God' (Psalm 139:23, 51:10).

The Bible in a year: Ecclesiastes 1–3; 1 Timothy 1

AUGUST 26 – SEPTEMBER 1

DAY 2

Contrite heart

A friend who asked the Lord to show her a picture of her heart, 'saw' an X-ray of a healthy-looking heart, but in one corner was a dark area of disease. 'I'll never have a pure heart,' she said sadly. 'I have so many weaknesses and failings.' Many of us who feel the same will find today's reading encouraging! Yesterday we were told it was the pure in heart who can live close to God in his holy place. As you read today, look out for another group who are just as welcome there …

Isaiah 57

Did you notice who are the people who can share God's holy place (v 15)? He knows consistent purity is impossible for us humans, but repentance makes us fit for his presence. In this passage God's heart is breaking over his people who constantly refuse to honour and obey him or love their neighbours as much as themselves. Instead they had turned to the occult (v 3), idol worship (v 6), ritual child sacrifice (v 5), orgies (v 8) and cynicism towards all that is good (v 4). In spite of all this, God's heart still yearns for them and is full of compassion (vs 13c, 18–19) and forgiveness (v 16).

Perhaps, like my friend with the X-rayed heart, you feel discouraged by all the mistakes, faulty thinking and bad habits that dog you constantly. So often we feel we must clean up our inner mess before coming close to God. He wants us to open our hearts to him, mess and all, and ask him right into the middle of that mess. Only then can he clean us up and make us pure enough to enter his presence. Will you do that today?

The Bible in a year: Ecclesiastes 10–11; 1 Timothy 2

AUGUST 26–SEPTEMBER 1

DAY 3

Ambitious heart

What drives you through life? The desire to succeed, find love, gain respect, be perfect, change the world, help others …? In today's passage the 'heart' is revealed as the engine that drives and motivates our plans. We all need goals, but the reason we make them is all-important. Hidden motives lie behind all our major life-decisions.

Imagine you had reached the end of your life. What would you most like to have achieved, and why would that give you pleasure?

Proverbs 16:1–25

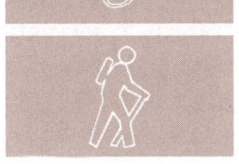

What do verses 1–3, 9 and 25 have in common? So many of these major life-plans are made because we want to feel good about ourselves. We think, 'I'll be a worthwhile person when I succeed.' 'I'll be safe if I find someone to love me.' 'Caring for others will win me respect and approval.' 'I'll be secure if I have plenty of money.' We forget that God longs for us to find our worth and security in him. Verses 5, 18 and 19 talk about proud hearts. We all know pride is a sin, but sin is a declaration of independence, the 'I'll do it my way' syndrome. Our self-confidence grows when we achieve our goals but self-confidence is just another word for pride. It is God-confidence we need; his approval is all that counts (v 7).

When you feel discouragement, stress and frustration, could it be because you are aiming at impossible goals that you, or someone else, have set rather than the agenda God has for your life? Are you trying to meet some deep need in your own heart or fulfil another person's hopes? When our greatest desire is simply to do our best to please God, life becomes as simple and enjoyable as he intended it to be.

The Bible in a year: Ecclesiastes 12; 1 Timothy 3

AUGUST 26–SEPTEMBER 1

DAY 4

Hard heart

Alf was a jack of all trades – builder, gardener, handyman and a good friend to me throughout my childhood. 'Alf, why are your hands hard, like leather gloves?' I asked him once. 'Years of blisters, cuts and bruises,' he replied. 'My skin's grown so thick nothing hurts anymore.'

Hearts can grow hard like Alf's hands. The Bible calls these 'calloused' hearts (see Isaiah 6:10). When people or events hurt us badly, we may grow new, tough skin over the wound. The more knocks life gives us the thicker our protective layers become. They keep us safe from further pain but they also separate us from others. A calloused heart is no longer soft and warm enough to love and receive love in return. Would you say that the painful events of your life have softened or hardened your heart?

Ezekiel 36:24–30

Years of abuse, rejection and victimisation had made Ann very hard. 'No one's ever going to get close enough to hurt me again,' she would say – but then she met Jesus. 'I want to love people like he does,' she said, 'but I never learned how to love and who could possibly forgive the stuff people did to me?' Today's passage helped her. She realised her heart was encased in stone so, humanly speaking, forgiveness was impossible. She needed a total heart transplant (v 26). Even a new heart was not enough – she also needed the Holy Spirit to guide and empower her (v 27).

Count the number of times the words 'I will' occur in the passage. What are you struggling to change about yourself? Are you trying to do this in your own strength? Which of these 'I wills' could you take as a personal promise to you?

The Bible in a year: Psalm 97–98; Song of Songs 1–2

AUGUST 26–SEPTEMBER 1

DAY 5

Praying heart

When you watch the TV news do you pray for the individuals involved in all those disasters? Or do you think, 'What difference could my puny prayer make?' We all underestimate the power of prayer. It is our greatest weapon against evil. It is also the best way of helping our family, friends, church and national leaders. Most of us believe that in our heads – but do you believe it in your heart by regularly acting on your convictions?

Lamentations 2:13–19

Time after time God's people turned away from him, got into trouble, then repented and returned – only to reject him yet again. Finally they refused to listen to the warnings of his prophets, and their land was left in ruins by enemy invaders (v 16). Yet God's heart was still so full of compassion that he sent a prophet to urge them to pray for the innocent children suffering in the national disaster (v 19). When my grandmother died, her minister, searching for inspiration for his funeral address, picked up her well-worn Bible. It fell open at today's passage and he noticed that verse 19 was heavily underlined. She prayed for her seven children and twenty-one grandchildren by name, daily, and always worked right through the list when she was unable to sleep at night. And how we have all benefited!

Look again at verse 19. Praying is not simply repeating words. If our 'heart' represents our thoughts, emotions, desires and personality, then pouring it out like water in God's presence means praying with all that we are; using our feelings, intelligence, willpower, creativity and spiritual energy. Are you concerned about someone you love? Then pour your heart out to God on their behalf.

Broken heart: Isaiah 61:1–3; Luke 4:14–22
God's heart: Isaiah 40:1–15

The Bible in a year: Song of Songs 3–4; 1 Timothy 4

Going deeper ...

At a conference for the wives of church leaders I challenged everyone to ask the Holy Spirit to show them a picture of their hearts. 'I saw a bruised, battered football, kicked between opposing sides in my church,' one of them told me. Another saw a porcelain ornament smashed by repeated hammer-blows. A woman who had recently been bereaved, couldn't see her heart at all – only an empty space where it used to be.

Before the days of computers, the captain of a ship at sea would always check his instruments, and note down his exact position at least once every twenty-four hours; drifting off course onto reefs or sand banks could be fatal. Whilst endless introspective 'naval gazing' is not helpful, I believe we should all check the position of our hearts regularly. The Holy Spirit can only convict us of sin if we give him permission to show it to us; we need prompt healing from the wounds others inflict if they are not to fester. Anger, resentment and self-pity must be dealt with quickly (Ephesians 4:26b) or they turn to bitterness and pollute our hearts more thoroughly than anything else can. So don't be afraid of asking for that snapshot of your heart.

When the prophet Elisha visited Jericho he was told that the water supply was dangerously polluted. He asked for some salt, and threw a handful down the well, after which the water was pure and sweet (see 2 Kings 2:19–22). If our hearts are 'the wellspring of life' (Proverbs 4:23), perhaps we should ask God to throw in a 'handful of salt' every time we feel hurt, angry or sorry for ourselves!

Forgiving heart

Conclusion

What does it mean to have a heart like God's? Recently, an old gentleman in a retirement home proudly showed me childhood photos of the son he adored. 'I would give him anything, but I haven't seen him for years,' he told me, tears filling his eyes. 'He got upset with me and I can't seem to put it right.' The anguish in his voice reminded me of the picture of God's breaking heart in Hosea 11. 'When Israel was a child, I loved him ... But the more I called to him, the more he turned away from me ... Yet I ... taught Israel to walk. I took my people up in my arms, but they did not acknowledge that I took care of them. I drew them to me with affection and love. I picked them up and held them to my cheek; I bent down to them and fed them ... How can I give you up, Israel? How can I abandon you? ... My heart will not let me do it! My love for you is too strong' (Hosea 11:1–8, GNB).

Because God so longs to lavish love, forgiveness and grace on us, he prizes these qualities in us. We think that the worst sins we can commit are murder, adultery or pride. Yet nowhere does the Bible say that if we commit these sins we will be cut off from God's forgiveness, although Jesus makes it clear that when we close our hearts to others and refuse to forgive we ourselves cannot expect forgiveness. Our failure to love others devastates the heart of God, because love is at the very centre of his being and he longs that love will also be at the centre of ours.

The Bible in a year: Psalm 99–101; Song of Songs 5–8; 1 Timothy 5

SEPTEMBER 2–8

Tantalising glimpses

Zechariah

Looking forwards and backwards simultaneously is what you have to do when you read Zechariah.

The backward look takes you to the sixth century BC; to the time of the Jewish exile in Babylon; to King Cyrus' liberation edict that spurred the return to Jerusalem; to King Darius' edict to rebuild the Temple in Jerusalem; and to the promises given through Zechariah which inspired and motivated the returnees.

Zechariah takes us to a time six centuries before the coming of Christ. From our perspective we are able to understand his messianic prophecies, and how they were fulfilled in Christ.

The *forward* look focuses our sights on the future; on the second coming of Christ – that glorious and mystical time when Christ returns to usher in the kingdom of God in its fullness.

Zechariah, along with Haggai and Micah – the three 'post-exilic prophets' – inspires and motivates the Israelites with the end vision of the glorious restoration of God's rule amongst them. The honour of the Lord was bound up with the rebuilding of the temple. For the Jews, to rebuild the temple was both an act of dedication and an act of faith. It symbolised the continuity of the present with the past, and expressed the longing of the community that the old covenant should still stand.

This week's readings cover eight visions given to Zechariah. Each offers a tantalising glimpse of what could be, if God were allowed to reign completely in their lives and communities. The message is as relevant for us in Africa today as it was then.

Jeremy Clampett is the National Director of Scripture Union in South Africa. He and his wife, Jenny, have four children.

SEPTEMBER 2–8

DAY 1

Jealousy

Before God gave his visions of future protection and plenty, there was one matter that had to be put straight. What was it? See verse 3. None of us can work for God without first restoring our relationship with him.

Zechariah 1:1–21

Zechariah is shown four riders on four differently coloured horses, standing among the myrtle trees in a ravine. Where have they been (v 11) and what clue does this give us of how God's concern for this world differs from the parochial view of the Israelites?

Zechariah then sees four horns followed by four craftsmen, whose business is terror and destruction. They symbolise the power of God. The surrounding nations are going to be routed by God's forces, predicts Zechariah.

God expresses his feelings for Jerusalem. What are they (v 14)? Jealousy or zeal (which have the same root) is an evil force when it considers only ourselves. Jealousy which considers others is a strong, positive force. God loves us so much that he cannot remain indifferent to indifference towards him. God is jealous of our loyalty, love and allegiance.

This passage shows that God has not abandoned his covenant with his people. Years later, he established a new covenant.

Peter explains this in 1 Peter 2:9: 'But you are a chosen people, a royal priesthood, a holy nation, a people belonging to God …' All who know and follow Christ are people of the new covenant, and can appropriate all the promises given through Zechariah.

Examine your relationship with God in the light of today's reading. Do you need to respond as the Israelites did in verse 6?

The Bible in a year: Isaiah 1–2; 1 Timothy 6

DAY 2

All we'll ever need

A believer who was plunged into poverty made the comment, 'I never realised what it meant to trust Jesus, until Jesus was all I had.' Zechariah promises a prosperous future, but it will be achieved through exercising complete faith and trust, not caution. There is no place for timidity when we determine to serve God.

Zechariah 2:1–13

The measuring line, already referred to in chapter 1:16, is stretched out over Jerusalem – but it is not going to be needed (v 4). The 'young man' holding the measuring line, the first step in the sensible process of building the walls to protect Jerusalem, is told that the walls are not going to be necessary. Why? Find two reasons in verses 4 and 5.

If ever there was a bright vision of the future, this was it! Jerusalem is promised prosperity (v 4), protection (v 5a), prestige (v 5b) and God's presence (v 11b). Zechariah makes another prediction that probably didn't sit too well with the nationalistic instincts of the Israelites. What is this overlooked promise (v 11a)? And what does it tell of God's heart for the surrounding nations?

Consider all the 'sensible' plans you have for your life in the light of the promises of God, and surrender them to him. Is it possible that your holding on to what you have and know, is preventing you from experiencing the abundance of God's blessing?

The Bible in a year: Isaiah 3–5; 2 Timothy 1

SEPTEMBER 2–8

DAY 3

Snatched from the fire

Have you ever felt unworthy of the task God has given you? As leader of Scripture Union in South Africa, I am constantly tempted to feel inadequate. Today's reading helps me realise that it is the false accusations of Satan that cause these negative feelings.

Zechariah 3:1–10

When we undertake a leadership role, or some project for the Kingdom, we must first be commissioned by God and cleansed by the power of his Spirit.

Joshua was given the office of High Priest, but just wearing the robes wasn't enough. There first had to be a deep inner transformation (v 4b) – he had to be anointed by the Holy Spirit for his leadership task.

Satan is the 'accuser' (v 1) of the faithful. The text doesn't specify his accusations, but he was probably pointing out all Joshua's past sins, and suggesting that he was way too sinful for priesthood.

Satan was absolutely correct – Joshua was way too sinful. Likewise, each of us provides more than enough convincing evidence of our unsuitability to be a child of God, let alone be a leader in his church.

But God has dealt with our sin and Joshua's, and Satan's accusations are meaningless. If we have allowed God's redeeming work in our lives, we, like Joshua, have been 'snatched from the fire' of judgement (v 2). Miraculously, when God looks at us, he doesn't see our sinfulness. To him, we are dressed in 'rich garments'. What a gracious God!

If the picture of peace and kingdom-rule in verse 10 appeals to you, pray for its realisation throughout Africa, this continent of conflict.

The Bible in a year: Isaiah 6–7; 2 Timothy 2

DAY 4

By my Spirit

God's work can only be done in God's way, and in his power. This is the message for Zerubbabel. It echoes the words of Psalm 127:1, 'Unless the Lord builds the house, its builders labour in vain.'

Zechariah 4:1–14

Zerubbabel is commissioned for his task of building the temple, as Joshua, in the previous chapter, was commissioned for his high priestly task. Zerubbabel is encouraged by the picture of him laying the cornerstone of the temple to the cheers of the people (v 7), and by the promise that his hands will both lay the foundations and complete the task (vs 8–10). The plumb-line in Zerubbabel's hand is the final act of the builder as the building is completed.

When God calls us to work for him, he makes all his resources available to us. More amazing, he sees in us the potential to achieve 'greater works' than his Son achieved on earth (John 14:12). God sees more in us than we see in ourselves. Look at the picture of Joshua and Zerubbabel (the two olive trees) – standing alongside the lampstand directly connected to its flow of energising oil (v 11). What impact do you think this had on them?

These verses are for anyone who has been called to serve God, but has lost heart. Do not despise 'the day of small things (beginnings)' (v 10). Let God show you the final outcome, and keep persevering.

Consider the challenges of your own calling, and repeat these words: "Not by might, nor by power, but by my Spirit," says the Lord Almighty' (v 6). Ask the Spirit to apply this to your own situation.

The Bible in a year: Psalm 102; Isaiah 8–9

SEPTEMBER 2–8

DAY 5

Under reconstruction

God is alive and active today, transforming lives and communities – as he did in Zechariah's day. He is still rooting out sin, setting his standards of right-living, sending his Spirit and restoring his church.

Zechariah 5:1–6:14

These last four, larger-than-life visions all indicate God's plans and purposes for his chosen people.

The flying scroll reminds me of a sky-banner over Newlands, huge and unavoidable. The words on the scroll proclaim the *standards* God expects amongst his people. Notice the sins he targets (5:3) – theft and dishonesty: seemingly petty in comparison with the more serious crimes of hijacking, rape and murder that plague South African society. God's policy of zero tolerance of even 'minor' sins indicates how high his standards are.

The woman in the basket is an *emblem of sin* (5:8). She is banished to Babylon (5:11), where wickedness is tolerated. God's desire is to banish sin wherever it takes root.

The four chariots (6:1–8) picture the *power* of the Spirit of God sent to all corners of the globe, which under the new covenant has great significance after Pentecost.

The crown for Joshua (6:9–15) elevates the status of the priesthood, and blends the functions of priest and king (v 12b), and pictures the restoration of his church. Up to then, the roles of prophet, priest and king were separated, following tribal descent. Zechariah is predicting that the priests, and not the prophets, will in future lead the people, which is exactly what happened.

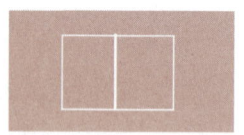

Fasting: Zechariah 7:1–14
Feasting: Zechariah 8:1–23

The Bible in a year: Isaiah 10–12; 2 Timothy 3

SEPTEMBER 2–8

Going deeper …

Repentance is changing our mind about God, ourselves and our sin. Zechariah's appeal to the Israelites is that they change their minds, repent, and be transformed by the renewing of their minds. The future looked bright for God's people – in the short term. The temple was later destroyed, and the rule of God ended. There was, and is, a solution. If the people of God had truly repented, everything would have been different.

Concerning God: they needed to realise how much he loved them, and how much grace and mercy he was (and always is) ready to shower on them.

Concerning themselves: they needed to realise that God saw enormous potential for good in them, and that when they drew close to God, he was able to use them for his work. God had a recipe for life which, if followed, would result in unprecedented blessing.

Concerning sin: they needed to recognise that sin was destroying the world, blackening the name and honour of God, and breaking his heart. They needed to accept that the problem of the sickness in the world lay within themselves.

The enduring message of Zechariah is still pertinent today. God's plan (Zechariah 8:20–23) was that his people should have a longing for him that would draw all nations to God. It remains God's purpose through his chosen people of the new covenant, who include Christ-followers in South Africa today.

Never the same again

Conclusion

The captivity was over. Cyrus had established the great Persian Empire, which had swallowed the Babylonian Empire and its king, Nebuchadnezzar. After Cyrus's untimely death, the crown had passed to Darius who, in his first months, had affirmed Cyrus's decree concerning the return of the exiles and the rebuilding of the temple. God used Darius's political motives for his own glory. Zerubbabel, the builder, and Joshua, the High Priest, were the men appointed to rebuild the temple, the outward symbol of the restoration of God's rule in their lives and communities.

In contrast to the pre-exilic prophets (e.g. Jeremiah, Amos) to whom God gave a message of curses and threats, the post-exilic prophets (including Zechariah) were given a message promising salvation and blessing. Such is the grace of God. His love flows from him either in *judgement* or in *mercy*. Which do you think is more relevant for South Africa today? Are we heading into, or out of, exile? Do we need warnings to heed, or promises to inspire us? Are we in the time of judgement or the time of mercy?

Sadly, the Israelites never realised their bright future. The temple, a smaller one, was built, but later destroyed, and the Northern Kingdom disappeared. God's rule over the two nations was gone for ever. Was Zechariah wrong in painting a rosy picture of a glorious future that did not materialise? No, his vision extended to Christ coming as man to live on earth, and even to the final ushering in of his kingdom.

The Bible in a year: Psalm 103; Isaiah 13–16; 2 Timothy 4

SEPTEMBER 9–15

Visions of destiny

These chapters – apocalyptic oracles concerning the future age – are probably the most mystifying passages of Scripture. I heard of a minister who, beginning his sermon series on Zechariah, admitted to his congregation that he 'didn't have a clue' what Zechariah was all about! He was referring to these last few chapters which we will read this week.

The first three chapters deal with Israel as a nation, outlining God's intentions for them. The second three deal with the international scene, and outline Israel's overlooked and never achieved international mission. These messages are divine revelations or 'oracles' which can also be translated as 'burdens'. This hints at the reason why the prophets brought such unpopular messages – they couldn't help themselves, they were merely divine messengers. The messages are also messianic. Jesus' entry into Jerusalem, his arrest, and his death are all foretold here.

The battle scenes show the catastrophe that will befall the Israelites on the military battlefield, but there is a victory won on the battlefield of human hearts, a victory that will signify the end of history. The political inter-play between rival nations takes on cosmic proportions, with the players being powers and principalities in the spiritual realm. Only the divine intervention of God will secure the victory. This will be the 'Day of the Lord' – a phrase mentioned fourteen times in the last three chapters – and when it comes, this world as we know it will be no more.

The nationalistic yearnings of the Israelites are shown to be inadequate. One cannot belong to the Kingdom of God by descent – only those who have allied themselves to the Lord will be saved. All who have defied God will perish. This is a powerful message to the people of South Africa today.

Jeremy Clampett is the National Director of Scripture Union in South Africa. He and his wife, Jenny, have four children.

SEPTEMBER 9–15

DAY 1

Jewels in a crown

Christ's victory is certain, and his intention is to draw continually to himself people who are alienated from him. Praise God for his power and grace.

Zechariah 9:1–17

Zechariah's oracle against several cities starts from the north – Hadrach (v 1) is the northernmost city mentioned – and the oracle works its way south until it rests on God's favourite, Jerusalem (v 9). With the exception of Judea, each of these cities and nations was destroyed, as predicted, by Alexander the Great in 330 BC and the years that followed.

The prophecy of the king entering Jerusalem on a donkey (v 9) is one of the clearest messianic prophecies in scripture, with its fulfilment recorded in the gospels (Matthew 21:5). The Passover crowds immediately saw the messianic significance of Jesus entering Jerusalem on a donkey, indicating that this messianic expectation was well known and accepted at that time.

The bright future of a rebuilt temple and a restored Jerusalem fades against the much brighter prospect of the rule of Christ in our lives and the coming of the Kingdom of God.

Reflect on verse 16: 'The Lord their God will save them on that day as the flock of his people. They will sparkle in his land like jewels in a crown'. How has this prophecy been fulfilled in your own life?

The Bible in a year: Isaiah 17–20; Titus 1

SEPTEMBER 9–15

DAY 2

Completely restored

The African proverb claims that a fish rots from the head down. If the leadership is rotten, the people will suffer.

Zechariah 10:1–11:3

The leaders – or shepherds – are condemned in verse 2. Clearly the people had suffered because of the weak leadership given by those meant to be the pastoral leaders. This is a challenge and a rebuke to anyone in a pastoral or leadership role.

Fortunately, God can overcome any human failing, and his promises in verse 6 to 'strengthen the house of Judah' (representing the Southern Kingdom) and 'save the house of Joseph' (representing the Northern Kingdom) stood firm, despite their lacklustre leadership. This was fulfilled by the amalgamation of the remnant of the exiles into one nation.

Here 'Judah' and 'Joseph' are a combined metaphor for the coming Kingdom of God, ushered in by Jesus. The prophetic arsenal issuing from Judah: the cornerstone, peg, battle-bow, ruler (v 4), also prefigure Jesus the Messiah. The peg may refer to the nail or hook in each Jewish home on which the items of most value were hung. The battle-bow illustrates the strength of our Lord. Passages like this hint at why the first century Jews anticipated a militaristic messiah, but with hindsight we can see how perfectly they describe his strength and power over sin and the forces of evil. The familiar metaphor of Jesus as the cornerstone is reminiscent of Psalm 118:22: 'The stone which the builders rejected is become the head-stone of the corner.'

When Jesus saves, he saves completely. Reflect on verse 6: 'They will be as though I had not rejected them', and thank God for the complete salvation he offers us.

The Bible in a year: Isaiah 21–22; Titus 2

SEPTEMBER 9–15

DAY 3

Good beats evil

Our battle is not against flesh and blood, but against the powers and principalities in the heavenly realms.

Zechariah 11:4–17

This oracle foretells Israel's dispersion in AD 32 and captivity by the Romans in AD 70. It paints the picture of Israel (the flock in verse 4) being sold out to occupying powers (the buyers in verse 5) by their worthless leaders (the sellers in verse 5).

A good shepherd takes over the flock in verse 7 and pastors them, saving them from slaughter and caring especially for the oppressed, suggesting the later saving work of Jesus, the Great Shepherd. The good shepherd in verse 7 uses two staffs – 'Favour' and 'Union', which suggest Christ's character (grace) and purpose (unity).

But the good shepherd is rejected (v 8b), as Christ was, and the flock sinks into self-induced destruction (v 9). God's grace is rejected (pictured in the breaking of the staff called 'Favour' (v 10), resulting in separation and disunity (pictured in the breaking of the other staff, 'Union' (v 14).

A foolish shepherd then takes over the flock (vs 15, 16), prefiguring the activity of Satan, whom we know as the 'Prince of this world'. Fortunately, Satan's ultimate destruction is foretold in verse 17. In a few, short, allegorical sentences, the cosmic battle between Christ and the devil has been illustrated.

Praise God that he is the stronger of the two, and that ultimate victory – already won by his death on the cross – is assured.

The Bible in a year: Isaiah 23–24; Titus 3

SEPTEMBER 9–15

DAY 4

The immovable rock

When we try to kick a brick out of the way, we only injure ourselves. We can't fight against God's purposes without damaging ourselves.

Zechariah 12:1–14

Jerusalem will be like an 'immovable rock' (v 3) against which all who attack it will injure themselves. But this will not be fulfilled without hardship and struggle. All the surrounding nations will besiege Judah and Jerusalem. God won't automatically give the victory – his people will have to fight the battle, enduring great suffering. Chapter 14:2 suggests that some will suffer captivity, rape and ransacking. Nonetheless, God's word is true, and he promises them (as he promises us) that 'The people of Jerusalem are strong, because the Lord Almighty is their God' (v 5).

The prophecy of verses 10–14, not fulfilled in any obvious way then, unmistakeably point to Jesus on the cross. Read John 19:34–37. The previous words concerning Jerusalem being 'an immovable rock for all the nations' (v 3) refer to the church of Christ. Reflect on Jesus' words in Matthew 16:18: 'On this rock I will build my church, and the gates of Hades will not overcome it.' Again, the prophet has leapt forward six or seven centuries to the life and work of Jesus, making the short-term victories and defeats of the early Israelites nothing more than a caption to the bigger picture of God's redeeming work in the world.

If you are resisting the work of God in your life, you are only damaging yourself. Yield your life to him, and begin to enjoy his power working through you, rather than pitting yourself against it.

The Bible in a year: Psalm 104; Isaiah 25–26

SEPTEMBER 9–15

DAY 5 False prophets

More than anything, God desires intimacy and friendship with his people.

Zechariah 13:1–9

It was national sin which brought about the Babylonian exile, and national cleansing was the necessary first step to ushering in national restoration. Coming clean before God is always the first, inescapable step in returning to God.

This passage pictures a fountain gushing out over Jerusalem (v 1), predicting the cleansing of sin and the removal of the false prophets from the land (vs 2–3). Note that the leadership is the first target of this purification. Those who accept responsibility over God's people need to know that God expects high standards from them, and that judgement will begin with them. God seems to hold the prophets accountable for the sins of the people.

The poem focusing on the shepherd (vs 7–9) returns to the shepherd theme, but in a more sombre way. The good shepherd will be killed, as Jesus was; and the sheep will be scattered, as were the Jews in the Dispersion of AD 32 – all over the world. Nonetheless, as always, God's promise stands, and a remnant will remain, of whom God will say: 'They are my people', and who will respond: 'The Lord is our God' (v 9). More than anything, God desires intimacy and friendship with his people.

What kind of relationship do you have with God? Does God say of you: 'This is my child'? And can you respond: 'The Lord is my God'?

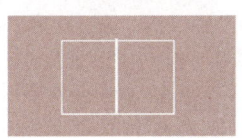

Cataclysm: Zechariah 14:1–15
Holy to the Lord: Zechariah 14:16–21

The Bible in a year: Isaiah 27–28; Philemon

Going deeper …

The minor prophets, including Zechariah, are hard reading. Why do we find it so difficult to understand them when, in their day, they were clearly understood, and changed the course of history? Here are some reasons:

The prophets spoke in oracles, which were not meant primarily to be read. They are transcripts of public speeches. They were also often not written as prose but as poetry, which falls more easily on the ear. To make matters worse, some translations print the words as prose rather than poetry. The divisions between oracles are sometimes unclear, and one oracle leads into another without the reader noticing. What makes this more confusing is that the oracles are often not in chronological order.

Many of the allusions: myrtle trees, measuring lines, priests' garments, lamp stands, flying scroll chariots, and crowns, were plainly understood by the Eastern reader, but are foreign and mystifying to the South African reader.

The modern reader is usually unfamiliar with the historical context of the sixth, seventh and eighth centuries BC, when the minor prophets lived. The rise and fall of the Babylonian and Persian empires; the dissolution, exile and return of the Jews; and Zechariah's frequent swapping between the Northern and Southern kingdoms, whose kings had like-sounding names, all contribute to making this difficult terrain.

Nonetheless, I hope that you have found that the message of Zechariah remains fresh and relevant to the people of Christ in South Africa today.

An unfinished symphony

Zechariah plays out like an unfinished symphony. God's purpose to restore his Lordship among his people and all nations was unfulfilled. The people longed for strong leaders, for wise leadership, but the prophets fell silent. They longed for God's blessing, but the priests did not lead them to this. Only in Jesus, the Prophet, Priest and King, are these longings satisfied.

There are common themes followed by the prophets, which we see in Zechariah: the holiness of God, the sinfulness of man, the necessity of repentance, the certainty of judgement and the indestructibility of God's grace. Prophets were original only in the manner in which they communicated: for instance, Isaiah went naked for three years and Ezekiel lay on his side staring at a clay model for three months. The message, though, was not their own, but God's. Prophets were to remind the people of what they had forgotten. They adopted three main styles: the lawsuit metaphor, in which God lays a charge and then issues a verdict; the message of woe, in which coming doom is announced; the promise of salvation, with its assurance of future blessing.

Zechariah fitted the classic mould of a prophet. Through him God promised salvation to the returned exiles in Jerusalem. They were meant to enjoy his blessing and be great among the nations. It should have been a beautiful tune, but the symphony remains unfinished. For its fulfilment, we need to look to the coming Christ, in whom all things come together.

The Bible in a year: Psalm 105; Isaiah 29–32; Hebrews 1

SEPTEMBER 16–22

How to live

Romans 11–13

Many people live with the dream of suddenly becoming very rich. The TV programme *Who Wants To Be A Millionaire?* has become an international hit by capitalising on this dream. National lotteries in many countries have appealed to the same aspiration. It's not so much possessing ridiculous amounts of money that appeals in itself, it's the fact that such wealth would be the doorway to a new lifestyle – a big home, a fast car, luxurious holidays and designer clothes. For all but a minuscule minority the dream will not become reality and they will never live the lifestyle.

The good news for Christians is that we are already incredibly rich. Our wealth does not consist of material riches, threatened by inflation, jeopardised by the uncertainties of the stock market and at risk of being stolen or spent. We have the spiritual riches of God's mercy. The first half of Romans explained in detail how we as sinners deserved nothing from God but judgement and yet how he has lavished upon us the spiritual riches of justification, reconciliation, the gift of the Spirit and the hope of glory.

This week we go on to look at the lifestyle we can live 'in view of God's mercy' (12:1). In short, it is a life of love: love for those who don't yet know God's mercy, love for our brothers and sisters in Christ and love for our enemies. Above all it is love for God our Father, which we show by pursuing his 'good, pleasing and perfect will' in a life committed to worshipping him (12:2). So let's forget the dreams of material riches we'll almost certainly never have and concentrate on living the life that goes with the spiritual riches we already have.

Martin Hodson is the minister of the Red Hill Baptist Church, Worcester, England. He and his wife, Becky, have three boys and live in a house full of toys, music and visitors.

SEPTEMBER 16–22

DAY 1

A faithful remnant

It's not difficult to think of reasons why God should have rejected us. It's harder to hold onto the truth that he has accepted us. Remember today that you are his: 'I have summoned you by name; you are mine' (Isaiah 43:1).

Romans 11:1–24

Most of us know what it's like to change our strategy, whether we're playing chess or trying to win an argument. Plan A isn't working, so we resort to Plan B. Some people thought that God had abandoned his Plan A, calling the Israelites to be his own people, in favour of Plan B, rejecting Israel and saving the Gentiles through faith in Christ. Paul explains that God has not rejected the Israelites (v 1). There is a remnant of Israel who are not relying on their heritage or works for salvation but on God's grace (vs 5–6). The rest are presently 'hardened' to the message of God's grace (v 7) but are not beyond recovery (v 11). God's plan of salvation is wider than Israel has fully understood. Their present rejection of God has created the opportunity to proclaim the riches of salvation to the Gentiles (v 12) but Paul hopes that his own people will be envious of the Gentiles in their new-found faith and seek Jesus themselves (v 14). Aware that this method of 'evangelism by envy' could make the Gentile believers think they have a superior place in God's purpose, he points out that if God's people were an olive tree then Gentile Christians would only be ingrafted shoots of a wild olive whilst the Israelites would be the natural branches (vs 17–24).

What is there about your life as a Christian that could make people who don't know Jesus envious? How could you 'boast in the Lord?' (1 Corinthians 1:31).

The Bible in a year: Isaiah 33–34; Hebrews 2

SEPTEMBER 16–22

DAY 2

Wisdom unsearchable

'I cannot tell why he whom angels worship/should set his love upon the sons of men' (WY Fullerton). We know that God loves us but we don't know why he loves us. Enjoy the mystery of being inexplicably loved.

Romans 11:25–36

While it may be comforting to think that someone else is showing us favouritism, this belief quickly leads to a feeling that we must therefore be better than others. Paul can envisage just such conceit growing among his readers if they continue in the mistaken belief that God has now rejected the people of Israel in favour of the Gentiles (v 25). Although many Israelites remain hardened to the gospel (v 28), the invitation to salvation is still open to them all. As with the Gentiles, their salvation will be by God's mercy and not as their right (vs 30–32).

How this will work out remains a mystery to Paul. He is not afraid to admit that he does not know the full details of God's plans. In fact, to admit this becomes an act of worship (vs 33–36). Who said our small human minds would be big enough to understand all God's plans? I have known people who believe they have to understand God fully and explain all his actions before they can worship him. This is an unattainable goal; their desire to master God's ways becomes an obstacle to worship. It's far better to have a humble spirit which says, 'Lord, I understand you sufficiently to know your mercy but I am human and cannot understand you completely.'

What questions about God and his ways remain unanswered for you? Some may trouble you, others may seem too big to contemplate. With them in mind, reread verses 33–36.

The Bible in a year: Isaiah 35–36; Hebrews 3

SEPTEMBER 16–22

DAY 3

Whole-life worship

In Old Testament times a burnt offering gave off an aroma that was 'pleasing to the Lord' (see Leviticus 1:9). In the New Testament it is the offering of our lives which is seen as pleasing to God. As you say again to the Lord today, 'I offer my life to you, to go where you lead and do what you ask,' know that he takes pleasure in you.

Romans 12:1–8

Sometimes when I'm leading a church service I hear myself saying, 'And now we'll have a time of worship.' Almost immediately I realise the inadequacy of this statement, and try to qualify it accordingly. Worship is the task of our whole lives, not just a slot in the Sunday service. It is not only bringing our words of praise to God in songs and prayers, it is offering our bodies, and everything we do in them and with them, to God (v 1). Such whole-life worship is a reasonable response to God's mercy but it will inevitably bring us into conflict with the worship patterns of this world, which cherish material prosperity, outward appearance and the possession of influence, rather than obedience to God (v 2).

Knowing that we are saved by God's mercy gives us a right approach to the worth of others, freeing us from delusions of superiority (v 3). It also gives us a proper understanding of the gifts God has given us all. They are not given to prove how good or effective we are; they are given to be used for the blessing of others and the glory of God (vs 6–8).

In what circumstances do you refuse to conform to the patterns of this world? Pray for strength to keep swimming against the tide.

The Bible in a year: Isaiah 37–38; Hebrews 4

SEPTEMBER 16–22

DAY 4 — No indifference

The car battery was almost flat and starting up was difficult. I put it on charge overnight and the next morning the engine started like it was glad to be alive! Ask God's Spirit to charge you up with enthusiasm for him. 'Restore to me the joy of your salvation' (Psalm 51:12).

Romans 12:9–21

The opposite of love is not hate but indifference. Here we are urged to resist indifference in our attitude to the Lord and to others. Notice the intensity of the words used in verses 9–11: hate, cling, devoted, honour, zeal, fervour. Some people are nervous about Christianity that is highly enthusiastic; the New Testament suggests that we should aspire towards just such enthusiasm, as long as it is rooted in the truth of the Word of God.

Refusing to be indifferent to others means noticing their practical needs (v 13) and being attentive to their emotions (v 15). In an increasingly mobile population, where work causes ever more people to move away from family and friends, there is a serious problem of social isolation, and a crying need for people who will be sensitive to the practical and emotional needs of their colleagues and neighbours.

We should not even be indifferent to the people who cause us hurt or offend us. We have no right to take revenge – that is stealing God's prerogative (v 19) – but we are not told simply to ignore them either. We must seek opportunities to do good to such people and demonstrate that evil does not have the last word (vs 20–21).

Can you think of anyone you are tempted to take revenge against? Make a conscious decision to forfeit your right to get your own back and plan to do them some good instead.

The Bible in a year: Psalm 106; Isaiah 39–40

SEPTEMBER 16–22

DAY 5

God's servants

Who are the powerful people in your world? As you picture them, imagine a shadow coming over them. You look up to see what is causing the shadow and there high above them you see the throne of God.

Romans 13

God has created certain institutions for the benefit of all society. These include marriage, family and government. The purpose of the government is to maintain law and order (vs 1–3); it is God's servant to keep society from drifting into chaos (v 4). This does not mean that governments are perfect (history makes this quite clear) but since their function is God-given it means that to keep a clear conscience a Christian will normally obey them and pay taxes as required (vs 5–7). There are times however when a government goes beyond its rightful powers, for example by banning worship or evangelism. Then Christians must remember Jesus' words, 'Give to Caesar what is Caesar's and to God what is God's' (Mark 12:17). From earliest times Christians have had occasion to challenge and disobey the authorities when they have overreached their proper authority (see for example Acts 4:18–20).

Christians are subject to a far more all-embracing law than any government could enact. The Rule of love (vs 8–9) sums up everything taught in the Old Testament law (v 10). The incentive to keep this law is stronger than the punishment of earthly governments: the day we meet Jesus will soon be upon us and we must be prepared for that by living lives worthy of those who bear his name (vs 11–14).

Pray for the government to act with wisdom and righteousness. Then pray for a particular politician and a specific political issue.

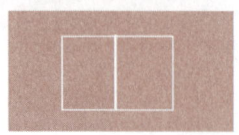

Politically correct: Mark 12:13–17
Prayer request: 1 Timothy 2:1–7

The Bible in a year: Isaiah 41–42; Hebrews 5

Going deeper …

I've lost count of the number of talks I've heard on spiritual gifts. In almost every case the emphasis has been on how these gifts can be recognised and used in the Christian community. This is partly, no doubt, because the longest passage in the New Testament on gifts (1 Corinthians 12–14) is about how to value them rightly and use them correctly when the church comes together. The gifts mentioned here are mostly ones that could come to prominence in a church meeting.

In Romans 12:6–8 there is another list of gifts: prophesying, serving, teaching, encouraging, contributing to the needs of others, giving generously, leadership and showing mercy. While all these gifts can and should be used to build up the church, they are not for the exclusive benefit of Christians. A gifted servant of others in the Christian community does not lose that gift in wider company. Someone gifted to encourage others in the church doesn't become a *dis*courager among his colleagues. A gifted leader in the church does not forfeit that gift when he is given authority over others at work. Someone who receives prophetic insights from God should not assume God *only* wants to speak to believers through them. Prophecy in the Old Testament didn't have that restriction. The church is to bring God's healing to a broken world. Spend some time in prayer, 'dreaming dreams' for God. How could you be an agent of God's love? The gifts God has given us are not simply to build up the church; they are channels through which the grace of God can flow into the needs of the world. Let's think how we can use our gifts for God's glory.

Obedience through faith

This week we have read a lot of dos and don'ts. If we put these into practice, we will certainly live a distinctively Christ-like life. Yet making obedience a priority can lead to the danger of legalism, where we begin to think that it is our obedience to the commands of God that makes us righteous in his sight, forgetting that we are 'justified by faith apart from observing the law' (3:28). Here are two principles to guide us away from legalism.

Obedience is the result of salvation, not the means to it. The obedience of Jesus to the point of death is what accomplished our salvation. It is a free gift we could never earn. We are made righteous through faith in him, and we obey God out of gratitude for what he has done for us. The purpose of our salvation is that we should live a new life for God's glory.

The freedom and motivation to obey these commands come from continuing in a living relationship with God. The essence of these commands is that we should treat others as God treats us. The more we get to know our Father, the more we will display the family likeness. The more we understand that God is gracious, loving and merciful to us, the more we will reveal those qualities. Our good deeds are not a way of catching God's attention but reflecting his glory.

The Bible in a year: Psalm 107; Isaiah 43–46; Hebrews 6

SEPTEMBER 23–29

Keep it going

Romans 14–16

Some time ago a salesman came round to try and sell us a vacuum cleaner. He gave us a thorough demonstration of its sucking power and a detailed (not to say long-winded) explanation of its benefits. Finally he promised us that an appliance of this quality would give us 'a lifetime of problem-free satisfaction'. (We weren't sure whether he meant our lifetime or the lifetime of the device!) Somehow the promise didn't ring true; he was offering more than he could deliver.

Anyone who believes that a problem-free life is possible needs to take a stiff dose of reality. In a world where everyone falls short of God's ideals there are many difficulties for us all to face. The same is true in the church, where we also fall short of God's ideals. So, in the final section of Romans, Paul faces up to some of the tough issues his readers will have to struggle with. There will be disputes among Christians over matters of conscience (14:1), they will have to bear with the failings of the weak (15:1), like him they may be hindered from doing what they long to do (15:22) and they may face persecution from unbelievers (15:31).

Paul is utterly convinced of the power of the gospel to reconcile us to God, but he is no super-slick salesman naively promising a problem-free life. What matters most is that we keep going with God through tough times and don't let these issues deflect us from the main purpose of God's kingdom (14:17). The personal greetings in the final chapter remind us of the importance of fellowship in all this; to keep us on the right track we have not only the Word of God and the Spirit of God but also the *people* of God.

Martin Hodson is the minister of the Red Hill Baptist Church, Worcester, England. He and his wife, Becky, have three boys and live in a house full of toys, music and visitors.

SEPTEMBER 23–29

DAY 1

Dealing with disputes

How would you describe the central core of your faith? Speak to the Lord with a few statements that begin, 'I believe …'

Romans 14

First-century Christians who were bound together in Christ by the primary truth of the gospel found themselves disagreeing over secondary issues such as the eating of meat (v 2) or the observing of sacred days in the Jewish calendar (v 5). Today we find ourselves disagreeing over such diverse issues as the role of women in leadership, the interpretation of Genesis chapter 1, whether Christians should drink alcohol and whether we should attend football matches on Sundays. Such 'disputable matters' will always be with us. Here we have some guidelines on how to live with such differences.

Firstly, we must not look down on people who have different views to ourselves (v 3) but respect the fact that they are acting with a clear conscience before God, their judge (vs 4, 10, 12). Secondly, everyone should be fully convinced in their own minds (vs 5, 23). It is too easy to accept second-hand opinions or do what we feel like doing without really exploring the issues and what the Scriptures say about them. Thirdly, we mustn't insist on our right to do as we prefer if it will be an obstacle to someone else's spiritual growth (vs 13–15, 19–21), yet this does not mean giving up our convictions (v 16). Fourthly, above all, we must keep the real priorities of God's kingdom in mind (vs 17–18) and not make a meal out of our differences (v 22).

Think of a disagreement you have with another Christian. Is it over a primary or a secondary issue? Which biblical principles have you applied as you live with the disagreement?

The Bible in a year: Isaiah 47–48; Hebrews 7

SEPTEMBER 23–29

DAY 2

Please yourself?

Jesus prayed, 'Not what I will, but what you will' (Mark 14:36). Consider the implications of this prayer for you today before praying it yourself.

Romans 15:1–13

Some people mistakenly see Christianity as an expressway to personal happiness and pleasure. They are looking for a 'therapeutic Christianity' that makes them feel better in all circumstances. There is certainly great joy in the Holy Spirit (see 14:17) as he reveals to us the depth of God's love and the privileges of being God's children, but this is in the context of an obligation to live for others. Pleasing ourselves is not a priority (v 1). Building others up (v 2) will at the very least mean hard work and persistent effort, and may lead to misunderstanding, opposition and rejection, as it did for Jesus (v 3).

This is a serious responsibility, but the good news is that God gives us endurance and encouragement (v 5).

How does he do this? Partly through the motivation that comes from being in unity with other believers who are also committed to building one another up (v 6); and partly through the Spirit continually bringing to our attention the example of Jesus who has accepted us (v 7) and who chose the tough path of servanthood (v 8), knowing that the outcome would be for God's glory (vs 9–12). The blessing in verse 13 is a reminder that living for others is too much to accomplish in our own strength. It is only when he fills us, we trust in him and the Spirit makes us overflow, that we can live this demanding life of building up others.

Make specific plans to do or say something that will build up someone else. Be aware of what this will cost you.

The Bible in a year: Isaiah 49–50; Hebrews 8

SEPTEMBER 23–29

DAY 3

Ambitious for God

God is with us every second of our lives. Quietly count out ten seconds. Then at the same pace say 'Father' ten times. Think about that exercise: there is never a moment when the Lord isn't there. Aim to think of God's presence with you every time you look at a clock or watch today.

Romans 15:14–22

Sometimes churches create a culture of dependency. Everything depends on the pastor or minister. A meeting can't take place unless he or she is there. The pastor is the only person anyone wants to hear teaching or preaching. Paul resists such hierarchical dependency on him as an apostle. He believes in the believers (v 14). He doesn't want to build an empire for himself; he wants the whole church to remember they are equipped by God for their own ministry. They may benefit from the exhortation of someone like Paul who is called to a life of proclamation (vs 15–16), but God has already given them all the gifts and wisdom to be the church he wants them to be.

Paul now reflects on his own ministry. It reads rather like an appraisal someone might receive at work today. Notice the clarity with which he answers the following questions. What has God called him to do (vs 15–16)? What has God not called him to do (v 18)? Where does his power come from? Where has God called him to serve? How effective has he been (v 19)? What is his ambition (v 20)?

Think through the questions Paul asks about his life with regard to your own life. If one of the answers seems particularly significant to you – perhaps because it surprises you or is difficult to find – let that be the starting point for your prayers.

The Bible in a year: Isaiah 51–52; Hebrews 9

SEPTEMBER 23–29

DAY 4

Planning ahead

Think of a time when you had to make a significant change in your life. How did you recognise God's will? Thank him for guiding you then and pray for him to lead you as you go about the ordinary things of today.

Romans 15:23–33

Many of us have a conservative streak in us; change doesn't come easily. Sometimes the Holy Spirit disturbs us by showing us that it is time for a new challenge. Paul had recognised that it was time for him to move on because his vision to be a pioneer missionary (v 20) could no longer be fulfilled in the Eastern Mediterranean where the gospel had now been widely preached (v 23). He felt God calling him to the unevangelised land of Spain, and to visit Rome en route (v 24). This call did not give him immediate liberty to forget his present commitments. He was entering a time of transition when important responsibilities had to be fulfilled before he could move on (vs 25–28).

Have you ever made plans, believing God was in them, and then things haven't worked out as you hoped? This is what happened to Paul. He did get to visit Rome, but only as a prisoner, after being arrested in Jerusalem. It seems unlikely that he ever reached Spain. He always knew that he would only visit Rome 'by God's will' (v 32) and God's will turned out to be different to what he envisaged. This must have troubled him deeply, yet he wasn't afraid to admit that in the end God's ways were greater than his understanding (see 11:33–34).

Ask the Spirit to show you clearly if he is leading you into any new area of service and, if he is, to give you the courage to move on.

The Bible in a year: Psalm 108–109; Isaiah 53–54

SEPTEMBER 23–29

DAY 5

Special people

Think of the church fellowship you belong to. Name some of your brothers and sisters in God's presence and give him thanks for the way he has used them to bless you.

Romans 16

Teaching about doctrine and lifestyle is best done in the context of fellowship. For the last fifteen chapters Paul has not been writing a textbook but writing to brothers and sisters for whom he thanks God and whom he longs to see face to face (1:8–12). He feels a deep sense of fellowship with the Christians in Rome because he has met many of them as they have travelled around the empire and now he expresses this fellowship by greeting them individually.

Imagine the impact on them as this letter is read out in the church when they hear their own names mentioned. This is more than a roll-call of people Paul has met. He takes the trouble to mention specific things about these people which have impressed him and advanced the gospel. Look at the variety of things he commends people for in verses 3–15.

When all the greetings are over this letter rises to a magnificent climax in an exclamation of praise (vs 25–27). The gospel is the gift of God, not the words of men and women. It has come through the Son of God (v 25), by the command of God (v 26), for the glory of God (v 27). Wherever God leads Paul next, whatever he has in store for the Christians in Rome, the purpose of their lives will be to give him glory.

Set aside time to write a letter to someone in the next day or so. As you write, make a point of mentioning specific ways in which their life has encouraged you.

Rome at last: Acts 28:11–16
Seize the day: Acts 28:17–30

The Bible in a year: Isaiah 55–56; Hebrews 10

Going deeper ...

If you are making plans, you've probably been struck this week by the way Paul announced his big plan to visit Rome and then Spain. Here are some things the Lord may be saying about your plans.

Don't be afraid of being ambitious. Paul certainly wasn't. Dream big dreams and pray for the courage and opportunity to turn them into reality. God is 'able to do immeasurably more than all we ask or imagine' (Ephesians 3:20).

Beware of selfish ambition. Make plans that will glorify God and bless others. James gives a cool warning to people whose elaborate plans amount to no more than schemes to make money for themselves (see James 4:13–14).

Plan with humility. Make plans based on how you believe God is leading you, but recognise that you don't have a perfect grasp of his will. Things may not work out as you intend, but that's not the end of the world. Proverbs 19:21 reminds us: 'Many are the plans in a [human] heart, but it is the Lord's purpose that prevails.'

Trust God. More important than your plans are God's plans for you. Whether your dreams materialise or evaporate, remember that God's plans for you are invariably good (Jeremiah 29:11). He has made you with a purpose and he will bring his plans for you to a glorious completion on the day of Jesus Christ (Philippians 1:6).

A great example

In the final chapters of Romans we have got to know Paul as a man. God is challenging us to learn from Paul as a person as well as from his teaching.

His focus on what is really important. He recognised that eating meat and observing sacred days are not worth dividing the church over. Although he is a brilliant thinker, not afraid of arguing for the gospel, he declined to heighten the conflict over these secondary issues. Some things are better kept between God and yourself (14:15).

His determination to proclaim the gospel. Despite recurrent illness he had preached the good news from Jerusalem to Illyricum (Albania/Croatia, 15:19), facing danger and opposition almost everywhere he went. This letter could have ended with the announcement of his retirement, but he is driven by a simple imperative: there are still people who don't know Christ, so his work is not over.

His love of other believers. It's easy to imagine Paul as a solitary, independent man, making lonely journeys to spread the good news. Romans 16 shows that this is far from the truth. He felt a great closeness to many believers he had worked with. He was not afraid to say that he loved them in the Lord and to affirm the significant part they had played in his ministry. Even as he writes he is surrounded by a group of co-workers.

In the light of Paul's example, ask yourself: Where am I focusing my efforts? What am I determined to do? Who are my co-workers. How do I demonstrate love for them?

The Bible in a year: Psalm 110–111; Isaiah 57–60; Hebrews 1

SEPTEMBER 30– OCTOBER 6

Joy despite everything

Philippians 1:1—2:18

Imagine you are in hospital, wired to drips and machinery because of a serious heart condition. The doctors tell you that you could die at any moment. While you are trapped in that bed streams of visitors bombard you with bad news. Work colleagues tell you how others are undermining your department, criticising you behind your back and deliberately destroying all you have built up over years. Members of your family worry you with problems that have occurred because you aren't there holding things together, and they seem too busy quarrelling to be bothered with you.

Suppose, as you lie there in that difficult situation, you decide to write to some old friends you have loved for years. The Greeks used to say, 'Everyone reveals his own soul in his letters.' I wonder what you would write? Most of us would probably unleash a torrent of worry, despair, negative thoughts, doubts about God's love, resentment and self-pity.

Over the next two weeks we'll be reading a letter that Paul wrote in similar circumstances. He was in prison, not hospital; he was chained to soldiers, not machines; execution threatened his life, not heart disease; and it was not the situation at the office which was causing him grief but upsets in the churches he had founded. He had no family, but the Christians who worked with him were quarrelling, criticising him and acting selfishly. Yet his letter to his friends in Philippi is one of the most joy-filled books in the Bible, full of peace and contentment. Everything in his life seemed to be going wrong yet he possessed an inexhaustible supply of supernatural, inner joy that was not linked to his outward circumstances. What was his secret and how can we have that joy, despite everything?

Jennifer Rees Larcombe runs a Christian charity called Beauty from Ashes which aims to help people who face bereavement trauma, rejection and loss of any kind. She is an agony aunt and has published twenty-three books. She has six children and loves gardening.

SEPTEMBER 30–OCTOBER 6

DAY 1

Connecting with joy

Imagine you are a diver, swimming effortlessly in a tropical sea. You are safe to explore the underwater world because you are firmly attached by an 'umbilical cord' to your support ship. Paul's supernatural joy came from knowing he was joined to Christ. When we are completely connected to Jesus all his strength and special qualities, such as joy, can pass into us. When we can trust Christ with every detail of our lives we float effortlessly in his love, like the diver in that tropical sea. But staying constantly connected to Jesus through our 'umbilical cord' is vital for our nourishment and security. Stop and ask Jesus if you need to be more closely connected.

Philippians 1:1–11

Another reason for Paul's joy was his attitude towards other people. Criticism and ingratitude smother joy. As he thought about his friends in Philippi he focused on their good qualities (vs 4–5), thanked God for them (v 3) and, rather than worrying about their failings, he simply trusted that God was working in them (v 6).

Verses 3–4 and 9–11 give us another clue to Paul's joy. The Philippian church was in grave danger from persecution (see v 29) and from false teachers (see 3:2). Paul changed his natural worry into prayer.

Recently I was so worried about one of my children my anxious thoughts felt like swarms of wasps inside my head! But when I brought the whole situation to God I experienced enormous relief and yes, real joy! We can't always help those we love, but prayer can do far more for them than we can!

Who are you carrying in your heart today (v 7)? Stop and thank God for their good points and let him deal with all the rest.

The Bible in a year: Isaiah 61–62; Hebrews 12

SEPTEMBER 30–OCTOBER 6

DAY 2

Joy is a choice

This morning felt chilly when I sat down in my rocking chair to pray. The fire beside me was just a cold lump of metal until I put the plug into the socket and switched it on. Through the flex poured electricity and soon the fire was pumping out warmth and comfort. Have you 'plugged' yourself into God yet today?

Philippians 1:12–26

Paul, stuck in death row, chained to a Roman soldier, with most of his 'friends' working against him could have been forgiven for a few negative thoughts but see verse 12! He was chained, night and day, to soldiers from a crack regiment in the Roman army. Knowing Paul, he would have talked about Jesus to every man who came on duty (v 13)! As they were posted all over the world they would have carried the good news with them. Friends who once left the preaching to Paul discovered they could witness too (v 14). In one week I visited two friends in different hospitals, both were recovering from cancer operations. One was full of fears and grumbles, the other looked radiant as she told me how God was using her situation to reach others in the ward. Joy has nothing to do with our outer circumstances but everything to do with the way we view them.

Paul could have allowed his joy to be smothered by the behaviour of other Christians (v 17) but instead he rejoices (v 18). So long as people met Jesus Paul didn't care who got the credit!

Look again at verse 18b. Paul says 'I will … rejoice'. Because I'm a born worrier with a tendency to depression I find I have to choose joy on a difficult day and choose not to be worried or sad. Will you choose to rejoice today – whatever?

The Bible in a year: Isaiah 63–64; Hebrews 13

SEPTEMBER 30–OCTOBER 6

DAY 3

Joy under pressure

Do you have someone in your life who constantly puts you down? Or perhaps they always argue, criticise, misunderstand? Maybe you are mocked or intimidated because of your Christian faith. Could you pause for a moment and bring your 'difficult people' to the Lord by naming them in his presence? Could you go further and ask him to bless them today? It will probably be very hard but this is how Jesus tells us to treat them (see Luke 6:28). In Matthew 5:11, 12 he also tells us to 'be glad' when we are mistreated by others because he has a big reward waiting for us in heaven.

Philippians 1:27–30

Paul was writing to a beleaguered church. Twelve years before they had seen him stripped and brutally flogged in their market place, then flung into a dungeon – just for talking about Jesus. They had been suffering the same kind of treatment ever since. Churches today are also beleaguered, if not by angry humans then by the powers of darkness (Ephesians 6:12). Unseen enemies try to split us, disillusion us and rob our faith. Paul tells the Philippians their only chance of survival is to stick together (v 27b); the same applies to us!

He gives them two other important tips for Christians in hostile societies. Firstly, don't let them see you're afraid (v 28). Secondly, it is not what you say that impresses people but how you act, so *live* your faith, don't just *preach* it (v 27a).

If you encounter one of your 'difficult people' today try to look beyond them, focusing your inner eyes on Jesus, who understands from personal experience how you are feeling. If you can do that you will begin to experience the joy of suffering with him (3:10).

The Bible in a year: Isaiah 65–66; John 1

SEPTEMBER 30–OCTOBER 6

DAY 4 — Joy through imitation

If you were offered a personal audience with the Queen of England I guess you'd take trouble to prepare yourself: bath, haircut, new clothes. Today we are going to read one of the most awesome passages in the Bible; it will carry us right into God's throne room. Take time first to get yourself ready …

Philippians 2:1–11

Paul knew that good relationships bring joy, yet he heard about squabbles and power struggles in the Philippian church. Notice verse 2. He doesn't say, 'You'll destroy my joy if you keep on quarrelling.' He says, 'You'll increase my joy by unity.' No one can take our joy away – that's our choice. No one can make us angry either, we are responsible for the way we react to their behaviour. But other people can add more joy on top of the joy we already have.

Church splits usually begin when people start using church activities for their own ends. Some love controlling others. They want power so badly that when they hit against others in church with the same goal sparks fly. Others use church involvement to gain the approval, respect and admiration they crave and are bitterly resentful when others gain greater popularity. Notice how firmly Paul talks to people like this (vs 3–4). Paul beseeches them – and us – to think about Jesus (vs 5–11). Realising what he did for us soon cures our pride. And there is no better way of increasing our joy than sitting and looking at Jesus. By the time Paul finished dictating this passage I guess he was positively shouting with joy!

Slowly reread verses 6–11, and let them relight your joy too, as the glory of Jesus seeps into your soul.

The Bible in a year: Psalm 112–113; Jeremiah 1–2

SEPTEMBER 30–OCTOBER 6

DAY 5

Killjoys

I guess Paul was sitting by an open window when he wrote today's passage. It was night and, against the dark sky, the stars stood out, bright, pure and beautiful. 'Our lives as Christ's followers should stand out in the darkness of this world like those stars,' he thought. Ask yourself, is my life so filled with joy that it shines like a star?

Philippians 2:12–18

Nothing dampens joy more quickly than grumbling! I used to conduct parties of holidaymakers abroad. Although we stayed in the same hotel the success of each week varied greatly. One group could have a marvellous time enjoying everything, but the next week's party might contain 'grumblers' who said the beds were hard, food boring and staff rude, and soon everyone's fun was ruined. Paul knew grumblers could wreck a church too, as well as being a bad advertisement for Christianity. Looking out of his window he told the Philippians that people who are full of joy, instead of grumbles, stand out like those stars sparkling in the night sky (vs 14–15). Holding out the word of life (v 16a) doesn't have to be done from a pulpit or a soapbox. An appreciative comment can be far more effective than ten sermons!

    Thinking negatively about situations and other people can quickly become a habit. Whether or not you feel it has for you, meditate on verse 13.

It is God's will and purpose to produce the fruit of joy in your life. Ask him to set you free from any negative mindset and then work with him by looking out for ways of encouraging and affirming others each day.

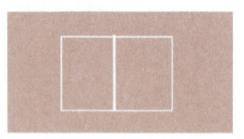

First impressions: Acts 16:12–24
Astonished by joy: Acts 16:25–26

The Bible in a year: Jeremiah 1–2; John 2–3

Going deeper …

When my best friend Rhoda developed liver cancer she was only forty-five. I was devastated, but when I visited her in hospital I found her radiant. 'I've been moved onto the launching pad,' she said happily. Rhoda loved the Lord with such passion she said with Paul: 'I want very much to leave this life and be with Christ, which is a far better thing … For what is life? To me, it is Christ. Death, then, will bring more' (Philippians 1:23b, 21, GNB). For many, dying doesn't worry them, but leaving loved ones does. Paul said, 'I am pulled in two directions' (1:23a, GNB).

Is it stepping into the unknown that worries us? Jesus can tell us more about heaven than anyone else – he's been there! His promise is that we don't have to go alone, he'll come back himself to take us there (John 14:2–3).

During the last few weeks of her life Rhoda so eagerly anticipated heaven that, the day before she died, she told me she could already see the beautiful colours. 'The turquoise is wonderful!' she said. 'Give my love to Jesus,' I whispered as I waved goodbye, envying her! Joy was her antidote to fear – and it was catching. So was Paul's when he told his friends, 'Perhaps my life's blood is to be poured out like an offering … I am glad and share my joy with you all' (2:17, GNB). Paul knew his reward waited in heaven (3:14) and like an athlete going for gold, he raced towards it! Is heaven your goal too? Spend some time praying through the issues this question raises, and then worship Jesus, who *is your life*.

Joy defined

How can we have joy despite everything? Joy is an inner, supernatural sensation, which is different from happiness because it has nothing to do with what is going on in our outer lives. It comes directly from Jesus himself, the source of joy through his Spirit. We cannot work joy up by ourselves; it comes when we deliberately decide to 'plug' ourselves into him. We can lose our joy when we become disconnected through unconfessed sin, holding anger in our hearts and refusing to forgive. It disappears when we stop looking to Jesus and become absorbed in self-pity, or while we are arguing with him over something he has allowed, rather than accepting his will.

A few years ago best-selling books urged us to praise the Lord for everything and rejoice whatever was happening. Obviously joy comes when we choose to look for the positive things in difficult situations, but I'm not sure it is right to expect someone to rejoice when their child is suffering terrible pain; when their husband runs off with their best friend or when the doctor says they'll never walk again. At times like these joy burns so low it's imperceptible! In my worst times of suffering I've often been conscious of little jets of joy, like candles in a long dark tunnel. They appear when I decide to believe God is still there, holding me tight and he will, ultimately, work everything out for my good (see Romans 8:28). Jesus endured on the cross by thinking of the joy *which lay ahead* (Hebrews 12:2). Everlasting joy is our reward too!

The Bible in a year: Psalm 114–115; Jeremiah 5–8

OCTOBER 7–13

Enjoying grace

Philippians 2:19–4:23

Paul did not e-mail his letter to the church in Philippi. It was carried, probably mostly on foot, by a man called Epaphroditus. Philippi, at that time, was a beautiful and prosperous city. Businessmen, made rich by the nearby gold mines, built mansions near the river and academics set up libraries in this centre of medical science. Soldiers thronged the streets, as Philippi was an important military base, strategically placed where two major roads intersected and the great Ignation Way cut through a mountain pass. Most important of all, Philippi was a Roman colony, populated by military veterans and their families who were fiercely proud of their Roman citizenship. They were more Roman than Rome itself as they reclined in their mosaic dining rooms, wearing the latest Roman fashions, sampling the latest Roman recipes, and discussing, in Latin, the news from Rome and listening to the current Roman pop songs!

This was the place where Paul founded the first church in Europe; and how he loved those people, calling them his joy and crown (4:1). He let them do something he allowed no other church to do – support him financially. Usually, when he settled in a city in order to found a church, he supported himself by tentmaking. He hated being a burden on anyone, but Philippi was different. You can trust people you love to do things for you.

They owed him nothing, he was with them only a few weeks, but during that time he taught them about grace (undeserved favour), and they longed to show grace by sending money to help him found other churches. When they heard of Paul's imprisonment they also sent Epaphroditus (the postman) to be his servant. The church was not wealthy, persecution robbed them of status, careers and property but still they wanted to show grace to the man who had brought God's grace to them.

Jennifer Rees Larcombe runs a Christian charity called 'Beauty from Ashes' which aims to help people who face bereavement trauma, rejection and loss of any kind. She is an agony aunt and has published twenty-three books. She has six children and loves gardening.

OCTOBER 7–13

DAY 1

Grace towards others

Who would you say shows you grace? By that I mean kindness you haven't paid for and love you haven't earned. Someone who thinks you're wonderful whatever you do – or fail to do; is always there for you, whatever time of the day or night you call them; and who would give you anything and everything they possess if you needed it. If you should be lucky enough to know anyone as full of grace as that, stop a moment, and thank God for them!

Philippians 2:19–30

Paul showed Timothy and Epaphroditus that kind of grace. Timothy was very young when he met Paul but he became Paul's companion (see Acts 16:1–3) and messenger, travelling between Paul and the churches he founded. Perhaps Timothy cared especially about the Philippians (vs 19–20) because he was with Paul when he first visited the city. Paul never treated him as a servant but as a son (v 22). Similarly, Paul does something very gracious for Epaphroditus by giving him a glowing testimonial. Who was he (v 25)? It would have cost the Philippian church a great deal to send Paul one of their slaves but what went wrong (vs 26–27)? When he got home to Philippi, people might have labelled him a quitter if Paul had not written as he did (vs 29–30). Actually, in a way, he had let Paul down – he wasn't the support Paul needed – but instead of resentment, Paul covers Epaphroditus's embarrassment with a mantle of grace.

Look back at the 'Prepare' section, and turn it the other way round. Is there anyone to whom you show that kind of grace? God longs for us to treat others as he treats us, so let's stop and ask him to help us show others his kind of undeserved and unearned love.

The Bible in a year: Jeremiah 9–10; John 4

OCTOBER 7–13

DAY 2

Grace versus good works

What is your greatest desire: a home; a loving spouse; children; an important, satisfying job? These are good goals but God's greatest desire is that we should desire him. He wants to be our grand passion. How much do you really want Jesus to be the centre of your life and to imitate him in everything you do, say and even think?

Philippians 3:1–11

Between writing verses 1 and 2 I imagine Paul being interrupted by a messenger suddenly arriving and saying the Philippian church was being split by teachers who were telling the new converts that it wasn't enough just to believe in Jesus and receive his forgiveness. They had to live perfect lives, and keep all the Pharisees' rules in order to get to heaven. Paul was furious (vs 2–3). What was he trying to say in verses 4–7? Look how he describes all his own good deeds (v 8). Paul's grand passion is clear (vs 10–11). Many of us would love to know the power of Christ's resurrection in our families, ministries and personal lives, but we are not so keen to suffer with him and act, and react, to others as he did the day he died. When my friend John lost his leg he was infuriated by hospital staff who tried to cheer him up with remarks about how good artificial limbs are. 'They didn't know how it felt,' John told me angrily. 'They even sent the hospital chaplain to do me good! I hated him on sight, until he pulled up his trouser legs, revealing *two* tin legs. After that I listened to everything he said!'

Can you make a list of the things in your life that cause you pain? Then see how many of them Jesus experienced too. Sharing the fellowship of sufferings (v 10) makes all the difference!

The Bible in a year: Jeremiah 11–12; John 5

OCTOBER 7–13

DAY 3

Remember who you are!

Does your Christian faith ever make you feel you don't fit with the rest of your world at school, college, work or even in your family? How does that make you feel? Ask yourself if your goal is to create a 'heaven on earth' for yourself and those you love, or whether you see your life as a journey towards heaven. If you feel uneasy about this, ask the Lord into that uneasiness.

Philippians 3:12–4:1

When Paul has finished dealing with those who were saying, 'You won't get to heaven unless you're perfect,' he turns his attention to another group in the Philippian church who said, 'God will forgive us whatever we do, so we can live as we like' (3:18–19). Paul calls them 'enemies of the cross of Christ' (3:18). He reminds the Philippians who they are (3:20). They were so proud that they were a Roman colony that they lived very separate lives from their Macedonian neighbours, but living by Roman standards, culture and law didn't make them Roman citizens. This had to be conferred on them by the Emperor. We do not have to live perfect lives to win our citizenship of heaven, but we live like a citizen of heaven to please our King and to be good ambassadors for him.

Look again at 3:13–14. Paul had caused terrible suffering to many Christians (see Acts 8:3). He could easily have spent his life bowed over with shame but he left his guilt at the cross and set his sights on heaven. Ask yourself if there is some failure or bad decision that makes you feel like a second-class Christian. If you've asked God to forgive you, then receive his forgiving grace. Show the same kind of grace to yourself – make the choice to forgive yourself too, and start enjoying your freedom!

The Bible in a year: Jeremiah 13–14; John 6

OCTOBER 7–13

DAY 4

Be different – for God's sake

Roman colonists felt safe because a garrison of highly trained soldiers guarded them and sentries would have surrounded their city day and night. In today's passage Paul tells the Philippian church that God's peace will guard their hearts and minds just like that (see v 7). Stop for a moment and allow this supernatural peace to surround you on every side, cover and support you. Let peace sink into your heart, softening your anger, comforting your fears and stilling all your restless thoughts. Sit and enjoy his peace for as long as you can.

Philippians 4:2–9

Being 'different' is tough for most humans. We feel safe when we can 'blend in' and feel accepted by our communities. But, as citizens of heaven, Paul reminds us we must be prepared to stand out like stars in the night sky (2:15). Today he gives us six tips for alternative living (vs 4–8). Which of Paul's instructions do you find most difficult? Look at the end of verse 3. When I think of just how many billions of people live, and have lived, on this earth I tend to feel as miserably insignificant as a speck of dust; but knowing that my name is firmly entered in God's special register of VIPs soon changes that!

Never before has it been harder to follow Paul's advice in verse 8. Books, TV, videos and the Internet bring horror, ugliness and sin right into our sitting rooms, and the papers are full of horrible stories that haunt our memories for days and arouse all kinds of fears. We can't separate ourselves from the world, and must see ourselves as part of our communities, but we can choose what we watch, read and listen to for entertainment. Consider prayerfully whether you should make any changes.

The Bible in a year: Psalm 116; Jeremiah 15–16

OCTOBER 7–13

DAY 5

The secret of happiness

Sit for a while and welcome the following words right into you: 'There is nothing you could ever do which would make God love you any more than he does; and there is nothing you could ever do which would make God love you any less than he does. He already loves you without limit! His love for you is everlasting, unearned, uncondemning and unchangeable.' Let the reality of this love bathe you in God's grace.

Philippians 4:10–23

How did Paul cope with the ups and downs of life (v 12)? When he stayed in Philippi he had two very different lodgings – the luxurious home of a rich business woman (Acts 16:14–15) and the local prison (Acts 16:23–24). Yet he was equally content in both (Acts 16:25). Most of us need to ask for God's help with being content.

As a prisoner Paul could not earn his money by tentmaking but prisoners *had* to provide their own food somehow. So he would have been particularly grateful for the gift from Philippi (v 16). But what pleased him even more (vs 17–18)? When we give, we always receive a blessing ourselves because God loves generosity. When a father sees his own good qualities and character traits displayed by his children, he's delighted. The God who loves to lavish grace on people, longs for us to do the same. The more we give to others, the more God gives to us so that we will have even more to give!

Look again at the two major statements about God's grace in today's passage (vs 13, 19). When we really allow ourselves to believe these two verses our lives will be completely changed. Why not write them out and stick them up somewhere as a reminder of God's grace.

Grace in action: 2 Samuel 9
Forgiving grace: Hosea 2:14–3:3

The Bible in a year: Jeremiah 17–18; John 7

Going deeper …

When I saw *Les Miserables* at the Palace Theatre in London I cried all the way through! I was moved because the story explains grace so beautifully: Valjean had been sentenced to years of hard labour for stealing a loaf of bread. When at last he was released no one would give him work or shelter because of his criminal record. Homeless, frozen and starving, he eventually knocked at the door of a priest where he was welcomed, treated with love and respect, given a good meal and a comfortable bed. But during the night he stole as much of the priest's silver as he could carry in his pockets and slipped away. By morning the police had caught him and dragged him back to the priest's door. They said, 'Look! He's stolen all your silver.' 'Oh no,' replied the gentle old man, 'He did not steal. I gave it all to him as a gift.' Picking up the two remaining candlesticks from his table he added, 'You left the best pieces behind, my friend. Take them too, they are yours with my love.' Bewildered by such grace Valjean staggered away determined to spend the rest of his life extending that kind of grace to others. God's grace not only gives us infinitely more than we deserve, it goes on giving without end.

Another illustration of grace is the story of John Newton. He was the cruel captain of a slave ship, yet during a terrible storm God met him, forgave and changed him. He later wrote: 'Amazing grace! How sweet the sound that saved a wretch like me. I once was lost but now am found, was blind but now I see.' Are you enjoying God's grace?

Fridge-door reminder

Because I receive so many letters every day, and some are rather long, I highlight the most important sentences. We have spent the last two weeks looking at one of the most remarkable letters ever written. Which verses are the most significant for you?

I decided to write my key verses out on little cards to stick on my fridge door. As I stuck them in place I realised that, together, they spell out Paul's philosophy of life. Jesus was all that mattered to him: 'For to me, to live is Christ and to die is gain' (1:21). 'I want to know Christ and the power of his resurrection and the fellowship of sharing in his sufferings, becoming like him in his death' (3:10). He knew he derived his power from Jesus: 'I can do everything through him who gives me strength' (4:13), and he trusted him for everything: 'My God will meet all your needs according to his glorious riches in Christ Jesus' (4:19). Because of this cast-iron belief Paul could sit happily in his prison, awaiting the death sentence, and write: 'I have learned the secret of being content in any and every situation' (4:12). His total trust in God's grace resulted in his experiencing 'the peace of God, which transcends all understanding' (4:7). Everything Paul needed was supplied without fail. Absolute peace and contentment were his on all occasions – because he put Jesus at the centre of everything. Every time I open my fridge door, I pray that I will be able to follow Paul's example (3:17). Will you join me?

The Bible in a year: Psalm 117–118; Jeremiah 19–22; John 8

God moves Israel forward

1 Samuel 1–7

I love stories – and love telling them. When I was a small boy I, for whatever reason, perfected the story of Ulysses and the Cyclops. I told it endlessly and people seemed to enjoy hearing it. I enjoyed telling it, and have throughout my life garnered stories which I use whenever appropriate. When a preacher says, 'Let me tell you a story,' the level of attention immediately rises, as people focus around the human interest.

History is the same. Old Testament history is a telling of stories which help us to see and respond to God in action. As we study these chapters from 1 Samuel, we will be pulled into the life of God's people as they are led forward from leadership by judges to leadership by kings. A difficult transition. So we have stories which seek to explain God's action in bringing the people of God another step of the way. Do remember that they are stories, and that the people of Israel (as was true in the Ancient Near East) could not read. Yet they listened, and because they were trained to do so, they remembered, and passed the stories on from generation to generation. Eventually they were written down – still to be listened to. They were exciting because they explained what God was doing, and that helped them not only to understand what he was doing, but also how they should respond to his activity.

One last comment. The passages for each day are long. Do not be daunted – read, listen and enjoy the stories, and then ask what God is saying to you. My small comments are less important than the stories themselves. For those who do not have time to read the whole passage on days 1 and 2, I have included an alternative, shorter reading.

Duncan Buchanan is the former Anglican Bishop of Johannesburg. He claims to have a passion – woodwork; a religion – rugby; and a faith – Christianity!

OCTOBER 14–20

DAY 1

Facing the impossible

How often have you faced terrible problems or insuperable barriers? The inclination is to give up – but that is not the way of God.

1 Samuel 1:1–2:10 or 1:1–23

The background is familiar. The godly family (1:3), the barren woman (Hannah, 1:5), the other wife who taunts (1:6), the puzzled husband (Elkanah, 1:8) who adores Hannah, and above all, the shame of having no child (1:7).

But it is the persistence which is impressive. Hannah's regular prayer is intermingled with her despair and weeping (1:10), but there is an ongoing belief that God will give her the child she desires. (It's very similar to the story of Abraham and Sarah: see Genesis 18:1–15, 21:1–7). The decisive moment for Hannah is her meeting with Eli in the House of God (1:9–18). His assumption of her drunkenness gives way to sensitivity and an ability to speak God's word to her.

Hannah's gift to God of the child (vs 27–28), and her great song of confidence in the majestic power of God (2:1–10), help us to see that even when the gift given to God is *really* costly, God uses it to further his purposes. Hannah's purpose for living has been brought to fruition and God continues to bless her (2:21).

Life is often very tough – and often unjust, but God keeps saying to us: 'Hang in there.' 'Don't give up.' 'Trust me.' Too often we quit just as God is about to act decisively. Faced with difficulties? Don't give up. And when God answers your prayer, don't hold it for yourself – give it away. That is real faith!

The Bible in a year: Jeremiah 23–24; John 9

OCTOBER 14–20

DAY 2

Facing the ugliness of humans

Do you cast a blind eye on the ugliness of the people around you? The people who use 'Jesus' as a swear word, who exploit others, or simply gratify their own wants, ambitions or cravings. Do you just let it pass because you do not want to 'cause trouble'? That is not the way of God.

1 Samuel 2:11–3:21 or 3:1–21

The focus of this passage lies in the contrast between the sons of Eli and the call of Samuel. Eli's sons exploited the people; but far worse, used the sacrifices of God's people for themselves (2:12–17). Even Eli's remonstrations with them are to no avail (2:22–25). They are corrupt, and happy to continue to be so. In contrast are the repeated allusions to Samuel (2:18, 26) and the man of God who came to warn Eli (2:27–36). The sad thing is that Eli *wants* to be obedient to God, yet is responsible for his sons' behaviour. As a result they will all be rejected.

The story of Samuel's call is wellknown (3:1–21). The important thing is the *listening* – Samuel hears (v 4); mistakes where it is from initially (vs 5–6); but then hears, not simply the call, but God's judgement on Eli and his sons (vs 11–14). The truth is usually painful, but if one can hear and act, it is wonderful. God's call is not to gratify Samuel, but to help Israel be aware of the presence and purpose of God. This is always so. God calls us, not to make us feel good, but to do his will.

Ask yourself if there is any situation which God is calling you to confront or in which you should intervene. Pray for strength to say and do the difficult things, and the humility to recognise that God is also chastening you in the process.

The Bible in a year: Jeremiah 25–26; John 10

OCTOBER 14–20

DAY 3

Trying to use God

One of the great heresies of history is to assume that God is on our side. All we can ever aspire to – is being on God's side.

1 Samuel 4:1–22

There is something infinitely tragic in all that happens in the events of this passage. It starts with the clashes between the Israelites and the Philistines (vs 1–2). Often the opposing armies took their gods into battle so that the power of the god would be available to them. Israel did not have a god (an idol), so what better than to bring the Ark, the great sign of God's abiding presence? They sent for it, thinking that with it, God's power would be available to them and in that power they would conquer (v 4). This caused joy for the Israelites and fear for the Philistines (vs 5–8). But God is not used. The Israelites are defeated, and Eli's sons killed, but worse still, the Ark is captured (vs 10–11). The news of the death of Eli's sons is bad enough for the old man, but it is the capture of the Ark which kills Eli (v 18). Eli had responsibility above all else for the Ark. Eli's daughter-in-law dies in childbirth on hearing, not of the death of her husband, but of the loss of the Ark (vs 19–20). Now God's presence (the glory of God) has been lost to Israel – and the Ark is in pagan hands.

Pray that your life will be focused on God (as we know him in Jesus); and that in listening to God you will seek to do only what he wants.

The Bible in a year: Jeremiah 27–28; John 11

OCTOBER 14–20

DAY 4

God cannot be manipulated

How often have you tried to bargain with God? To say, 'Lord, if you do this, I promise to do that'? I have long since realised I cannot bargain with God; and anyway, when God fulfils his side of the bargain, I usually forget mine.

1 Samuel 5–6:16

The Philistines were not a unified nation. Rather they lived and ruled in city states, each with its own leadership and way of life. So when the Ark goes to Ashdod (5:1–8) God acts against Ashdod, both in terms of disease (tumours and probably rats) and by reducing their god, Dagon, to rubble. As the Ark goes to Gath and Ekron, God's power, and his ability to induce panic, become apparent. God alone has power.

The Philistines' victory has become a major disaster, and God (without Israel) reduces the Philistines to panic and chaos. He does not need his own people, he is capable of manifesting his power as he wills (5:9–12). So the Ark must go back, and reparation must be paid. The gold tumours and rats are not only reparation, but also protection from further scourges (6:4–6). With relief the Philistines send the Ark back (6:10–12). The people of Beth Shemesh (Israelites) are delighted – offering sacrifices and rejoicing that the glory of God has returned to Israel (6:13–15).

The church often sets up programmes, not so much to glorify God, as somehow to control God's grace. We want to be successful and show others how successful we are. That is idolatry. God requires obedience and humility, not success. Pray that your efforts are in response to God, and not for yourself.

The Bible in a year: Psalm 119; Jeremiah 29–31

OCTOBER 14–20

DAY 5   **Prophet and judge**

All of us have gone through a crisis of some sort, and as we emerged from it, we were all aware of the need for new ways of living, of relating to each other, our context, and especially to God. This is what happened to the Israelites.

1 Samuel 6:19–7:17

We start with a strange little passage, probably explaining why the Ark got to Kiriath Jearim and stayed there for an extended period (6:19–7:2). The implication is that we are to treat God with respect and not see him as an imposition. At this point Samuel makes a reappearance, and he does so as prophet and judge. We must be clear about these two terms. The prophet represented God to the people in a particular situation. The judge interpreted the law of God, so that the people could live consistently godly lives. Samuel, as prophet, challenged the Israelites to return to God from their idolatrous ways (vs 3–4). The prophet's task was to keep them focused on God.

The assembly at Mizpah was to recommit themselves to God (vs 5–6). The Philistines wanted to take advantage of the Israelites being in one place (v 7). The leadership and intercession of Samuel were enough for God to act on his people's behalf, and the Philistines were not only defeated but, at least for a while, subdued (vs 10–14). Then we see Samuel as judge – patiently and conscientiously going from place to place, interpreting the law and helping the people to be godly in their day to day lives (vs 15–17).

Have we returned to the Lord with all our hearts and resolved to serve him only (vs 3–4)? Our lives are complex. The crises of today move to the regular patterns of tomorrow. But we can trust God to be in all of our situations.

Strength in weakness: 2 Corinthians 4:7–12
Keep going: Titus 2:11–14

The Bible in a year: Jeremiah 32–33; John 12

OCTOBER 14–20

Going deeper …

As Israel moves into a new phase of its existence, in spite of seemingly impossible odds and situations, God is not only in control, but he is guiding his people to face new challenges and changes in history.

So Hannah, dependent on God, receives her child and, as is so often the case, other children follow. Eli, a really godly old man, dies without a dynasty because he cannot control the wilful corruption of his sons. The Israelites have to face the horror of the loss of the Ark, because they believe God is available to be used. The Philistines learn that God is greater than any other 'god', as they suffer plague and pestilence. The Israelites are reminded that following God is the only way to a peaceful and productive life. Abandoning him brings turmoil!

Leadership involves accepting God's authority, often (as with Samuel) from an early age. It means confronting evil in whatever form it emerges, and serving God by serving his people. God calls us gently, but once we are aware of his call, we must go forward in love and confidence in the God who is there. God is supreme. The abiding lesson the Israelites had to learn and relearn in each generation, was that *following* the Lord God is the only way to full and abundant life.

The abuse of the holy

At various times in history, the people of God have fallen into moral decline. When that happens, the people who suffer most are the ordinary people. The tragedy is that the things of God are abused and exploited for gain. One of the things that worries me most is to see the leadership of the Church assume status, authority and power in the name of God. They assume that what they say is right; that their interpretation of Scripture is the only one; that their word is to be obeyed. They brook no criticism and accept not even the slightest negative assessment. They put themselves above any form of condemnation and become aloof and arrogant.

That is an abuse of the holy – God's special gift to the church. God sets the church aside to be humble, obedient, listening to and following Christ. God calls us to be servants. Christ's way of love, humility and listening to the Father and his people is the only way.

God's church is holy – set aside as the vehicle of God's love and grace. We are not to abuse it. Money, relationships, attitudes to others are all sacred, to be used for the enhancement of God's work in his world, so that we can be *different for God*. Do we want to join God in that work?

The Bible in a year: Psalm 119:25–48; Jeremiah 34–37; John 13

OCTOBER 21–27

Can there be a king in Israel?

1 Samuel 8–12

These chapters deal with a question which is fundamental for all of us. The issue is the nature of authority. The background, firmly held by the Old Testament writers, and particularly the prophets, is that there is only one king in Israel, and that king is God. As the movement from judges to kings takes place, there is a clearly expressed anxiety, probably felt by many in Israel, and expressed by Samuel. The worry is that the desire for a king is actually a rejection of God.

The only model they had was that of the surrounding kings, who acted with an autocracy foreign to Israel. Israel had judges (Samuel was the last of them) who seemed to exercise both a spiritual and a political role. The basic belief was that the judge was essentially a leader designated by God, whose authority was to do what *God wanted* in obedience to him. He was also responsible for interpreting the covenant law, thus leading the people to true godliness. Because the Israelite model of kingship was of one who did what *he wanted*, there was stiff opposition to it. Yet the people were looking for a leader who could help them hold their own against the other nations. The problem, which Samuel saw clearly, was that it was a short step to accepting an absolute monarch and effectively rejecting God as the true king of Israel.

Having said all of that, these chapters are quite confusing. Different attitudes about kingship are expressed. The people want a king, against Samuel's will; yet God tells Samuel to anoint Saul as God's chosen one. Saul also acts against Nahash, the Ammonite, in a style similar to the judges, giving another slant to the narrative.

Duncan Buchanan is the former Anglican Bishop of Johannesburg. He claims to have a passion – woodwork; a religion – rugby; and a faith – Christianity!

OCTOBER 21–27

DAY 1

We want a king

I don't know about you, but I often want something because 'everyone else has it'. I forget whether it is right or important, I just want it. So it was with the Israelites.

1 Samuel 8:1–22

There are three players in this little drama: the people, Samuel and God.

The people feel the need for change (vs 1–3, 19–22). The reasons are not wholly bad. Samuel's sons are unworthy (v 3) and they need a dynamic leader (v 20). Samuel himself feels rejected (v 7), but like any good leader, he prays.

God knows that, in moving in this direction, the people were wanting to be like the surrounding nations (v 20), but equally they are following the pattern of apostasy which has been their way from the moment they left Egypt (v 8).

God recognises the sense of inevitability about their request. All he tells Samuel to do is warn them of the consequences of their request (v 9). The people will be exploited and abused; there will be no true justice and they will suffer. In this Samuel again acts as prophet (vs 11–18).

The people's will prevails, however, and the stage is set.

Sometimes so-called 'progress' is a process of going backwards. Society's pressures are not always the best. 'Wanting to be like all the other(s)' (v 20) can lead us away from God. Like the Israelites, we are called to be different. We must look carefully at the implications of our decisions.

The Bible in a year: Jeremiah 38–39; John 14

OCTOBER 21–27

DAY 2

Saul meets Samuel

God chooses people who least expect it. He chooses you to be an agent for his purposes – in small and big ways.

1 Samuel 9:1–26

This is a strange passage. The donkeys are lost, so Saul goes with a servant to find them (vs 3–4). When Saul wants to turn back, it is the servant who knows about Samuel and who encourages Saul to see him (vs 5–10). Samuel now takes over. His vision from God has prepared him for Saul's coming (vs 15–17), so he is ready to give him hospitality, reassure him about his father's donkeys and nudge him towards a new way of life for himself and indeed for his whole family (v 20).

There is more to follow, which we will look at tomorrow. What we need to see here is that God's planning is meticulous. All is in place. The lost donkeys pry Saul loose from the family. The servant is ready to point to Samuel; Samuel is ready to welcome Saul, prior to anointing him king. Nothing is left to chance – and, as always, God's timing is perfect.

God does prepare things. What we need is the patience to trust God; to give him space to do what is necessary. Then great things happen!

The Bible in a year: Jeremiah 40–41; John 15

OCTOBER 21–27

DAY 3

Samuel anoints Saul as king

The patience to wait and be prepared always gives way to God's action, which can change history. Look at your life and see where this has happened to you.

1 Samuel 9:27; 10:27

The moment has come. Saul is anointed, set aside for God's purposes. Certain signs confirming God's initiative will follow (10:2–7). He is given the wonderful promise that the Spirit will come upon him and he will become a different person (v 6). God changed Saul's heart (v 9) and all the signs were fulfilled. How gracious of God to choose and empower Israel's king, despite their rejection of him in favour of an earthly king (8:7). The kingship is still secret, though it is a foregone conclusion when Samuel calls an assembly at Mizpah. Drawing lots (vs 20–21) is a way of discerning God's will, but since Saul has already been designated and anointed by God, it is simply a public confirmation of what God has done. Saul displays pleasing humility before his public acclamation (vs 16, 22). He also shows commendable restraint in the face of the cynicism and contempt (v 27).

All that God has set in motion has come to fruition. God is the God of history – and he has set things in motion in your life. Pray that you will be open to his equipping and empowering so that they will come to fruition.

The Bible in a year: Jeremiah 42–43; John 16

OCTOBER 21–27

DAY 4

Saul and the Ammonites

We left off yesterday saying that God is a God of history. History is not an idea. Concrete events which help us to focus on God are the content of history.

1 Samuel 11:1–15

Clearly Nahash was a cruel king who impressed his authority through fear. Gouging out eyes is an awful way to suppress people (v 2), so when he besieged Jabesh Gilead they pleaded for mercy (v 1). So confident was Nahash that there would be no help for Jabesh Gilead from the Israelites that he allowed them seven days (v 3). Saul – who was not acting at all like a king, ploughing a field (v 5) – heard of their plight. God used this desperate situation to galvanise Saul into action. The Spirit came upon him, giving him the courage and authority to dispatch the limbs of two oxen as a way of calling the tribes to war (vs 6–7). The Lord endorsed Saul's call to arms (v 7b), and the tribes responded (vs 7b–8). Nahash and the Ammonites were soundly defeated (vs 9–11). This event established Saul's authority, and from this time onward he was effectively king (vs 12–15), though unifying the tribes was a matter which Saul found very difficult, and did not fully achieve.

So often interruptions in our ordinary, everyday routine are of the Lord. Do not resent or resist them; they are divine interventions that may take you to new visions and endeavours. Ask God for the courage, like Saul, to be proactive.

The Bible in a year: Psalm 119:49–72; Jeremiah 44–46

OCTOBER 21–27

DAY 5

Samuel says goodbye

It is a sign of real insight and humility when people know it is time to step down. Most of us want to hold on too long, and as a result what has flourished withers.

1 Samuel 12:1–25

As Samuel steps down, we sense in him a feeling of betrayal (vs 1, 2). Perhaps this is why he seeks to justify his past actions, wanting assurances that he has acted in a godly manner (vs 3–5). Be that as it may, what a wonderful example Samuel is to us, in South Africa, of the right use of authority. Samuel goes on to show that the judges, of which he is the last, have saved Israel through the power of God (vs 6–11). But, he points out, when Nahash came on the scene, instead of accepting another judge, they wanted a king (vs 12–13). Samuel's act of bringing thunder and rain shows that he, the judge, is still the instrument of God (vs 16–18). Samuel ends his speech with a touching assurance of his prayers and ongoing teaching (v 23), and warns the people that they must continue to avoid idolatry, despite having a king; and stay constantly subject to the true King of Israel – God.

How have you reacted to change in South Africa? Change brings with it dangers and insecurities. Perhaps the worst is to want to go back to the past. Pray that you will live confidently in the present. Are you prepared to follow Samuel's example (v 23) and promise to pray earnestly for our nation?

Be prepared: Mark 1:14–15
Why are you afraid?: Mark 4:35–41

The Bible in a year: Jeremiah 47–48; John 17

OCTOBER 21–27

Going deeper ...

These are crucial chapters in the history of Israel. They form the narrative of how Israel switched from a judge to a king. They keep in balance those who want the kingship and those who believe that, in accepting the institution of king, God is being pushed out as the central figure in Israel's history. With an earthly king, rather than a judge, Israel would move into apostasy. The king would act as though he could do what he liked. The basis of Israel's history and theology is that God is King. Israel is a theocracy and anything which pulls them away from God's sovereignty is dangerous, and should be rejected.

The clash which ensued between prophets and kings in Israel's history always centred on the king being disobedient or following other gods. The kings, designated as God's representatives on earth, too often did as they pleased, and it was left to the prophets to represent the true monarch – God. Samuel saw what was coming and, in spite of God's reassurances, he found it difficult to let the change happen. The lasting impression from these chapters is that, while the people got their way, God, and certainly Samuel, were less than happy with the outcome. The sobering thought is that God permitted a course of action even though ultimately it led to disaster. We have the ability to choose; the Lord will not force himself upon us. If we insist on sidelining God, we too are courting disaster.

Change

Conclusion

None of us really looks forward to change on a large scale. Small changes are fun: a holiday, an occasional meal out, a room rearranged, a change in routine. These are stimulating and help us to appreciate the 'normal'. But changes which shake the roots of society and create unexpected imbalances are different.

We are experiencing such change in our own country, and we want to escape the corruption and violence. These changes involve attitudes and mind-sets; they involve new ways of seeing and doing things. They place enormous pressures on our spiritual and moral resources. During times like these it is not surprising when moral values and ethical behaviour are abandoned. People look for stability and call on the leadership to create a new morality. History is full of such circumstances.

People have not changed radically over thousands of years. Modern technology, while offering exciting possibilities, opens the way to different styles of corruption, dishonour or violence. New ethical and moral problems are created. 1 Samuel underlines the fact that change can be resisted or accepted, or sometimes it just happens, but it is monitored and influenced by God.

We look to God. God alone is the stabilising force; he alone is the rock on which society can be built. He gives us the moral fibre to deal with new situations. God is the one on whom we rely, and as we focus on him, we make the difference in society which leads to the new morality and love which we seek.

The Bible in a year: Psalm 119:73–96; Jeremiah 49–52; John 18

OCTOBER 28– NOVEMBER 3

Praying for change

Nehemiah

Transformation is a word on everyone's lips. Last year saw the holding of the Transformation Conference in Cape Town when delegates shared how prayer had transformed three crime-ridden cities in South and North America and Africa. It was marvellous to see on film the way God had totally changed these cities through repentance and unified prayer. We in Southern Africa can only dream of cities where everyone has water and electricity; where women and children can walk in safety; and where jails are empty. We just feel so powerless, looking at the crime, need and human suffering around us.

Nehemiah was confronted by just such a city, desperate for transformation. The facts were depressing – Jerusalem's wall was in ruins and had been for years. The temple was defenceless and the people were in disgrace. He had no resources: no modern cranes or front-end loaders to construct the wall, merely a group of untrained men and women and a high priest! It was a gargantuan task.

However, Nehemiah knew God. He was a man of real prayer, used to talking and walking with his heavenly Father. He was faced with a seemingly impossible task, yet he asked the Lord for his plan, and then implemented it with boldness and effectiveness. God, as he always does when we ask him for help, came through for Nehemiah and the people of Judah. They prayed for success and they got it. Their society and community life in Jerusalem were transformed.

Nehemiah shows us that no matter how desperate or impossible things seem to be, change is possible. Are you ready to pray for transformation in Southern Africa?

After qualifying at the University of Cape Town, Alison Bourne was a social worker for many years. She is currently Pastoral Assistant at Christ Church, Kenilworth, where her emphasis is the promotion of intercessory prayer.

OCTOBER 28–NOVEMBER 3

DAY 1

Praying for the impossible

Are there situations in your own family or our own country which break your heart or seem hopeless to you? Are there people or situations you'd love to see changed, but you cannot begin to imagine how this could happen?

God uses ordinary Christians working with him to accomplish seemingly impossible tasks.

Nehemiah 1:1–4

When Nehemiah heard about the walls of Jerusalem being in ruins, he was heartbroken. He knew that having broken walls made the inhabitants of the city vulnerable and defenceless. Walls, in those days, meant being able to live in safety. As a Jew he felt shame that the city that housed the temple was unprotected by a wall. He himself could do very little to change the situation. He was miles away in Susa. He had some influence with the king, but no real power.

And so Nehemiah sat down and wept. He mourned; he prayed and he fasted. He knew, despite his despair, that when we come before God with a problem, difficulties fall into perspective and we are shown the right course of action. Nehemiah's remarkable story shows us how God uses our prayers to achieve his purposes:

- God puts a burden on our hearts or shows us a special need.
- The Holy Spirit prompts us to pray to the Father who always has a solution.

How does prayer change our perspective about a problem? Why do you think God wants us to be his partners in prayer – surely he can solve problems without our help? Is the Holy Spirit laying a particular burden on your heart?

The Bible in a year: Lamentations 1–2; John 19

OCTOBER 28–NOVEMBER 3

DAY 2

Prayer that works

Are you an intimate friend of God? Are you confident about approaching him with your prayers and requests? How should you do this?

Nehemiah 1:5–2:10

Nehemiah had spent many hours talking and walking with God. He had an intimate relationship with him – he understood his nature and character. He knew that God keeps a covenant of love with those who love and obey him.

Nehemiah shows us that he was serious about rebuilding the wall. He persevered in prayer: he prayed for some days (1:4) and he prayed day and night (1:6). He also prayed spontaneously in emergency situations (2:4–5), but just like us he was afraid (2:2). However, he knew that he could confidently bring all these prayers to God, because he had had previous experience of the gracious and loving nature of God. 'And because the gracious hand of my God was upon me, the King granted my requests' (2:8). Without God, our work is in vain. God is our strength, power and the giver of good gifts.

Nehemiah, faced with a daunting situation, shows us how we can pray effectively. He praised and thanked God (1:5). He confessed and turned from his, his family's and the country's sins (1:6–7). He reminded God of his promises (1:8–9). And he made specific requests (1:11).

Are you battling to pray for a situation that seems hopeless? Use Nehemiah's prayer to help you – perhaps writing down your prayer. Persevere; admit your fears to the Lord; focus on the character of God who is loving and longs to answer you.

The Bible in a year: Lamentations 3–5; John 20

OCTOBER 28–NOVEMBER 3

DAY 3

Stategising for success

Have you ever thrown yourself into an activity with wild enthusiasm without much thought? Suddenly it all falls apart, and you think, 'What went wrong?' Before we start something, we should ask God what he wants us to do.

Nehemiah 2:11–20

One can imagine the scene – the moonlit night and Nehemiah on his horse, picking his way through the ruins of the wall. His aim was to see for himself what needed to be done. All the time, the gracious hand of the Lord was upon him (v 18). He assessed and he observed, and he made his plans, initially keeping them secret to make sure that they were the right plans. Nehemiah received the vision for rebuilding the wall from God. Then he shared the vision and challenges with the people and leaders to incorporate them in God's plan. The Holy Spirit impressed the vision on their hearts and there was unity of purpose – and so God could accomplish his task through them.

God wants us to achieve his purposes in the most effective way. His plans really are perfect, and he is very keen that we know what they are! How do we find out what they are? We need to ask him in prayer. We also need to use our God-given common sense: our ability to observe and assess situations. Having a God-given plan keeps us on track and we don't lose heart when things get tough.

Have you asked God whether he has a plan to solve your pressing problem? Nehemiah needed many others to make his plan work. Do you have a vision that you should share with others?

The Bible in a year: Ezekiel 1; John 21

OCTOBER 28–NOVEMBER 3

DAY 4

When things go wrong

When things go wrong, as they almost inevitably do, we often become exhausted, and lose sight of our goal. Lack of energy for the task often indicates that God is not in control, or that the enemy wants to discourage us.

Nehemiah 4:1–23

Nehemiah's task was incredibly ambitious. Yet it was accomplished by ordinary men and women – some working, some guarding – in a mere fifty-two days. However, they soon faced ridicule (vs 2–3), and finally the threat of attack (v 8). The builders were also overwhelmed by all the rubble, and soon became exhausted and started to complain (v 10). Nehemiah kept on praying (vs 4–5, 9) and asked the Lord for his plans to guard the walls and strengthen the people's morale.

This is a picture of the spiritual battle we face when completing any task, and how God always helps us. Satan wants us to become exhausted and distracted – he wants us to stop praying, and will attack us at our weakest points. We must be like watchmen (Isaiah 62:6–7) on the walls, always alert to the plans the enemy is making to hurt and discourage us. We have to keep focusing on God and his plans for us, and we have to use his weapons, and the authority we have in the name of Jesus to overcome the plans of the Evil One. Be like Nehemiah who told his people not to be afraid, to remember the Lord, and to fight (v 14)!

Ask God to show you how to deal with criticism and how to cope when your plans go awry. Put on the armour of God (Ephesians 6:10–18).

The Bible in a year: Psalm 119:97–120; Ezekiel 2–3

OCTOBER 28–NOVEMBER 3

DAY 5

Real faith

God is not only interested in our spiritual lives. He wants our faith to affect the way we live and interact with others.

Nehemiah 5:1–19

Nehemiah continued to lead the people – showing sensitivity and concern for them, but also exhibiting an amazing ability to organise and motivate them. He not only knew what God wanted him to do, but he continually talked to God. He was in communication with him on a daily and hourly basis, putting God's plans into action.

Nehemiah was also a leader who would not tolerate sin in his people. Some Jews were exploiting those who had returned from exile. They were charging them exorbitant interest rates on loans, and when they were unable to pay, forcing them to sell their fields and eventually to sell their children into slavery (vs 4–5). Nehemiah became very angry and stopped these practices (v 6–11).

Once he became Governor, he made sure he did not place onerous demands on the people, and continued working on the wall himself (v 14–16). He was committed to the welfare of all his people, especially to the poor in the city. In fact he shows us that fairness to the poor is central in our walk with God. Nehemiah also knew that any sin is absolutely abhorrent to the Lord and he urged his people to walk in the fear of God.

God will not answer our prayers if we have sin in our lives. Often when we are so busy and caught up in our own plans, we stop talking and walking with God. Are you in this position?

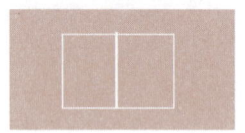

The praying church that saved Peter: Acts 12:1–19
Praying in the Holy Spirit: Jude 1:20; Romans 8:26–27

The Bible in a year: Ezekiel 2–3; James 1

Going deeper ...

Nehemiah was undoubtedly a great leader, used by God to make an impossible dream come true. However, he could not have done what he did without the people of Jerusalem. They, with all their different talents and gifts, actually did the building work and made the dream come true.

Fortunately, God has given us each other. Just as the people worked together to complete the wall, so every member of the Body of Christ must work together so that things can work effectively. The body needs you – it can't complete its work without you (1 Corinthians 12:12–28)! Unity is a precious thing in God's sight. We draw strength from one another and, it renews and revitalises our ministry and work. Unity is an attractive quality which draws others. It does not always mean agreeing with everything, but our ultimate purpose is the same. 'How good and pleasant it is when brothers live together in unity' (Psalm 133:1–3). In fact, God bestows his blessing where there is unity!

Transformation is conditional on unity, because God delights in unity – it's on his heart for us. We can't do it alone. He cannot answer our prayers for South Africa unless we are united in Jesus.

Are you guilty of criticism of others in the church or of spiritual pride?

Are you committed to unity in your church and across denominational barriers?

Instruments in God's hands

Nehemiah knew about earthly power – he'd seen it as cup-bearer to King Artaxerxes. He was then made Governor of Jerusalem where he could have reaped the rewards of his position. Yet out of reverence for God (5:15) he treated the people considerately, because he knew that the demands were heavy on them (5:18). He used his power and authority to sort out the shocking practices and sin of a section of the community. But Nehemiah knew even more about heavenly power. He knew that going to the Lord in prayer releases God's power in our lives. God can transform any situation, if only we will ask him! John Wesley said, 'God will do nothing on earth except in answer to believing prayer.' If we don't, he can't! God needs our prayers, he needs us to work as his partners to bring about his purposes and plans for our country. Does your heart bleed when you see men begging on the side of the road or see photographs of a sixteen-year-old girl dying of Aids?

We, like Nehemiah, are born for a time such as this. God has not made a mistake. God calls us to repentance, to unity, to seek his face, so that his plan for our cities and country can be established. The problems in South Africa are enormous, and we will face resistance in both the natural and spiritual realm. But our God is waiting on us to turn 'to him who is able to do far more abundantly than we can think or imagine, according to the power that is at work within us.' May his power at work within us change South Africa.

The Bible in a year: Psalm 119:121–144; Ezekiel 6–9; James 2

A new king in Israel

1 Samuel 15–16; 2 Samuel 5–7

The chapters for this week are highly selective because the events leading to David being acclaimed king are lengthy and fairly involved. The result is that we are looking at a tiny part of the picture.

The reality is that Saul could not cope with the kingship – and was caught in moods of depression. The music of David lifted his spirit, but David's presence and friendship with Jonathan caused huge jealousy for Saul. As a result, David ran for his life into the desert and spent time as the leader of a band of brigands. They lived dangerously, and certainly not legally, and Saul spent a good deal of time searching for David in order to kill him. On two occasions David spared Saul's life. David also formed an alliance with the Philistines.

The death of Saul and his sons was dramatic. By then David had established a rule in the southern part of Israelite territory. It took a while for him to become king of all the Israelites. It was after the assassination of Ishbosheth, who had succeeded Saul, that David was asked to rule over the whole territory.

David, like the rest of us, was a flawed person. His relationships with women were doubtful. He was deceitful in his dealings with the Philistines. He let Joab, his general, do his dirty work, and it was sometimes very dirty. He was weak with his children, which led to Absalom's revolt. But he had one characteristic which allowed history to judge him as the greatest king of Israel: he wanted to be obedient to God. And when it was shown that his behaviour was not worthy of God, he admitted his sin and repented. That is what made him great.

Duncan Buchanan is the former Anglican Bishop of Johannesburg. He claims to have a passion – woodwork; a religion – rugby; and a faith – Christianity!

NOVEMBER 4–10

DAY 1

Saul's disobedience

We often find ourselves rationalising the easy way out. Saul did, and it effectively cost him the kingship.

1 Samuel 15:1–16; 24–34

One of the most difficult elements to understand in the practice of ancient Israel was the command that in victory all living things were to be sacrificed to God (v 3). This seemingly barbarous custom was aimed at protecting the Israelites both physically and spiritually. God knew that the corrupt, idolatrous religious practices would threaten his relationship with his people. When Saul defeated the Amalekites, the saving of the best of the livestock, as well as Agag the king, seemed to make sense (vs 4–9).

Yet this act of disobedience raised the anger of God, and therefore Samuel. Samuel had no alternative but to confront Saul and convey God's message of judgement and rejection (vs 13–16). Saul's repentance was not enough. This had happened before. In the previous event, it was Saul's impatient sacrifice prior to a battle, rather than waiting for Samuel (13:3–14). On both occasions we can feel sympathy for Saul, but each time it was an act of disobedience.

God's rejection of Saul (vs 24–29), no matter how penitent he may have been, focuses us on Saul's impetuosity and inadequate leadership. No wonder he sank into deep depressions. An essentially good man, he could not cope with the weight of kingship under God.

Sometimes God's commands are difficult to understand – his ways are not ours. But sin enters human experience through disobedience, and ongoing disobedience in our daily lives mars our relationship with God and keeps us from fully doing his work.

The Bible in a year: Ezekiel 10–11; James 3

NOVEMBER 4–10

DAY 2

God is not interested in looks

It amazes me how much time and money is spent on making our image good. Clothes, hair, make-up, all help us believe that we are creating a good impression. But what of our attitudes, values, and concerns? They make up the people we really are.

1 Samuel 16:1–23

Surely verses 1–13 contain one of the best-known stories in the Old Testament. Samuel was seeking for a new king for Israel. All of Jesse's sons were splendid people: mature, able, of great stature. But that was not enough. What of their inner qualities? When David, the youngest, was finally called, the Lord told Samuel that he was the one with the right inner qualities (v 12) – and David was anointed as the next king. The Spirit came upon David as he was anointed (v 13), as it had upon Saul (10:9–10).

Verses 14 to 23 dwell on Saul's depression and David's skill as a singer and musician. They also explain how David entered Saul's court, and eventually befriended Jonathan. David's ability to soothe Saul is a delightful insight into what was to be a turbulent relationship between them. How sad verse 14 is! Saul started with such promise and potential. But he was disobedient and God's Spirit left him and he became the victim of depression.

Those whom God chooses he enables and equips. How sad it is when people who have been anointed and used by the Lord, forfeit their calling, because – like Saul – they are disobedient. Rather than being critical, let's examine ourselves, for 'there, but for the grace of God, go I'.

The Bible in a year: Ezekiel 12–13; James 4

NOVEMBER 4–10

DAY 3

David takes over

Action should always follow appointment. Status on its own is idolatry. So we look at David's actions following his being made king of all of Israel.

2 Samuel 5:1–25

David was initially king over Judah, reigning in Hebron. Only at the death of Ishbosheth, Saul's son, was he asked to reign over the northern tribes. This, in many ways, was the climax of David's life, for he was at last not only God's king but also the people's choice (vs 1–3). His first act was to take Jerusalem. The water shaft was always the vulnerable point in ancient towns – and that is how Jerusalem, considered otherwise impregnable, was captured (v 8). It was the perfect place for the capital of a nation that had just been consolidated (vs 9–11). Verse 12 expresses the ideal of David's reign, but sadly verses 13–15 suggest that the model of Baal kingship was not far below the surface.

While David had been an outlaw (1 Samuel 21–30) he had used his rebel status to take refuge with the Philistines. As king his task was to rid Israel of the Philistine oppression. Under God's direction, he did this very successfully (vs 17–25).

David is like us in so many ways. He wanted to do good, and often did, despite the fact that he was a flawed person – as we saw in the introduction. A key to his success was that David regularly 'enquired of the Lord' (vs 19, 23). God uses us, flawed as we are, when we seek his will for our lives and are obedient to his leading.

The Bible in a year: Ezekiel 14–15; James 5

NOVEMBER 4–10

DAY 4

Endings and beginnings

Each movement forward in our lives signals an end of things and a new way ahead. Frequently we want to hold on to the past and keep comfortable. Not so David.

2 Samuel 6:1–23

The Ark had, after its return from the Philistines, been resting in the house of Abinadab. Now David, in order to identify his kingship with the presence of God as symbolised by the Ark, took the Ark from Abinadab's house on its way to Jerusalem. Uzzah's 'familiarity' with the holy object had a terrible consequence, and David was both fearful and angry (vs 6–9). The Ark was lodged with Obed-Edom, and blessings fell on his household (vs 10, 11). This encouraged David to continue the procession three months later, with rejoicing, dancing and sacrifices (vs 12–15) and a final feast of joy (vs 17–19).

Michal, Saul's daughter and David's wife, rejected David's protestations of joy (v 16). She probably also recognised that her father's house had been finally rejected, now that the Ark was housed in the city of David. Her bitterness made it impossible for her to share her husband's joyful worship (v 20), and no doubt contributed to her remaining childless (v 23). The spontaneity of David's dancing may have been vulgar, as Michal suggested (v 20), but the crucial factor was that David, with true integrity, cemented the religious and political future of his reign under God, by bringing the Ark to Jerusalem.

To be oneself is important. To live by other people's agendas means we are prisoners of their values – and God comes second to human prejudice and values. Is the Lord calling you to 'loosen up' in your worship of him?

The Bible in a year: Psalm 119:145–176; Ezekiel 16–17

NOVEMBER 4–10

DAY 5

Good intentions, bad ideas

We often have good ideas, and get excited about them. What is more difficult is being prepared to give them up because they are not actually the right ideas. It takes courage to do that.

2 Samuel 7:1–17

We have seen in the readings this week David's initiatives to establish a stable monarchy. At this point he lived in 'a house of cedar' (v 2). His rule was stabilised and there was not only peace, but he had gone a long way to pushing the borders of Israel further than they would ever be. Now, surely, was the time to build a temple. Nathan agreed (v 3) until he received a revelation from God which made David back off (vs 4–17). There is an important distinction here. A tabernacle is a desert construction. Even when it appeared permanent, it was nevertheless understood to be mobile and flexible – as were the people of Israel in the desert. A temple on the other hand was a permanent structure in which a god lived, and was pagan in origin. God promised rather a Davidic dynasty (house) which would outlast buildings and would be a permanent sign of God's presence amongst the Israelites. The point is, God cannot be trapped in a building – even a building as grand as Solomon's temple – because God cannot be used and manipulated, only loved and obeyed.

'I have been with you wherever you have gone' (v 9). God is the God of your history, with all its twists and turns. Trust him to continue to shepherd and protect you.

David and the Messiah: Luke 1:67–79
God sends us out: Matthew 28:16–20

The Bible in a year: Ezekiel 18–19; 1 Peter 1

NOVEMBER 4–10

Going deeper …

We saw at the beginning of the week how David was a flawed person. He was a shrewd politician, yet his whole desire was to serve God. That, and his spontaneity make him very attractive. Unlike virtually all the other kings in Israel and Judah, he was prepared to accept the word of God from the prophet when he was tempted to stray from the right path, or indeed when he actually did what was contrary to God's will (2 Samuel 11–12).

What is important in all of this is that David allowed Israel's 'desert religion' of flexibility and movement to continue. He himself set about establishing the nation of Israel in relation to the neighbouring nations, particularly – initially – the Philistines. The other nations which surrounded Israel were to follow later.

Obedience to God, both practically and spiritually, is at the heart of our faith. They merge in a person like David. He could ask God about whether to go into battle, just as easily as he could hear Nathan and pray a prayer of repentance (Psalm 51). That surely was at the heart of David's charisma. In spite of his sinfulness; in spite of his rather dubious dealings with his 'gang' in the desert, as well as with the Philistines; in spite of his trying to make his religious activities bolster his political status; he was a person who ultimately saw himself as under the authority of God. He did not simply do what he wanted. That is what made him great, and in the future the house and lineage of David would bring us face to face with the Messiah.

God keeps his promise

Conclusion

Throughout this week's passages, we have been reminded that God is the God of history. That is easy to say. It has its origins in God's revelation at the burning bush where, in giving his name, 'I AM' (Exodus 3:13–14), he makes it clear that faith in God means constantly interpreting history – our history. For Moses it meant living by faith and believing that, through the Exodus, he would save his people. In David's context, it meant looking at the events surrounding him and believing that God does keep his promises. God promised peace and rest from his enemies; a place for his people and a great name for David. David, more than anyone, was instrumental in bringing the surrounding people into the ambit of Israel's borders. He made sure that a resting place for the Ark was established. Jerusalem was the capital of this small empire, and more important, the spiritual home for all those who worshipped and followed God.

So it must be with us. God has promised us, in Jesus, a special relationship with himself as his sons and daughters. He promises that he will be with us to the end of time. God *does* keep his promises, but his expectation from us is obedience and risk – moving out into society to make known through the way we live and relate to others, the wonderful presence of God. That requires courage, faith and perseverance.

The Bible in a year: Psalm 120–122; Ezekiel 20–23; 1 Peter 2

NOVEMBER 11–17

Why do Christians fast?

Matthew 6, 9; 1 Peter 5; Acts 13; David 1

Have you ever fasted as a deliberate spiritual discipline? I have, and I know it's not easy missing even one meal, when we are used to having all the food we want. Yet fasting is a spiritual discipline often practised in Scripture, and was modelled and taught by Jesus. Protestant churches have rather neglected it, but fasting is making a comeback. More and more churches and groups seek God in prayer with fasting. Corporate fasting is often mentioned in reports of revival and community transformation. Congregational fasts are common in some church communities. It's as though God has tapped his people on the shoulder and said, 'Remember fasting?'

There are many Biblical stories of fasting, and we'll look at some of them this week. The best known is probably Jesus' forty day fast (Luke 4:1–13). It followed his baptism; concluded with his temptation by Satan (when he said, 'Man does not live on bread alone'); and served as a prelude to his public ministry. Paul and the early church also practised fasting (Acts 13:3, 14:23).

Fasting is a *symbolic* act: a *spiritual* more than physical discipline. It is a lot like baptism or communion: an outward physical sign used to signify something inward and spiritual. Without the inward reality, the sign is meaningless at best, idolatry at worst.

Fasting is simply our hunger for God and his righteousness expressed through abandonment, specifically the abandonment of normal good things, as we pursue ('Draw near to' – James 4:8) the One who pursues us. Like all symbols, its meaning is best grasped as we experience it.

John Hewitson is a cardio-thoracic surgeon at the Red Cross Children's Hospital in Cape Town. He is married to Di and they have a son, Joshua.

NOVEMBER 11–17

DAY 1   'Then they will fast'

Jesus established a new kingdom on earth into which we who are saved are welcomed. We are welcomed as his friends (John 15:15) and fellow-workers (1 Corinthians 3:9). Friends seek each other's company; go out of their way for each other. Fellow-workers work together! We are also called his 'bride'. He is our Bridegroom.

Matthew 9:14–17

John's disciples and the Pharisees fasted, but Jesus' disciples did not (v 14). Fasting was generally a sign of mourning for sin or desperation over one's situation. Jesus explains that when the Bridegroom (Messiah) is present (v 15) at the wedding reception; it is inappropriate to 'mourn' (fast). The absence of fasting by the disciples was a sign of the presence of God in their midst.

But Jesus says the time will come when he is 'taken from them; *then* they will fast'. According to Jesus we are now living in the time for fasting: while he is 'away' and until he returns at the second coming.

The unshrunk cloth and new wine (vs 16–17) speak of new ways for the new kingdom. We are now Christ's co-workers. Fasting is no longer just personal mourning, but mourning with God for the things on his heart rather than on ours. We fast and pray to seek his presence, his will and his solutions.

Are you a friend and co-worker of Jesus? Consider choosing a time for a short fast, say from one meal, when you will pray instead of eat. Tell him now that you are available for this. Wait for a moment in his presence with the request that he begin to burden your heart with his burdens.

The Bible in a year: Ezekiel 24–25; 1 Peter 3

NOVEMBER 11–17

DAY 2

Who, me? Fast?

The Sermon on the Mount (Matthew 5–7) is like Jesus' 'manifesto'. It is an outline of what he stands for and a description of how his disciples should live. In today's reading from this manifesto, Jesus speaks of three 'acts of righteousness' (v 1) which he clearly expects of his disciples.

Matthew 6:1–18

Notice that in verses 2, 5, and 16, Jesus introduces each 'act of righteousness' with the words: 'When you …' He clearly *expects* us to be giving, praying, and fasting! They are not optional extras! But he criticises the Pharisees who took great pride in their devotion: their 'acts of righteousness' were done in a blaze of publicity to boast of their piety (vs 2, 5, 16).

Jesus isn't against public prayer. He himself often prayed in public. If people know you are fasting, that in itself isn't wrong. Jesus is saying, 'Do not let pride be a part of your motivation.' Acts of righteousness are empty when our motive is to be known and admired for them. But if we fast with a 'pure heart' (right motives), Jesus promises that our Father *will* reward us (v 18).

Consider how to start living up to Jesus' expectations of a private life of giving, prayer, and fasting. Tell him that you want to, and ask him to help you by giving you his heart of compassion. Tell him you want to give as he directs; pray for his will and his concerns; and fast for his presence.

The Bible in a year: Ezekiel 26–27; 1 Peter 4

NOVEMBER 11–17

DAY 3

Fasting brings humility

'Whoever exalts himself will be humbled, and whoever humbles himself will be exalted' (Matthew 23:12). Humility pleases God; he exalts the humble. Biblically, fasting is inextricably linked to the command to humble ourselves. It has always been the way God's people humble themselves. We humble ourselves to seek his face, and to understand his will, rather than to express our own.

1 Peter 5:5–11

The command here (v 6) is to humble yourself. The Bible never says, 'Ask God to humble you.' We take the initiative. David said, 'I humble myself through fasting' (Psalm 35:13). Fasting is one way to humble yourself. Notice in verse 5 that God 'opposes the proud'. When pride is your motivation, God himself will oppose you! But if you are humble, God gives you grace (v 5b). He grants you his empowering presence to enable you to succeed.

We are also told to resist Satan (v 9). Pride is behind many temptations (as it was in Jesus' temptation); we can resist by humbling ourselves. Then God himself will 'make (us) strong, firm and steadfast' (v 10). In humbling ourselves we confess our reliance on God. Peter says, 'Cast all your anxiety on him' (v 7). 'Cast' is a strong word meaning 'hurl with force'. Get rid of those anxieties – the things that tear you away from relying on God.

Talk to God about the phrase 'he cares for you' (v 7). Make it personal: 'You care for me.' Almighty God himself cares for me! Care indicates his heart-attitude toward me. I hurl all my anxieties to him.

The Bible in a year: Ezekiel 28–29; 1 Peter 5

DAY 4

Fasting together

Corporate fasting was a normal part of early church life, and has been down the centuries. There are many biblical examples of the power of united prayer and fasting. We saw how in Matthew 6:16–18 Jesus instructed us not to fast with public display or to let pride be a part of our motivation. But Jesus was not excluding corporate fasts, and the early church clearly understood this.

Acts 13:1–5

The disciples at Antioch were together fasting and worshipping (v 2). They were not praying for something; not wanting something; but worshipping, spending time in God's presence, listening to him; and fasting was a natural part of the process. They heard God tell them to 'set apart' Barnabas and Saul. So then they fasted *and* prayed, and Saul and Barnabas were commissioned by the church to launch their missionary work (v 3).

Fasting can give us a heightened awareness of the voice of God, of his gentle prompting. So we fast to hear and understand God's will, his ways and his solutions, not to demand our own way. We should never look on fasting as a way to 'twist the arm of God'.

Corporate fasting is often easier. There is support and accountability. It's easier to battle 'the flesh and the devil' when we're not alone. Ask God to grow the habit of prayer and fasting amongst your Christian friends. Consider arranging with a friend or a small group to set aside a particular meal to fast and pray in unity.

The Bible in a year: Psalm 123–125; Ezekiel 30–31

NOVEMBER 11–17

DAY 5

'Daniel' fasts

The principle of fasting is self-denial, not starvation! It is a meaningful symbol of your humility and seriousness about seeking God's presence. Thus most people, while fasting, permit themselves at least water, often more. Partial fasts taking only juice, tea or milk are popular. One can also include nourishing drinks, or just cut out 'choice foods' like desserts. Such fasts are sometimes called 'Daniel' fasts.

Daniel 1:3–17

The king wanted the young men to rely on a special diet for strength (v 5). Daniel decided rather to rely on God. He had faith that God would honour his choice. And God did (v 15). But he honoured their faith, not their fast. The fast was a *symbol* of their self-denial and willingness to rely on God. God responded, giving them wisdom and strength (v 17).

As an old man Daniel again followed this kind of fast when praying for the restoration of Israel. He wrote: 'I ate no choice food; no meat or wine touched my lips; and I used no lotions at all until the three weeks were over' (10:3). Again, God responded and answered his prayers.

Choose an evening, a meal, a day or even just an hour to pray while denying yourself food or something else. Self-denial can be applied as a fast to many things: drinks (coffee, tea, etc.), sweets, television, telephones, music, the internet. Choose something sufficiently important to you to be a meaningful symbol of self-denial whilst you pray.

A nation saved: Esther 4:1–17
A city repents: Jonah 3:1–10

The Bible in a year: Ezekiel 32–33; 2 Peter 1

Going deeper ...

Fasting is often abused. It is not, as the Old Testament prophets pointed out, simply a way of ensuring that God answers our prayers. It is a symbol of what is going on inside us: a deep hunger for God, for his presence, and not for his assent to our will. For God, the denial of any appetite for the sake of spending time with him, or for him in ministry, is a 'fast' — and something that pleases him more than a skipped meal.

In Isaiah 58 (entitled 'True Fasting' in the NIV) God says that *how we live* is the real test of the authenticity of our fasting (vs 3–7). If, in spite of fasting, we are 'gluttons' in other ways, or mistreat employees (v 3), or are irritable and contentious (v 4), or neglect the poor and needy (v 7), then our fasting is *not acceptable* to God! We cannot substitute religious discipline for righteous living (see Jesus' criticism of 'the hypocrites' in Matthew 6:1–18). Of course, fasting in penitence for an unrighteous lifestyle is good, as long as we are committed to changing that lifestyle.

God is concerned that the hungry are fed and the oppressed are liberated. In Isaiah 58 he calls this 'feeding and freeing' his 'chosen fast' (v 6). Fasting is meant to awaken us to the hunger of the world, not just our own hunger. When you fast with humility he will 'guide you always; he will satisfy your needs in a sun-scorched land and will strengthen your frame. You will be like a well-watered garden, like a spring whose waters never fail' (Isaiah 58:11).

'You are my portion'

Jesus specifically gave instructions about 'when' you fast not 'if' (Matthew 6:16). The question is not 'Should I fast?' but 'When and how should I fast?' Fasting is a biblical way of humbling yourself before God and expressing your total reliance on him. Don't be tempted to fast in an attempt to get what you want. Be willing to submit to God's will. Fasting is not a tool to force God to act. Jesus' teaching on fasting calls for a radical orientation towards God; it calls for a real, authentic, personal relationship with God; for spending time waiting on him to discover his will and ways. The Father will reward you, but don't try telling him how to do it!

Biblically, the commonest fast was one day. There is no 'formula fast' that is the 'right' way to do things. Fasting is about the condition of your heart, not the number of meals or days. Fasting is a symbolic act, a *spiritual* discipline. It simply means denying (sacrificing) yourself *so that* you can pray or worship, or minister for God. Going without food but not praying is just dieting!

When we fast our hunger (physical) is turned into prayer (spiritual). 'Yes Lord, as I feel the hunger, I acknowledge that's how I am spiritually. I am *hungry* for you, to hear from you, to be empowered by the Spirit, to know your will. No Lord, I will not give in to these bodily desires before I have spent this time with you – you come first. 'You are my portion, O Lord' (Psalm 119:57).

The Bible in a year: Psalm 126–128; Ezekiel 34–37; 2 Peter 2

NOVEMBER 18–24

Divine intervention

Ezra

There is much gloom and doom about the state of South Africa. Crime on the streets and corruption in high places seem to be the order of the day. Human life is cheap and the strands of the hoped for 'rainbow nation' seem as far apart as ever.

The nation of Israel was in an even worse situation. They had been defeated and exiled to Babylon, some 1 500 km from their beloved Jerusalem, which lay in ruins, as did the temple which symbolised God's presence. There seemed no chance of their ever being restored to their land. However, just when things seemed hopeless, God intervened. Weak and helpless the Israelites might have been, but God was still sovereign, and the might of the Babylonian Empire was no obstacle to his restoration programme. The Babylonians were swept aside by the Persians, and the stage was set for the Israelites to return to their land.

The book of Ezra is just part of the story, which starts in 2 Chronicles and continues in Nehemiah. It seems that all three books had the same author, possibly Ezra himself. It is the thrilling story of Divine activity overruling human failure; of God using gentile kings and governors, Jewish leaders, prophets and priests. Ezra himself is described as a 'scribe'; but he was far more than someone who just recorded things: he was a teacher, an unfolder of the meaning of God's will (as we shall see in chapters 9–10).

God does intervene in the affairs of men. As we read about his restoration of Israel, let's continue to trust him to intervene in our land.

Alf Friend is the National Bible Ministry Co-ordinator of Scripture Union. He retired from headmastering in 1998.

NOVEMBER 18–24

DAY 1

Unexpected moves

Sometimes the challenges we face are huge. People and circumstances seem insurmountable, and we are tempted to throw in the towel before we've even begun. No doubt the Jews in exile had similar feelings. But God had a surprise for them!

Ezra 1:1–11

The Jews must have wondered how Jeremiah's prophecy that they would return to Jerusalem after seventy years (Jeremiah 29:10) would ever be fulfilled. They were still in captivity and in no position to make it happen. But God had Cyrus up his sleeve! King Cyrus conquered Babylon in 539 BC, and immediately issued a decree that the Jews should be allowed to return to Jerusalem to rebuild the temple. Why this extraordinary action? Very simply: 'the Lord moved the heart of Cyrus' (v 1). The Lord can 'move the heart' of the most unlikely person. He is sovereign and uses whom he pleases.

There was nothing grudging about Cyrus's permission to the Jews: anybody could go; their neighbours were instructed to provide them with lavish gifts (v 4); and he returned all the temple valuables to them (vs 7–11). When God moves the heart, there are no half measures! But the Lord's work did not end with Cyrus. He opened the way through a pagan king and then *moved* his own people: 'Everyone whose heart the Lord moved – prepared to go up to build the house of the Lord' (v 5).

The Lord moves whoever he pleases, whether saint or sinner. Are you prepared for him to move in you? And more important, to move when and where he directs you?

The Bible in a year: Ezekiel 38–39; 2 Peter 3

NOVEMBER 18–24

DAY 2

First things first

In our busy lives it is difficult to prioritise. Which calls on your time carry God's stamp of approval?

Ezra 3:1–13

The Jews have settled down in Israel (v 1). What is their first priority? Surely to build the temple – that is what they have come for. Instead the priests immediately begin to build the altar (vs 2–3) and offer sacrifices to God (vs 3–6). This before they have even started on the temple foundations (v 6). It could be argued that there would be plenty of time for sacrifices once the temple was built; weren't they putting the cart before the horse? No indeed! The altar and its sacrifices were central to Israel's relationship with God. So first things first: restore the relationship then the building.

It was not all plain sailing. They soon ran into opposition from the locals, but they were not put off. They were *fearful*, but they remained *faithful* to their task (v 3). And then it was time to start on the temple. They went about things systematically: financing craftsmen; securing building materials (v 7); contracting the right people, the Levites (or priests), to supervise the job (v 8). Having delegated responsibility, the leaders didn't just sit back and relax: they got stuck into the work themselves (v 9).

At last the foundation was complete, and what rejoicing there was (vs 10–11)! Amid due pomp and ceremony they praised the Lord for his goodness and his love which 'endures for ever' (v 11).

Has the Lord called you to a specific task? He has equipped you, but he expects you to be organised, bold and hard-working.

The Bible in a year: Ezekiel 40–41; 1 John 1

NOVEMBER 18–24

DAY 3

Highs and lows

So often after euphoric highs (like the celebration of praise in chapter 3:11) we plunge into the realities of life and our joy evaporates.

Ezra 4:1–5, 24; 5:17

No sooner had the building started than the opposition appeared (4:1–2). Their first strategy was infiltration. Accepting their offer would have meant compromise, as their religion was a synthesis of Jehovah and pagan worship. So Zerubbabel and Jeshua would have nothing of it (4:3). Next came psychological warfare (4:4–5). It was a sustained attack, lasting some sixteen years. Resisting a brief onslaught is one thing, but coping with sustained pressure is another. Initial strength and enthusiasm eventually gave way to weariness and lethargy. The enemies' aim was subtly to discourage. And they succeeded, bringing the work to a halt (4:24).

But help was on the way. The prophets, Haggai and Zechariah, suddenly burst on the scene and challenged the Jews' commitment (5:1). Apparently some of them were building themselves luxury homes instead of restoring the temple (Haggai 1:4)! Revival broke out, and the building recommenced. Even the prophets rolled up their sleeves and got stuck in to the work (5:2)!

Next it was bureaucracy in the form of the local governor, Tattenai, that reared its officious head (5:3–4). Who gave you permission? What are your credentials? The leaders' bold and lucid reply (5:11–16) resulted in a letter being dispatched to verify their story (5:6), and the building continued.

'But the eye of their God was watching over the elders of the Jews, and they were not stopped' (5:5). This is the secret of the builders' success – and yours as well.

The Bible in a year: Ezekiel 42–43; 1 John 2

NOVEMBER 18–24

DAY 4

Patience wins the day

Nobody is beyond God's sovereign will and purpose. Yet so often we feel that he is incapable of working in our personal situation!

Ezra 6:1–22

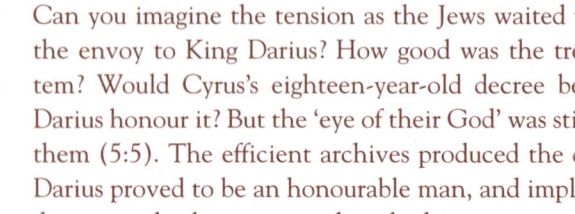

Can you imagine the tension as the Jews waited for the return of the envoy to King Darius? How good was the treasury filing system? Would Cyrus's eighteen-year-old decree be found? Would Darius honour it? But the 'eye of their God' was still watching over them (5:5). The efficient archives produced the document (v 2). Darius proved to be an honourable man, and implemented Cyrus's decree to the letter, even though this meant extensive financial commitment (vs 8–10).

Yes, God was still at it. Nearly two decades after he had moved the heart of Cyrus (1:1), he did a similar job on Darius (v 22). God also had Tattenai in hand. Ever the perfect bureaucrat, he now couldn't do enough to help the Jews (v 13). At last, over two decades after construction had commenced, the temple was completed (v 15). It hadn't been easy, but they had persevered.

Perhaps we can learn something from this story about our dealings with civil authorities. Sometimes they can be so frustrating and slow, and we become highly agitated, especially when there is injustice or God's work is adversely affected. Plodding, prayerful patience often pays off. Explosive impatience seldom honours the Lord; protest should be a last resort.

How do you feature when it comes to perseverance? Personally, I find it exciting to start a new venture, but my staying power is poor. Jesus said: 'He who stands firm to the end will be saved' (Mark 13:13).

The Bible in a year: Psalm 129–131; Ezekiel 44–45

NOVEMBER 18–24

DAY 5

The Lord's hand

Are you feeling out on a limb at the moment? The Lord's hand is still on you.

Ezra 7:1–10, 27–28; 8:21–23, 31–34

There is a gap of nearly sixty years between chapters 6 and 7. Artaxerxes I is now king, and at last Ezra himself appears on the scene. He was a priest and scribe with an excellent pedigree (vs 1–5), and a learned academic (vs 6, 10). He probably would have had some official position in Babylon, possibly Secretary of State for Jewish Affairs. But Ezra was no dusty divine. Forsaking his cloistered, academic security, he set out on the risky 1 500 km, four-month journey to Jerusalem (vs 8–10).

Ezra's distinguishing feature was not his learning, but the fact that 'the hand of the Lord his God was on him'. These words occur no fewer than five times in today's reading (7:6, 9, 28; 8:22, 31). It was the secret of his success with Artaxerxes (vs 6, 28), and ensured protection along the way (vs 31, 32). But Ezra, like the rest of us, had moments of doubt. He had assured the king that they did not need an escort as God would protect them (v 22). But as the dangerous journey, carrying very valuable articles (8:24–27), was about to begin, he wished that he had not been so adamant. His subsequent action at the Ahava Canal is a clue to his closeness to the Lord, despite moments of doubt. He proclaimed a fast, and he and his fellow travellers humbled themselves and prayed for safety for three days (vs 21, 23).

'The gracious hand of our God is on everyone who looks to him' (v 22). Make time, as Ezra did, to look to him.

True repentance: Ezra 9:1–15
Sighing in the rain: Ezra 10:1–17

The Bible in a year: Ezekiel 46–47; 1 John 3

Going deeper …

Why did God allow the Israelites to be defeated by King Nebuchadnezzar and exiled to Babylon? Jeremiah had repeatedly prophesied that this would happen, and made himself very unpopular by recommending that Israel surrender to Nebuchadnezzar, as the only way to save the nation (Jeremiah 27:6–11). The problem was Israel's repeated idolatry. After endless warnings God finally lost patience and banished them from their land.

The exile had its desired effect: as C Campbell Morgan points out, they 'never set up an idol again'. It was at this time that the Pharisees first appeared. They were a divine movement whose role was to make sure that the worship of Jehovah remained pure. At its inception Phariseeism was a good thing, yet some 480 years later Jesus had only scathing criticism of them (Matthew 23).

What had gone wrong? What had started out as a movement to enrich and enhance worship ended up enslaving the worshippers. It replaced the spirit of worship with the letter of the law. Worship became an outward show, and the rules became more important than the people they were meant to serve. As Jesus retorted: 'The sabbath was made for man, not man for the Sabbath' (Mark 2:27).

Sadly, history repeats itself. So often what starts out as a movement of God ends up enslaving instead of liberating. Man and his teachings take centre stage, and the work of the Spirit is sidelined. We need to be constantly alert!

'He made it again'

The heading is a quotation from a wonderful object lesson that God gave to Jeremiah. He went down to the potter's house at the Lord's bidding, and watched the potter moulding a pot. The pot was a failure, so the potter took the clay and 'he made it again … as seemed best to him' (Jeremiah 18:4, AV).

This story sums up perfectly the theme of our readings this week. The purpose of the object lesson, given to Israel before their exile, was to assure them that God could remould them: 'Can I not do with you as this potter does?' (v 6). At that stage Israel would not accept the offer: 'It's no use. We will continue with our plans' (v 12). So they went into exile. But God's promise still stood, and Ezra and Nehemiah tell us the story of how God began to remake the pot that had been marred.

We serve a gracious God, a God of infinite patience who does not write us off when we fail. He is a God who gives us another chance, as he did to Jonah after his disobedience: 'Then the word of the Lord came to Jonah a *second* time' (Jonah 3:1). The Lord comes again and again offering to remould us into 'something beautiful for God'. He continues to say to us, 'Like clay in the hand of the potter, so are you in my hand' (Jeremiah 18:5). He waits for our response.

The Bible in a year: Psalm 132–134; Ezekiel 48; 1 John 4

NOVEMBER 25– DECEMBER 1

The time has come

John 17–19

When we look around us, nationally and internationally, the signs are there. Obviously every day is a day closer to the return of our Lord Jesus Christ. Spiritually speaking, the twigs are budding and summer, it would seem, is imminent. The day or the hour is unimportant, but the clarion call of the prophetic trumpets needs to be heeded. Jesus taught us to pray 'thy kingdom come', because it's God's ultimate desire that Jesus returns to govern bodily. But it's almost a stuttering and stammering hope we hear. In some quarters it's almost a dead expectation, as Christians are intimidated by the world's cynicism.

Popular modern theology is all about the *utility* of the cross, stressing the *work* of Christ rather than the *person* of Christ. What he *did* for me has become more important than what he *is* to me. Christianity is now jolly good fun, so what's the rush for heaven? Christ has done all the suffering, so that we can now enjoy all the benefits – like a spiritual Country Club!

But it's God's will that Jesus returns. We need to believe it, pray for it and get excited about it. Jesus had two missions. The first was to die on the cross, pay for sin and restore the spiritual link with our Father in heaven. 'The time has come,' said Jesus (John 17:1), and as always the timing was perfect. The second is to return, rule and bring judgment on all dissidents. That time will come, for sure! In the meantime, very simply the major challenge is to get people to repent and be 'born again'. Time is short and lives need to be challenged and radically changed.

Peter Pollock is a former South African cricketer and selector and father of Shaun Pollock, the current Proteas' captain. Peter Pollock Ministries has an effective and wide-ranging ministry in South Africa.

NOVEMBER 25–DECEMBER 1

DAY 1

A world of difference

John 17 really is the Lord's Prayer (rather than the prayer Jesus taught his disciples in Matthew 6:9–13). Consequently Jesus' requests were prompted by the Spirit and most certainly answered by his Father. All he requested has already happened or will take place.

John 17:1–19

'I am not praying for the world, but for those you have given me' (v 9). Jesus knew with certainty that the gospel would face opposition. Just as he was given a tough time by the politicians and religious leaders, so would those who followed him. Worldly kingdoms and nations are mere pawns; simply a means to an end. 'My kingdom is not of this world,' Jesus told Pilate (John 18:36), and 'flesh and blood cannot inherit the kingdom of God' (1 Corinthians 15:50). God's kingdom is for those who have died to their own kingdoms! Sadly, nationalism and patriotism bring division. That's why the gospel is guaranteed to bring discomfort to its adherents. Jesus would no longer be around, so he asked that his name and his word protect the believers in a hostile environment (vs 11–12).

Jesus' church needs to be around. The world is the believers' platform. But Jesus sought protection for them against the Evil One whose wiles would constantly buffet them. The true rewards are not on earth but in heaven, so beware those who dish out religious accolades! But his sheep will be recognised by their lives, love and joy that are beyond this world's understanding.

Pray that you may know the peace that the Father's protection brings (v 11). And trust him for a 'full measure of (Jesus') joy'.

The Bible in a year: Daniel 4–5; 1 John 5

NOVEMBER 25–DECEMBER 1

DAY 2

Real unity

We live in a world of pretence and nowhere is it more plastic than in the area of unity, where we are continually 'walking on egg shells' trying to convince everyone, including ourselves, that the brotherhood of man is a biblical doctrine!

John 17:20–26

Jesus prayed that we should 'be one' (v 21). I have travelled much, both as a cricketer and evangelist, and have stayed in many homes and met many people across the globe. Cultural and colour differences are perceptibly absent when the fellowship involves true believers. There is an immediate warmth and unity of the spirit.

Spiritual unity transcends all the natural 'people' barriers. It cannot be imitated and this makes the devil furious. Unity of the Spirit is *divine* and is based on our unity with the Father and Son (v 23), while unity of common cause and like minds is *human*. The latter is so fragile because minds change so often as do politically expedient causes.

Until the end times the church will house both wheat and tares (Matthew 13:24–30). The Holy Spirit will finally separate believers and unbelievers. Until then they will live side by side, but they will never find true unity. Rest assured, however, that politicians will continue to brandish national pride and patriotism as the demagogue of unity.

Marvel afresh at the unity you have with Jesus and the Father. Your relationship with your fellow believers is rooted in this. Ask the Lord to help you to recognise his grace in others, and to give you patience and gentleness in your dealings with them.

The Bible in a year: Daniel 6–7; 2 John

NOVEMBER 25–DECEMBER 1

DAY 3

The ultimate betrayal

Betrayal is so common these days. Newspapers and magazines highlight it daily. Greed, revenge, a grievance, the temptation of financial reward, all too easily expose this ugly side of human nature. So why should we be surprised at Judas, the ultimate biblical example?

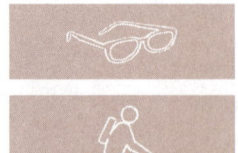

John 18:1–11

Judas was a genuine, called disciple. He was also the treasurer, a position of trust, but he became a traitor. Clearly it's not position, placement or perception that count. Deep inside he had a weakness, which Satan exploited, and he succumbed with the help of the influential Pharisees.

Maybe Judas felt that Jesus was not utilising his power and influence strongly enough in bringing political change. Maybe he felt that he had a better plan. There is no doubt, once Satan had entered him, that he believed he was doing right – the classic deception! Even the vilest dictators, like Hitler, believe in their mission. Maybe it does shatter us that someone so close to Jesus could have been led astray and betrayed. But I believe it's a profound warning. He needed to keep his eyes on Jesus and not on himself. It's so easy to get caught up in one's own agendas.

When Judas finally realised what he had done and how he had been 'conned' by the Pharisees, he was remorseful. He was desperately sorry and this brought depression and self-pity that led to suicide and eternal damnation. Too often we go that route when what is required is repentance.

Have you recognised and owned up to your sin? Being remorseful is not enough; forgiveness comes only after genuine repentance.

The Bible in a year: Daniel 8–9; 3 John

NOVEMBER 25–DECEMBER 1

DAY 4

A turning point

From time to time, we all experience incidents and episodes that affect us profoundly. Peter's denial of Christ was the turning point in his life.

John 18:12–27

Peter had made a fool of himself a few times. One comment caused Jesus to reply, 'Get behind me Satan.' In the garden he drew a sword and cut off Malchus's ear (v 10). Peter had vowed loyalty and support (John 13:37), yet when the crunch came he denied Jesus three times (vs 17, 25–27). But there is no doubt that Peter loved and adored Jesus. His heart was in the right place, and that's what counts. In the other three gospels, the writers record that, after his denial, Peter wept bitterly. It was a passionate response indicating the type of relationship he had with Jesus. His heart-felt realisation of what he had done registered massively.

Peter had once been persuaded to go out fishing by Jesus (Luke 5:4–11). Suddenly he had looked with amazement into a full net! Jesus had moved into his area of expertise and Peter was astounded. His response to the revelation was to cry out, 'Go away from me, Lord; I am a sinful man.' Jesus responded by telling him that he could now become a fisher of men. To serve Jesus requires passion and a clear understanding of sin. You can't preach about or understand the love, grace, mercy and forgiveness of God except as a 'saved sinner, totally repentant and utterly grateful'.

We can deny the Lord through our lifestyle, our actions and our silence. Ask the Lord to keep you passionate – never forgetting your first love, and single-minded in your service for him.

The Bible in a year: Psalm 135–136; Daniel 10–12

NOVEMBER 25–DECEMBER 1

DAY 5

The wrong choice

Life is about choices. We are all part of the decision-making process, but sadly education prepares us for just about every decision except the most important of all – our response to Jesus Christ. And the world does its level best to relegate this decision to mere religious preference!

John 18:28–19:16

'Give us Barabbas' (v 40), shouted the mob. The 'world' chose Barabbas, and sadly still does. This notable prisoner, half-robber, half-revolutionary, was the alternative to Jesus. It was decision time and Jesus got the thumbs down. The motley, ignorant rabble had been roused by political, social and religious manipulation. Pilate knew that Jesus was innocent (v 38). But such was public pressure that he yielded to political expedience (v 12–16).

No man can evade taking responsibility: the time of choice always comes. Typically, Pilate tried to exonerate himself by washing his hands in public (Matthew 27:24). We invariably try to excuse ourselves and blame others, but it doesn't work. Blood is not washed off easily. The ignorant masses responded defiantly, almost shaking their fists at God, 'Let his blood be on us and our children'(Matthew 27:25). No more reckless cry was ever uttered. The voice of the people is very rarely the voice of God. AW Tozer once wrote: 'The masses are always wrong! The number of the righteous is small; be sure you are among them.'

Ask the Lord to give you the discernment to recognise the difference between his truth and popular opinion. Pray for the courage and conviction to stand for that truth irrespective of the consequences.

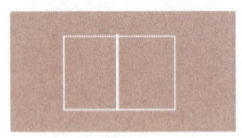

Gospel never popular: John 17:14
A precision plan: John 17:1–26

The Bible in a year: Hosea 1–2; Jude

NOVEMBER 25–DECEMBER 1

Going deeper …

At Pentecost Peter delivered one of the greatest sermons ever preached (Acts 2:14–41). He told the gathered crowd, 'You, with the help of wicked men, put him to death by nailing him to the cross' (v 23). It is vital to understand that each one of us put Jesus through the agony of Gethsemane and Calvary. Jesus didn't just die for the sins of the 'world'. He also died for my 'transgressions' and 'iniquities'. Jesus went to the cross and there he became my personal Lord and Saviour. Jesus opened the way for us to become intimate with our Father in heaven.

I once had a very special experience at the Garden of Gethsemane in Jerusalem. In a profound moment I came to understand that Jesus had in fact died very specially for me. I, through my sin and iniquity, had nailed him to the cross. But as he looked down at me from the cross, his response was loving: 'Father, forgive (him) because (he) does not know what (he) is doing.' My life was never to be the same again. Don't blame everyone else: Pilate, the Romans or the Jews. I am to blame – that's the essence of sin. Acceptance of guilt and the consequences of sin are vital in restoring our relationship with God. It's the key to revival.

The faith message

'They have obeyed your word … they know that everything you have given me comes from you … they knew with certainty … they believed' (John 17: 6–8). What a wonderful summing up of faith: 'They have obeyed your word.' The importance of obedience in an age that has gone overboard on grace, cannot be stressed enough. The challenge is to submit to the Lordship of Jesus and do what he says. 'Do not merely listen to the word … Do what it says' (James 1:22). We need to be promise keepers, not promise makers and promise breakers.

Our society is so obsessed with freedom that we have got into bondage. Anarchy and rebellion now parade as liberty! Ironic isn't it? Jesus requires faith that in turn establishes obedience. If you believe, you listen. Unfortunately, contempt for God's laws is rife; and we wonder why lives don't change and the church has no power. Knowing with certainty is not something you can teach. It starts with a decision of the heart and will, not just the mind. I have counselled people who freely admit that they should believe; they know that the Gospel is true, but confess that personally they just can't take that step of faith. At least they are honest.

Billy Graham's turning point came when his friend told him that the Bible needed up-dating. He chose to believe absolutely in God's Word. He was also accused of being 'naïve' in this intellectual and highly scientific world. The accuser was Sir David Frost, of TV fame. Billy Graham's child-like certainty disturbed him in a world where, 'although they claimed to be wise, they became fools' (Romans 1:22).

The Bible in a year: Psalm 137–138; Hosea 3–8; Revelations 1

DECEMBER 2–8

New beginnings

John 19–21

I usually like new beginnings. There's a freshness and anticipation about what's ahead, the edge of excitement in the unknown, the chance for a clean start … But then again, new beginnings imply old endings! Letting go of the old way is sometimes harder than we expect.

When it comes to new beginnings with Jesus I guess we'd all like to say we're eager and ready. But what if that means Jesus not being quite how he was before? What if it means not being sure where he will turn up next? What if it means being challenged to trust in new ways? This week the disciples are challenged by the new beginning of relating to a resurrected Jesus. They experience the roller-coaster ride of ecstatic joy – and hardly daring to believe. They tell excited stories – and hide fearfully behind locked doors. They want to see Jesus again – and they doubt that it is really him. They wonder if Jesus will want to see them again after the way they've treated him – and they discover that he does!

Perhaps you can identify with some of their ups and downs. Sometimes it's just as we've got comfortably into a routine of spiritual life that Jesus says, 'Don't hold onto that. I've something new to show you.' Let this week be a chance to grow in your relationship with the resurrected Jesus. Start where you are: excited, cautious, doubtful, eager, sceptical, reaching out … Jesus will meet you just as he met each disciple. You'll need to be alert though. He turns up unexpectedly in all sorts of places! Even on the most ordinary of days he'll be there somewhere just waiting to add a joyful surprise if you recognise him.

Sheila Pritchard is now self-employed after twenty years of lecturing in spiritual formation at the Bible College of New Zealand. She enjoys encouraging others in their spiritual journey through teaching, writing and personal mentoring. She also enjoys walking the beaches and bush tracks in beautiful New Zealand.

DAY 1

'It is finished'

Being relaxed and open prepares us to be receptive to what God wants to communicate. So relax into your chair and deepen your breathing. As you breathe slowly in and out pray: 'Speak, Lord, I'm listening.'

John 19:17–37

Before there can be a new beginning there has to be an ending. That's a hard reality at times. Letting go is not easy, especially if we are letting go of something that feels essential to our life. I wonder what feelings were contained in Jesus' gasped statement: 'It is finished' (v 30). Was it a cry of triumph? Was it an exhausted sigh of relief? Was it a moment of darkness, feeling all was lost? Perhaps we tend to read it as a cry of triumph because we know this ending led to a wonderful new beginning. Maybe Jesus was in touch with that too, but I hold open the possibility that in his real humanity he might have felt the anguish of an ending much as we do. Remember that Matthew records Jesus crying: 'My God, my God, why have you forsaken me?' (Matthew 27:46).

We will never know all that Jesus felt at that moment. We do know that through all the devastating events that led to the end of his earthly life Jesus maintained a bedrock trust in God. Through the eyes of those watching this was the worst possible ending anyone could endure. By God's grace and power it was about to become a far better beginning than anyone could imagine!

A prayer: 'Lord, help me to trust that each of my endings leads to a beginning filled with your grace and power. Amen.'

The Bible in a year: Hosea 9–10; Revelations 2

DECEMBER 2–8

DAY 2

Where is he?

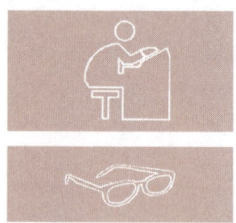

Place any concerns or distractions in the care of God and settle down to find the still place within you where the Spirit dwells. Rest there for a few moments.

John 19:38–20:18

Are you the kind of person who jumps to happy conclusions easily? Or are you one who carefully puts all the data together and comes to a reasoned conclusion after careful thought? What conclusion would you come to when faced with an empty tomb? With whom do you most identify – Peter, 'the other disciple' or Mary (see 20:2, 6–8)?

In his years of ministry, Jesus had a habit of surprising people, but nothing could be more surprising than a dead man turning up alive in the cemetery garden! I find myself identifying with Mary all the way. It didn't appear to cross her mind that the empty tomb might be good news, not bad. She wept for the loss of the Jesus she had known (20:13), unaware that a new, more wonderful experience of Jesus was at hand (20:16–17).

The historical death and resurrection of Jesus happened only once. Mary experienced it all first hand in a tangible way. Yet I think the same pattern is played out again and again. We weep at our empty tombs of loss and disillusionment, wondering where Jesus has gone. Perhaps when we turn away from the empty place and listen through our tears we will hear Jesus call our name from a new direction. The resurrected Jesus is not limited to our expectations of how and where we should find him.

Is there an 'empty tomb' in your life which you are seeing as bad news? Ask the Spirit to help you turn around and meet Jesus in a new life-giving place.

The Bible in a year: Hosea 11–12; Revelations 3

DECEMBER 2–8

DAY 3

Seeing and believing

On a scale of 1–10 where would you place your level of peacefulness? Open yourself to receive the peace of Christ more fully today.

John 20:19–31

Poor old Thomas often gets a bad press as being 'the doubting disciple' (vs 24–25). But wait a minute. All the rest of them were huddled in fear in a locked room before Jesus arrived (v 19). Does that make them superior? I don't think so! I'm very glad the disciples were such ordinary human people. Then and now, fear and doubt are two of the biggest obstacles to recognising the resurrected Jesus.

The disciples had the privilege of seeing, hearing and touching the physical person of Jesus risen from the dead (vs 26–27). No doubt we sometimes wish it could be the same for us! When fears and doubts assail us where are we to look for assurance that Jesus is alive and present? Strange as it may seem I think we have even more options than the first disciples. Firstly, we have a whole library recording the presence of God in the lives of people throughout history. The covenant promises of God are set out clearly. We can count on the Word of God! Then we have the very Spirit of Jesus within us to lead us into truth and give us personal experience of his presence and power. We don't have to wait in a locked room, or be in the right place at the right time. By his Spirit Jesus is right here, right now, at every moment. Peace be with you! Reach out and believe!

Receive Jesus' special blessing because you are one who has not seen and yet has believed (v 29). Give thanks for all that strengthens your faith.

The Bible in a year: Hosea 13–14; Revelations 4

DECEMBER 2–8

DAY 4

It is the Lord!

Pray for some 'spiritual windscreen wipers' to clear the haze from your vision and give you a renewed ability to recognise Jesus in the activities of your day.

John 21:1–14

After a traumatic time it can be a comfort to go back to doing something familiar. What are your places of retreat when you are confused or stressed? What activities can you slot into on 'automatic pilot' if you need to? Such things can be a welcome blessing. However, that comfortable familiarity may sometimes blind us to seeing Jesus in the ordinariness of it all.

The disciples hadn't quite got used to this resurrected Jesus. Was he or wasn't he really here again? I get the feeling Jesus was training them to expect him at every turn – by turning up unexpectedly! Jesus made his presence felt on this ordinary and rather unsuccessful day by making a suggestion they'd heard once before (vs 4–6; see also Luke 5:4). Suddenly the light dawned! It really was Jesus. He was the same – and yet different. And that was the problem. They couldn't quite put their finger on it but they had to learn all over again to recognise and trust him. Having breakfast together on the beach helped a lot (v 12)!

We too sometimes find it hard to recognise Jesus. His character is consistent but he turns up in many unexpected places! The trick is to expect him to be there and look out for that extraordinary presence in an ordinary day.

Eat your next meal with a conscious awareness that Jesus is present. Talk with him about how he has been present in the last twenty-four hours. Go out expecting to experience his presence in the day ahead.

The Bible in a year: Psalm 139; Joel 1–2

DAY 5

Yes, Lord, I love you!

Spend a few quiet moments 'just being' with Jesus. Get a sense of him sitting alongside you in companionable silence.

John 21:15–25

Have you ever felt a sense of shame and despair so deep that you wondered if you would ever be free? If you have you'll know something of what Peter was feeling. I meet people quite often who wonder if God could ever look on them with love again. They feel a terrible separation from God because of something they have done – or something that has been done to them at the hands of others. Their grief is enormous. I'm sure God grieves too when we don't realise how generous his love is.

Just a few days before Peter had strongly, emphatically and repeatedly denied any connection with Jesus. What could be more terrible than that? Reflect for a moment on anything you feel has caused separation between you and Jesus. Could anything be more serious than an outright denial? I don't think so! Now join Peter in finding out the generosity of Jesus' love. Jesus sought Peter out for a walk along the beach. There were no words of reproach or disappointment. Instead Jesus gave Peter an opportunity to reaffirm his love (vs 15–17). A rather chastened Peter was not boastful in his affirmation. He knew his frailty now. This probably equipped him to be better able to take care of the lambs and sheep of God's flock. Peter was not just forgiven, he was appointed to partnership in the work of Jesus!

Write a letter to Jesus thanking him for the generosity of his love for you and affirming your love for him. What partnership task can you join him in?

A new creation: 2 Corinthians 5:11–21
A new path: Isaiah 43:14–21

The Bible in a year: Joel 3; Revelations 5

DECEMBER 2–8

Going deeper …

I'm inviting you to go on your own walk on the beach with Jesus as Peter did (John 21:15–19). I'll describe how to do this in prayerful imagination and how to go out and 'walk the meditation' on a beach or some other outdoor setting.

Become as still inside as you can … Tune in to what it feels like to anticipate going for a walk with Jesus – just the two of you. Are there things you feel nervous about? Are there topics you are afraid he may bring up that you'd rather avoid? Do you have questions you want to ask, or things you want to say? Now get a sense of Jesus inviting you to come walking and set out together … Let Jesus begin the conversation. What does he say to you? How do you respond? Let the conversation continue as long as it needs to. It will be a personal conversation for you. It may or may not follow the same lines as Peter's time with Jesus. Trust the Spirit of God to lead you as you listen and respond.

When it is time for the walk to end, sit down with Jesus and be quiet together for a time. Then let him bless you and send you out into what lies ahead. When you have finished your meditation it would be good to note down in your journal the things you want to remember. Going for walks with Jesus and conversing as you go is a wonderful way of praying. You can do it often.

New every morning

Conclusion

Can you recall the beginning of your relationship with Jesus? Is there a special memory of God's love or a touch from the Holy Spirit that brought new joy? Sometimes a new experience stands out with a vibrancy and energy that makes the whole world look different! It is as if we have stepped into a new reality. And of course that's exactly what has happened! An encounter with the living God does put us in touch with a source of life and energy that is different from mere human resources. The trouble is that when the 'newness' wears off it is all too easy to sink back into a level of living that takes it all for granted. When that happens we forget the wonder of what we knew so clearly at the beginning.

This week we have been with people who experienced the new beginning of life with the risen Jesus. And that is just what is available for you and me every day! Try taking a few moments when you wake to say: 'Today I will meet the risen Jesus! Today I live by the power of the Holy Spirit within me.' Then step out of bed into a day filled with that reality.

Every day truly is a new beginning. One of the best ways to see every day with that vibrant newness is to recognise that it could be the last day you have. As part of my prayer every morning I say: 'This is a good day to die. This is a good day to live.' This helps me to value the wonderful gift of a new day and to live it with that expectant edge of meeting Jesus whether in life or in death and resurrection.

The Bible in a year: Psalm 140–141; Amos 1–4; Revelations 6

DECEMBER 9–15

God's book of remembrance

Malachi

There are many unique things about this small book of four chapters. Obviously, it is the last book in the Old Testament. Less obvious is its nature as being a bridge between the Old and New Testaments. It provides an excellent vantage point for you to look back on the whole story of Israel, and forward to the hope of the coming of Jesus. The Israel of Malachi's time was sandwiched between the past activities of God and the promised future activity of God. Yet nothing was happening in their day. Within the nation, people were becoming impatient, indifferent and religiously arrogant. God was not delivering as expected, and this vacuum provoked different responses in his people.

In the light of this situation, our theme this week focuses on *how to live when God is silent*. During those silent times, Satan, the master tempter, aims to blur our vision of God's love, and lead us into spiritual unfaithfulness. We are going to realise that, though Satan tempts, God tests, in order that our faith might shine like pure gold. Be ready to be confronted, corrected and redirected, as you seek to follow the God of whom Isaiah said: 'Truly, you are a God who hides himself, O God of Israel, Saviour' (45:15).

A note on Malachi's structure: It is structured around a dialogue form of accusation (God), interrogation (people) and refutation (God). The seven defiant words of the nation reveal a soul that is suffocating in religious pride. The Messenger of the Lord addresses the defiant and recalcitrant citizens, and in the end focuses his promise on the righteous remnant of believers. (You will find it really valuable to read through the book in one sitting, if you have time.)

Paul Hartwig is a Baptist Minister who is presently taking a break from pastoring to complete his PhD through the Baptist Seminary in Cape Town.

DECEMBER 9–15

DAY 1

The love of God

Today we start with the most profound truth in the Bible. It is an unconditional fact that needs to be meditated on daily. This reality needs to take over our internal processing system and revolutionise our life. Are you ready for this priceless diamond?

Malachi 1:1–5

'"I have loved you", says the Lord' (v 2). These four simple words can change your life! Let's highlight two things. Firstly, notice the past tense, 'have loved'. Secondly, notice the speaker, 'the Lord'. This scripture reveals the *fact* and the *source* of the love you are subject to. It is 'there' regardless, and it flows from one who does not lie. Notice how these words serve as a heading for the whole book. Further, God substantiates his love by comparing Israel's status with that of their neighbour, Edom. Whilst Edom was a wasteland (v 3), Israel had been partially restored. 'I the Lord do not change. So you, O descendants of Jacob, are not destroyed' (3:6). God has always provided external evidence for his love. There is no ground for any accusation.

Can you feel the rock of God's love under your life? It is there: firm, stable and secure. Nothing needs to be added or intensified. He loves you now as much as he ever has or ever will do. Also, it is God's love, unique, strong, and full. Begin to worship God by thanking him for his care and consideration – even if he seems to have forgotten you. As you begin in faith, you will start to understand, for the Bible says: 'By faith we understand …' (Hebrews 11:3).

The Bible in a year: Amos 5–6; Revelations 7

DECEMBER 9–15

DAY 2

King of the nations

Today we deal with the offerings we give to God. The Bible makes it clear: firstly, that we have a responsibility to worship God; secondly, that we must do this with all we are and all we have; and thirdly, that spiritual apathy nauseates God. In what condition are your offerings?

Malachi 1:6–14

The priests were getting slack with the quality of the offerings given to God. What do you think the root of this was? Verse 6 pinpoints the problem: contempt for God. Notice what religious distortions this produced. They gave God what they did not want – flawed offerings of sick, blind and 'cheap' animals (v 8). Notice God's response in verse 10. Compare this with Isaiah 1:10–15. It's all or nothing! Finally, note that his name IS great (the NIV misleadingly uses the future tense) among the nations – verses 11 and 14. God has people all over the world and is not dependent upon us for his worship or mission.

These verses are the equivalent of Jesus' message to the Laodicean church in Revelation 3:15–16. If you are 'lukewarm', you are jeopardising your faith. The best response is to turn from compromise and do all you need to do to honour and love God, as he deserves. Make sure you have a clear conscience toward God. 'Offer your bodies as living sacrifices, holy and pleasing to God' (Romans 12:1). Make sure you are on the altar.

The Bible in a year: Amos 7–8; Revelations 8

DECEMBER 9–15

DAY 3

Marital faithfulness

Today we consider our relationships. The whole law is summed up as: 'love your neighbour as yourself' (Matthew 19:19). Spiritual breakdown first shows its face in relationships. Ask the Lord to reveal to you the importance of your relationships and how he feels about them. Particularly consider how religious offerings are rendered ineffective through any type of marital breakdown.

Malachi 2:10–16

This section has an affinity with Matthew 5:23–24. The offerings at the altar are rendered ineffectual through interpersonal discord. God looks at the heart. Purity of heart and inward integrity are of greater value to God than external purity. Faithful love is essential in all relationships. Marriage is described here as a covenant (v 14). God seeks a love that goes far beyond what can be expected or deserved within a relationship. God, who personifies this, recoils at any form of treachery – '"I hate divorce (literally 'putting away')," says the Lord' (v 16).

Consider the relationships you have at present. God calls you to translate your spirituality into the 'stuff' of human relationships. Make that your focus. Make your relationships the arena where your faith is spelled out. Ask God for more love, whilst you sow the measure that you already have. Lastly, verse 16 exhorts us to watch over our spirits diligently, alert to any intrusive selfishness.

The Bible in a year: Amos 9; Revelations 9

DAY 4

A refiner's fire

All of us tend to make Jesus a compatible, 'user-friendly' Saviour. Our Scripture today reveals that he is not a conformist, but rather a transformer of men. We must be willing to co-operate with his refining process. In doing so you will hopefully gain a fresh understanding into why God watches you so closely (Job 7:17–20). Will you submit to his work or resist?

Malachi 2:17–3:5

Verse 2 describes the coming Messiah with two graphic images. He is like a fiery furnace and a washing detergent. Praise God that we are not on a bonfire or a pyre: we are not being consumed but refined. There is a beneficial purpose in all we go through. I have heard it said that the 'sitting' in verse 3 refers to the process whereby the refiner scrutinises and refines the alloyed compound until he can see his own reflection in the purified silver. If this is so, we can link it to the New Testament which discloses God's ultimate purpose as fashioning us in the image of his Son.

Cloak in prayer all those uncomfortable things in your life. Do not leave a thing untouched by the hands of prayer. Thank God again that your pains are birth pains and not rigor mortis! As you arise in this faith, be a light of hope to others who are suffering.

The Bible in a year: Psalm 142–143; Obadiah

DECEMBER 9–15

DAY 5

The victory crown

As you begin the day, remember that Jesus said there are only two roads in life – one is broad and spacious, the other is narrow and cramped. The important factor, though, is the destination of the roads. Death or life: you choose. Prepare to make the right choice and take the right road in your faith.

Malachi 3:13–4:3

The 'Day of the Lord' is coming (v 1). On this day he will openly divide humanity into two camps – see verse 18. Observe the end of the two roads in verses 2 and 3: total consumption or total restoration. Note who receives the crown: it is those 'fearers' of the Lord (v 16). The Lord recorded their behaviour under circumstances when God seemed absent (v 14) and promises to reward them on the last day of history. The Divine Secretary takes minutes of our lives – neither the good nor the bad escape him and he will reward us accordingly. In the introduction we saw that Malachi is a bridge. Consider the scene of verse 2: is it not a fitting introduction to the New Testament?

We need to pray for a renewed mind to see life the way God does. We only see a small part of the picture. He is not limited by time and space and sees it all at once. Ask God to give you an eternal frame of mind, so that you will live each day in the light of eternity.

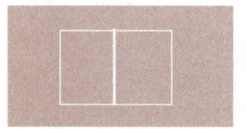

God's store house: Psalm 31:14–20
Your Father who is in secret: Matthew 6:1–18

The Bible in a year: Jonah 1–2; Revelations 10

DECEMBER 9–15

Going deeper …

The book of Malachi was written about 100 years after the return of the Israelites from the exile in Babylon. The prophecies of Isaiah, Jeremiah and Ezekiel had foretold a period of unprecedented renewal and restoration after the exile. Their words fuelled the returnees to rebuild the temple and return to the Law of God. Yet, as time went on, they saw only a partial fulfilment of these promises. After 100 years of unrequited expectation and hope, how do you think they felt? In the vacuum of delay, a rift started to appear amongst the people. Some became reckless and forsook their former hope, whilst others held on and even died in hope. Their hope only materialised some 400 years later when Jesus was born of the virgin Mary. What a story!

How do you cope with disappointment? Does your tender hope mature, or does it shrivel up and die? Romans 5:3–5 threads the development for us. Turn to it and notice how *hope* is not the first or middle virtue, but the goal to be desired! Hope does not let us down because it is hitched to a God who loves us with all the fulness of his 'godness'. Praise his name!

God takes notice

Conclusion

'And the Lord listened and heard' (Malachi 3:16). This is our theme verse for the week. The picture is not one of a vindictive God, gleefully piling up a list of all your sins. Here the focus is rather on a gracious God who has a surfeit of love that disproportionately enriches our lives as we faithfully persevere. With every choice we make to side with God and do what is right, he takes notice and 'hears' us.

This verse is a fitting prologue to the New Testament. There we read that the God-fearers of Israel received the Messiah and the religious professions rejected him. They finally 'received one blessing after another' (John 1:16), whilst the arrogant came under the curse of the Lord. All this shows that we serve a God who is not unjust or indifferent, but who actively engages with us even when we are unaware of him.

The only appropriate response to such grace is faith expressed in thanksgiving. Let your life be encompassed by a chorus of thanksgiving. As your feet are planted on the rock of God's love, give your Father thanks for what he has done, is doing and will do. As you articulate your faith – even in 'cold' circumstances – the Spirit will begin to warm you and download some of those blessings that the Father has stored up for you.

The Bible in a year: Psalm 144; Jonah 3–4; Micah 1–3; Revelations 11

DECEMBER 16–22

Busyness

2 Thessalonians 3; 1 Timothy 6; Matthew 11; Ezekiel 44; Colossians 3; Psalm 23; Isaiah 32; John 15

We live in the stress epidemic. Hurry, worry, and being busy are seen as normal, especially for the urban dweller. (I wonder where forest rangers go to get away from it all?) The stress that accompanies busyness is regarded as the number one killer of adults, with links to cancer, heart disease, high cholesterol, ulcers and other digestive system disorders, vitamin deficiency, domestic violence and road rage.

But do I hear you say: 'I'm a Christian, and that stuff can't come near me'? I have bad news for you. The laws of living life are universal. Busyness and stress happen to Christian and non-Christian alike, and they affect us all in the same way. Jesus had to admonish his people strongly to 'quit worrying' (Matthew 6:25–34). He did not teach that work was bad, only that we should be trusting while we work. He was suggesting an attitude of humility and faith, which believes that God is the author of our destiny, and not we ourselves.

Trust in God is the *basis* of productivity, while the work that emerges from that trust is what will actually *make* us productive. So our refuge should be in right living, respect for God's Word, and respect for the principles of the Kingdom of God as they apply to our mundane lives. I hope that our readings and meditations this week will help you to handle the many facets of your life with sanity and victory.

After pastoring churches for many years, Costa Mitchell is now the Regional Overseer of the Association of Vineyard Churches in South Africa. He is based in Cape Town.

DAY 1

Contentment is a state of mind

Have you ever felt the sense of futility reflected in Psalm 127:1–2a and Ecclesiastes 2:22, 23? Does your work routine, or the sheer weight of hard work demanded of you, get you down? Bring it to God today, and let him reassure you. Read Psalm 127:2b and Ecclesiastes 3:13. Own these promises as gifts from God.

2 Thessalonians 3:6–13; 1 Timothy 6:6–10

In Genesis 3:17–19 work was made a part of the conflictual relationship between humanity and the rest of creation. The struggle to conquer creation reminds us that all is not well in our world while we are out of relationship with God. So we have to work, or 'sweat', to earn our bread, and Paul reminded the Thessalonians that this was their duty (vs 6–10). Idleness is as much of a problem as busyness!

In modern life we tend to become self-reliant, and then covetousness takes over. Bread is not enough – we want jam as well! Our desire for the marks of success becomes insatiable. A bumper sticker sums it up: 'He who dies with the most toys, wins!' The result is a frenetic lifestyle, or non-stop busyness. 1 Timothy 6:9–10 reminds us that we are called, even in our careers, to 'seek first his kingdom and his righteousness' (Matthew 6:33). We need to set boundaries for our busyness, or physical and mental burnout will do it for us.

Lord, you have called me to godliness and contentment (1 Timothy 6:6–8). I bring you my mindset and commit my situation to you, confessing that your provision is enough for me. I choose to measure life in terms of quality rather than quantity.

The Bible in a year: Micah 4–5; Revelations 12

DECEMBER 16–22

DAY 2

Partnership with Jesus

Jesus was an artisan before he began to preach, and thus he sanctified work as part of a holy life. Today he invites us to make him our partner in all aspects of our lives. Give him thanks that he loves your career as much as your spiritual life.

Matthew 11:28–30

In this passage Jesus uses the analogy of oxen being yoked to the plough (v 29). The yoke was a wooden collar, which went over the top of the ox's neck, with a leather harness fastening it to the plough. There were yokes that involved only one ox, and others that were designed to enable two oxen to pull the plough together. In the latter case, the oxen needed to harmonise their efforts. Pulling out of harmony would result in strain, inefficiency, and even injury. To work in harmony would halve the load and double the efficiency, and produce 'restful work'.

Jesus is inviting us into a partnership with him, where he pulls alongside us and facilitates our work, making it lighter than it would otherwise have been. His language at the end of the passage could be translated: 'To be yoked with me is easy, and the burden carried with me is light.'

Jesus, today I confess that when I am weary and heavy laden, it is because I so often insist on working alone, rather than in partnership with you. Restore in me the rest you give when I work alongside you.

The Bible in a year: Micah 6–7; Revelations 13

DECEMBER 16–22

DAY 3

An audience of one

God is omniscient. He knows and sees everything. We need to remind ourselves that we live under his scrutiny, and then put ourselves there deliberately: 'Lord, go where I go today, look on my life with grace, and sustain me.'

Ezekiel 44:10–18; Colossians 3:22–24

What is meant by 'ministering before (or to) the Lord' (Ezekiel 44:15–16), and how does it counteract busyness? Much of our busyness occurs because we do not have clear boundaries. This allows others to dictate how we spend our time and energy. Like the priests, we are called to a singular focus, to an audience of One.

The command in Colossians is given to 'slaves' (v 22), who did not have the luxury of setting their own agenda! They had to do whatever their boss told them to do. Paul, however, shows them how to turn their tedious employment from busyness into peacefulness. It is by creating a boundary around everything they do, putting it in the context of worship, or devotion to the Lord (v 22–23). By so doing, they will glorify God and they will be freed.

In Ezekiel 44, working *for people*, even in the area of 'ministry', is seen as a judgement God imposed on the Levites because of their idolatry (vs 10–14). The alternative, to which those who had remained faithful to God were invited, was to enjoy intimacy with God himself in what they were doing (vs 15–16).

Who are you working for? Become conscious of Jesus as your 'boss' today. The result will be a day, and a life, without sweat (Ezekiel 44:18)!

The Bible in a year: Nahum 1–3; Revelations 14

DECEMBER 16–22

DAY 4

The causes of busyness

Look at every activity, or field of activity, that makes up your life. Bring them, one by one, to God in a commitment of 'your way' to him. 'Lord, take my moments and my days; take my feet, my head and hands. Let them serve you today.'

Psalm 23:1–6; Isaiah 32:1–8,15–20

Busyness is not a state of being: it is a state of mind. It is an attitude, or a collection of attitudes, manifesting itself in: too much to do; not enough time; no clear plan; no timetables or boundaries; no attempt to prioritise; a chaotic or disorderly existence. Many people are like a cowboy I once read about who ran into the corral, jumped on his horse and rode off in all directions! Remember that you are meant to be a sheep that is led (Psalm 23:1–3), not a vehicle that is driven.

Just as busyness is a state of mind, so is peacefulness. Peace is not having nothing to do; it is doing whatever we do with a sense of direction, wisdom and confidence. It is a sense of harmony between all the parts and functions of our lives (Isaiah 32:2). It is being *appropriate* in our activities: resting when we need rest, and working without stress, because we have a Good Shepherd.

Lord, I repent of my pride and self-reliance, and of my neglect of prayerful planning. When I take my marching orders from you, the pace is peaceful, manageable and growth producing. Today, in you, I choose to rest in my work, and work peacefully, without stress or busyness.

The Bible in a year: Psalm 145; Habakkuk 1–3

DECEMBER 16–22

DAY 5

Practical steps to change your life

We are called, in today's reading, to be branches that bear fruit. This means letting God's life flow through us, and being conscious of his presence. Take a moment to 'practise his presence'.

John 15:1–11

Let us look at practical ways of implementing a peaceful life. Firstly, perhaps you can set an alarm on your watch or PC to remind you to focus on Jesus for two minutes in every hour. Use the time to thank him for his partnership, and to commit the next hour to him. Ask for his wisdom in the decisions you have to make, and in implementing these decisions. Breathe, and relax in him.

Secondly, know your calling. The job we are doing in our working hours, is not just a job, but is the fulfilment of God's will or calling on our lives. Be grateful that Christ has called you to the work you are doing, whether you are a mom, working in an office, running a company, or repairing leaky pipes. Jesus has sanctified all of life, including work, and made it the place in which we can serve him and encounter him.

Thirdly, identify and plan according to your priorities. Set goals; decide what you need to do to accomplish them; and establish a strategy for spending time, energy and money according to that plan.

Do the exercises above, writing down a daily and weekly plan and timetable for your life. Present it to the Lord with a fresh determination to live 'on purpose' and in peace.

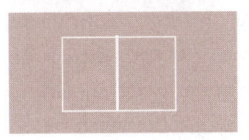

Curiosity kills people: Ecclesiastes 1:12–18
Single-mindedness: Philippians 3:4–16

The Bible in a year: Zephaniah 1–3; Revelations 15

DECEMBER 16–22

Going deeper ...

We have explored several antidotes to the busyness trap over the past few days. I find it helpful, in all attitudes and behaviour, to reflect on God himself as a model for my Christian mindset. We are to be 'imitators of God' (Ephesians 5:1). What an encouragement it is, therefore, to discover that God is himself a God of rest. He rested from his labours (Hebrews 4:10), and invites us to imitate him. He made the Sabbath for humanity, to celebrate his own enjoyment of rest! (Exodus 20:8–11). Does this mean that God has been idle since he finished his creation? No, it means rather that he works with the confidence and peace that his sovereign plan will be fulfilled. He works without being worried; without panic; without being busy.

With regard to salvation, Paul and James have sometimes been seen to be in conflict, because whereas Paul says: 'By grace you have been saved, through faith ... not by works' (Ephesians 2:8–9), James says: 'A person is justified by what he does and not by faith alone' (James 2:24). Is this a contradiction? No. They are attacking the same problem from opposite sides. Paul's enemy is self-reliant 'workaholism', whereas James is attacking empty, lazy faith. If we apply the principle of salvation to our working lives, we realise that we are called to neither laziness nor busyness, but work which issues from a secure, peaceful dependence on the God of our destiny.

First things first!

Conclusion

While lecturing, a professor pulled out a wide-mouthed jar and set it on the table in front of him. He produced about a dozen fist-sized rocks and placed them, one by one, in the jar. When no more rocks could fit inside, he asked, 'Is this jar full?' Everyone in the class said, 'Yes.' He reached under the table and pulled out a bucket of gravel. Then he poured in the gravel and shook the jar, causing the gravel to work itself down into the space between the rocks. He asked once more, 'Is this jar full?' By this time the class was on to him. 'Probably not,' one of them answered. He reached under the table and brought out a bucket of sand. He poured the sand into the jar and it filtered into the spaces between the rocks and the gravel.

The lesson? If you don't put the big rocks in first, you'll never get them in at all. What are the big rocks in your life? Your God. Your spouse. Your children. Your close friends. Your education. Your dreams. A worthy cause. Time for yourself. Your health. Remember to put these BIG ROCKS in first, or you'll never get them in at all. If you sweat over the little stuff (gravel, sand), you'll fill your life with little things and you'll never have time to spend on the big, important stuff (big rocks).

So ask yourself this question: What are the 'big rocks' in my life? Then put these in your jar first '... and all these things will be given to you as well' (Matthew 6:33).

The Bible in a year: Psalm 146–147; Haggar 1–2; Zechariah 1–2; Revelations 16

DECEMBER 23–29

Christmas presence

Luke 1–3

I have warm, fuzzy-edged memories of magical childhood Christmases. We sang of snow and sleigh bells, despite the shimmering heat of an Australian summer. On one occasion our tree was only a spindly pine decorated with foil milk-bottle tops, but to me it was a festive masterpiece. On Christmas morning, the stocking at the end of my bed would be bulging with wonders, which my mother had painstakingly gathered at the sales or sewn late at night from scraps of fabric. I remember a particularly lean year where the gifts were mostly pencils and notebooks I needed for school – but even they were exciting to the youngest of five children, because they were brand-new, and all mine.

What memories does Christmas evoke for you? For some, this time of year brings joy, but for others it is regret. Some people will feel weighed down by memories of family conflict or tragedy, or an aching loneliness. Some will be angered by the commercialism and greed that has overtaken this Christian festival.

In the end, though, Christmas is much more than the sum of all our memories and expectations. It goes far beyond a family celebration or a retail event. It is about the entrance of the almighty, eternal God into human history, on an astonishing rescue mission. It is about a gift a million times greater than the most opulent present. It is about a peace far beyond any human ceasefire. It is about Jesus. It is about love on a scale we can barely imagine.

Come with me on a journey through the Gospel of Luke. Allow your heavenly Father to deepen your joy or quieten your anger or heal your loneliness. Meet Jesus, the reason for Christmas.

Belinda Pollard is a freelance journalist and editor based in Brisbane, Australia. She writes news and feature articles for publications in Australia and the USA and has edited numerous books including Bible commentaries and biographies.

DECEMBER 23–29

DAY 1

Divine humanity

Once I spent a night wrestling with God because I felt that he was asking me to do something that I simply couldn't bear. Have you ever felt that obedience to God was just too costly?

Luke 1:26–38

Mary was probably only a young teenager when this heavenly visitor came calling. I think I would have reacted with similar fear and puzzlement (vs 29, 34). God's message of reassurance to the frightened girl is moving (v 30). I admire her ready submission (v 38) to the news of a pregnancy that would make her a social outcast. In Mary's time, unmarried mothers could even be executed for adultery.

The centre of today's reading is Jesus. The child to come has already been given a name that means 'The Lord is salvation'. Great Jewish kings of the past have been called sons of God, but this child will be *the* Son of God (vs 32, 35). His kingdom won't be limited to the temporal, political world – it will be eternal (v 33). And although the concept baffles us, Jesus will be the child of a human being and Almighty God, with both divine and human natures. God created this world, and he can transcend its natural laws whenever he pleases (vs 35–37). Up to this time, God's great love for humankind had driven him to pursue us from above and around us, but now he reaches out from among us. He, amazingly, is one of us.

Your Saviour is all-powerful, able to turn the world upside down. What difference will that make to you today? Your Saviour is a human being, who understands your fears and failings and joys. What difference will that make to you today?

The Bible in a year: Zachariah 3–4; Revelations 17

DECEMBER 23–29

DAY 2

Peace child

For many of us, there are times when we wish we could be more certain of God's existence or his love for us. What do you think God should do to prove himself? Let your thoughts lead you into prayer.

Luke 2:1–20

This is a cosmic event on a tiny scale. The eternal God bursts into human history, but he does it through the birth of a child to a poor teenager, in an obscure backwater of the Roman Empire. The conditions are so desperate that there isn't even a cradle available, and she has to place her new-born in a feeding trough (v 7). There is an appropriate heavenly fanfare to herald the arrival of the King (vs 9, 13), but the only ones to see it are a group of lowly shepherds.

Jesus was born in the hometown of King David (see 1 Samuel 16:1), because the long-awaited Christ/Messiah would come from the line of David (vs 4, 11; see also Micah 5:2). The witnesses don't fully understand what is in store for this small baby, but they know it will be something big, so they praise God (v 20) and ponder (v 19). We have the advantage of knowing how the story ends. This new-born would grow up to bring glory to God, and peace between humankind and God (v 14) – by dying on our behalf.

God didn't come to earth and stay in a palace, living luxuriously among rulers and priests. His Kingdom doesn't work that way. No matter how unimportant we might be in the world's eyes, we are precious to him, and he can do mighty things through us.

The shepherds couldn't help talking about what they had heard and seen (v 17). What would you like to tell people about Jesus?

The Bible in a year: Zachariah 5–6; Revelations 18

DECEMBER 23–29

DAY 3 — Promised child

I used to wonder why my Russian friends didn't smile for photographs, until it started me wondering why I do smile! Think of some of the ways that cultural characteristics have made you the person you are, and how this affects the way you think about God.

Luke 2:21–35

Jesus was a Jew. That might sound obvious, but I frequently overlook the implications of it. I forget that my Old Testament is the Bible Jesus read. I forget that my Saviour and Lord came first of all to save his own ancient people. In this short passage there are no less than five references to the requirements of the Jewish Law (vs 21–24, 27), and three references to Jesus' impact on the future of Israel (vs 25, 32, 34). If I really want to know Jesus, then I need to get to know him as Jesus of Nazareth, born into a devout Jewish peasant family, the fulfilment of a nation's hopes.

For a thousand years, the Jewish people had been waiting, yearning for the Messiah, the world-saver, that God had promised them. The godly Simeon instantly recognised the answer to this promise in a tiny baby. Simeon understood that Jesus would not be universally accepted by his people (v 34). They wanted the short-term answer of a political revolutionary who would live to break the yoke of Rome, not an eternal Messiah who would die to destroy the human race's bondage to sin. But even their rejection was part of God's design, so that he could extend his rescue plan to the whole planet (v 32).

Think of some of the ways God has used cultural differences to bring blessing in your life.

The Bible in a year: Zachariah 7–8; Revelations 19

DECEMBER 23–29

DAY 4

In his father's footsteps

When you were a child, what did you want to be 'when you grew up'? How does that compare to the course your life actually took? Spend some time thinking about the way you can see God's direction in your choices.

Luke 2:39–52

Imagine the anxiety of Joseph and Mary (vs 45–46, 48). 'Misplacing' a child might seem irresponsible to us (v 43), but in the extended families of the Ancient Middle East, a child was cared for by everybody, and Jesus was on the verge of Jewish adulthood anyway.

Jesus' attitude to his parents is one of obedience (v 51), in full accord with the Jewish law. So why did he wander off without telling them? Theologians struggle to find the correct way to reconcile the knowledge that Jesus was divine and without sin (see Hebrews 4:15) with the fact that he was a real human child. Perhaps he didn't realise his absence could scare his parents. Or he may have been showing them that his higher obedience was to his heavenly Father.

At the tender age of twelve, Jesus had wisdom and understanding beyond his years, and was growing in approval with God and people (vs 40, 47, 52). 'In my Father's house' (v 49) also means 'about my Father's business'. To Jesus' hearers, that would mean carpentry (see Matthew 13:55). Joseph was not Jesus' biological father, but he had raised him as his own son. It seems that Jesus did indeed go into the carpentry business (see Mark 6:3) – while he was preparing for his heavenly Father's business.

Because of Jesus, God is now your Father too. What does it mean for you to be 'about your Father's business'?

The Bible in a year: Psalm 148; Zachariah 9–10

DECEMBER 23–29

DAY 5

No compromise

To many in our world today, Jesus is just another guru. What is he to you? Worship him.

Luke 3:15–22

John the Baptist was the most outstanding prophet of his time. His message was hardly a comfortable one, but people flocked to hear it (see 3:7). Even the highest levels of government were rattled by his pronouncements (vs 19–20). Everyone began to speculate: could this be the one (v 15)? John could have used the situation for his own glory, but his answer was firm and honest. He was just the bulldozer clearing a path for the Messiah to walk in, as predicted (see Isaiah 40:3). Impressive though John's career was, he recognised that compared to the Messiah he was nothing (vs 16, 17) – a domestic kitten making way for a roaring lion.

The baby of Bethlehem is now an adult, and the baptism marks Jesus' official commissioning. Heaven opens when this man prays (v 21)! God declares that Jesus is his Son, his beloved only Son, his delight (v 22). Everything to this point has been preparation, but now the real work of the Messiah begins.

Just as John preached good news (v 18) but also rebuked sin (v 19), Jesus' gospel has a flip side. He has come to gather his followers to himself, but also to declare the penalty for rejection of God (v 17). The baptism Jesus offers will bring the remarkable gift of the Holy Spirit to human beings, but also the pain of purifying fire (v 16). The gospel can't be good news unless it includes the destruction of evil.

Because Jesus is representing you to the Father, heaven now opens when you pray. Let that thought inspire you to pray now.

Without fail: Matthew 2:1–18
Fresh start: Isaiah 11:1–10

The Bible in a year: Zachariah 11–12; Revelations 20

Going deeper ...

I am often overwhelmed by the cost of the cross to God. But I seem to have to work harder to grasp the cost to God of 'the incarnation' – becoming human.

In Isaiah 6:1–5 the prophet is in the ancient Jewish temple when he sees a terrifying vision of God's majesty. Isaiah doesn't even describe God himself, just the throne room with its awe-inspiring creatures, thunderous voices and swirling smoke. God is beyond description. Isaiah's instinctive response is fear that he must instantly die, because he has seen God. Now reread Luke 2:1–20. Think about the contrast between Isaiah's vision of God in the temple, and the visible God in Bethlehem. God found a way to appear before us without terrifying us ... but at what cost?

What did it mean for the immortal, all-powerful God to submit to the limitations of mortal, human flesh? This was not even a grown man, but a helpless baby who needed an adult to make all his decisions for him. God knew that the only way to save us was for a sinless human to die in our place. Only God is sinless, so this person had to be both God and human. I can't begin to imagine how that could have worked, or to comprehend the massive love that drove God to do it.

Respond to God's gift of himself at Christmas. Use your imagination. Express your thanks and wonder in a way that means something to you, and to him.

Reality check

When I'm trying to survive the Christmas shopping panic, I'm always delighted to spy a nativity scene in a window. At last – emerging from the red-and-white blur of Santas (inflatable, plaster or cardboard cut-out) – a reminder that Christmas is actually about the birth of Jesus. These nativity scenes are usually appealing in their stylised simplicity: the rustic stable, the serene woman and man draped in elegant robes, the charming animals, the cute baby in the hay.

The realistic version probably wouldn't sell well: a sweaty, exhausted teenager, relieved to have survived her first childbirth, and delighted with her new-born; a dishevelled and equally relieved man; a helpless baby wrapped in strips of cloth, lying in a feeding trough because there isn't anywhere else, doing the normal baby things like sleeping and crying. The Bible doesn't mention a stable or animals.

I still like to see nativity scenes, even if they're a bit inaccurate. I still put a sparkly angel at the top of my Christmas tree, even though I know that if the real thing appeared, it would undoubtedly scare me half to death. And even though society seems at times to have completely lost the plot of Christmas, I find their desire to celebrate something, anything, an encouraging sign of a longing for hope.

We can use these captivating Christmas symbols to point our neighbours to the solid, reality, the Jewish Messiah, the divinely human Son of God, the remarkable baby who was born to die, the one who alone can make peace between God and man.

The Bible in a year: Psalm 149–150; Zachariah 13–14; Malachi 1–2; Revelations 21

DECEMBER 30

How good is our God

How do you feel as you look back over the year? Has it been one of happiness and fulfilment? How has your relationship with the Lord progressed?

Psalm 147:1–11

Do you share the Psalmist's sentiment in verse 1? He sounds ecstatic: 'How good … pleasant and fitting to praise him!' He goes on to give good reasons for his excitement.

The Lord has been *acting* on their behalf. Notice the verbs in verses 2 and 3: 'builds', 'gathers', 'heals', 'binds'. He is no remote, impersonal deity, but a 'hands-on', concerned Father. What a good thought to take with us into the new year! He also praises God because he *controls* the stars (v 4) and nature (v 8). Surely we can trust ourselves to the One who numbers the stars! This God also has infinite *intelligence* (v 5), but amazingly 'he suffers fools gladly', paying special attention to the humble (v 6). There's no IQ test needed to become his child! Finally, the Psalmist praises the God who *provides* (vs 8–9). If God 'clothes the grass of the field … Will he not much more clothe you?' (Matthew 6:30).

What is it that pleases this wonderful God? Does he delight in physical strength and beauty (v 10)? Fortunately not. Many of us would find it difficult to please the Lord if that were the case! He takes great delight in our devotion and faith (v 11).

Have you delighted the Lord this year? Make time to take stock of your relationship with him. He has done so much for you, and wants you to put your hopes for 2003 'in his unfailing love' (v 11).

The Bible in a year: Malachi 3–4; Revelations 22

DECEMBER 31

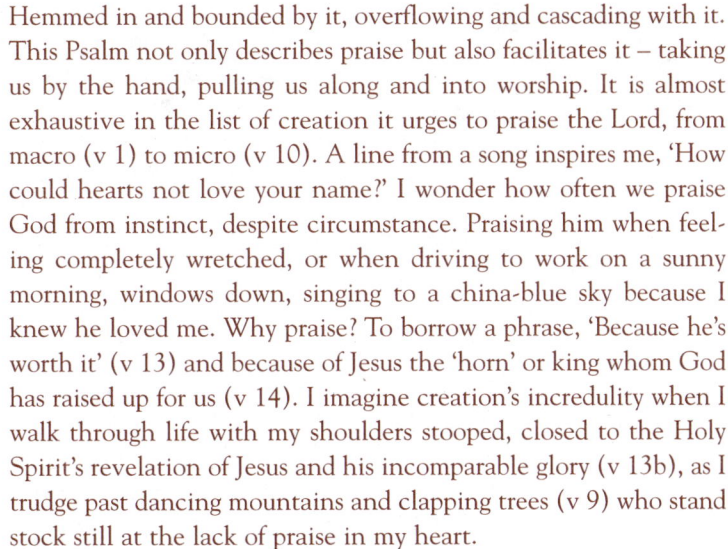

365 Days of praise

'He has fashioned you – so you are very precious in his sight. He will protect what he has made and bless you. Trust him.' (Anon)

Psalm 148

Hemmed in and bounded by it, overflowing and cascading with it. This Psalm not only describes praise but also facilitates it – taking us by the hand, pulling us along and into worship. It is almost exhaustive in the list of creation it urges to praise the Lord, from macro (v 1) to micro (v 10). A line from a song inspires me, 'How could hearts not love your name?' I wonder how often we praise God from instinct, despite circumstance. Praising him when feeling completely wretched, or when driving to work on a sunny morning, windows down, singing to a china-blue sky because I knew he loved me. Why praise? To borrow a phrase, 'Because he's worth it' (v 13) and because of Jesus the 'horn' or king whom God has raised up for us (v 14). I imagine creation's incredulity when I walk through life with my shoulders stooped, closed to the Holy Spirit's revelation of Jesus and his incomparable glory (v 13b), as I trudge past dancing mountains and clapping trees (v 9) who stand stock still at the lack of praise in my heart.

New year can seem like an 'artificial' time for some of us. For others it's a watershed, a new start, a chance to refocus and rededicate our lives. Perhaps 2002 has been a difficult year, perhaps a good one. Why not think about (re-)committing yourself to a life of praise?

'Jesus, how could hearts not love your name? This new year, teach me to praise my Father in heaven no matter what, and to remember that I'm close to your heart' (v 14).